WHO
KILLED
THE
KOORIES?

BY THE SAME AUTHOR

The Land Boomers (1966)
Australia in the Victorian Age (3 vols, 1971–76)
That Damned Democrat (1981)
Historical Records of Victoria (7 vols, 1981–90)
Australia: A History in Photographs (1983)
Australia: Spirit of a Nation (1985)
The Exploration of Australia (1987)

Michael Cannon

WHO
KILLED
THE
KOORIES?

William Heinemann Australia

First published 1990 by William Heinemann Australia
22 Salmon Street, Port Melbourne, Victoria 3207

Edited by Beryl Hill
Designed by Andrew Cunningham
Typeset in 11/14 Bembo by Leader Composition Pty Ltd
Printed in Australia by Australian Print Group

National Library of Australia
cataloguing-in-publication data:

Cannon, Michael, 1929–
  Who killed the Koories?

  Bibliography.
  Includes index.
  ISBN 0 85561 370 X.

  [1]. Aborigines, Australian – Treatment. [2]. Aborigines,
  Australian – Government relations. [3]. Massacres –
  Australia – History. I. Title.

994.0049915

CONTENTS

Conversion of Measurements

At the time of white settlement of Australia, the imperial system of weights and measures was in use. The system continued unchanged until decimal currency was introduced in 1966, followed by the gradual adoption of metric units from 1970.

Money

The standard unit of currency was the pound (£).
£1 comprised 20 shillings each of 12 pence. The penny could be divided into 2 halfpennies or 4 farthings. A crown equalled 5 shillings, a half-crown was 2s. 6d.

At the time of the adoption of decimal currency £1 = $2. The value of money in the early nineteenth century is not comparable with values in the late twentieth century.

Weight

The imperial pound (lb) was the most common unit of mass.
1 lb = 454 g
1 lb comprised 16 ounces (oz); 14 lbs = 1 stone; 8 stones = 1 hundredweight (cwt); 20 cwt = 1 ton (1.01 tonnes).

Length

The foot was the standard measure of length.
1 foot (ft) = 30.48 cm.
There were 12 inches in a foot; 3 ft in 1 yard; 1760 yards in a mile (1.61 km).
1 chain = 100 links = 66 ft = 20.177 m.

Area

The standard measure of land area was the acre.
1 rood = 40 perches = 1210 square yards = ¼ acre = 0.101 hectares.
1 acre = 10 square chains = 0.4046856 ha.

For large areas the square mile was the unit.
1 square mile = 640 acres = 258.9988126 ha.
Smaller areas were measured in square feet or square yards.

Capacity

The pint was the basic measure of liquids.
1 pint = 568 mL.
8 pints = 1 gallon = 4.55 L.
Spirituous liquor was often measured by the gill, which was a quarter pint = 0.142 L.
The bushel, equivalent to 8 gallons (36.40 litres), was used as a measure of grain, produce, etc.

Author's Note

Once upon a time, in a less sensitive age, it would have been unnecessary to comment on the terminology used in this book. Today it seems desirable to explain why certain stylistic decisions were made.

I have used the word 'Koories' in the title because it is euphonious, value-free, and conveys to modern readers a sense of the universality of Aboriginal experience. However, the word appears nowhere in the source materials on which this book is based. These materials give a truer rendition of attitudes in pioneering days by referring indiscriminately to Aborigines, natives, blacks, lubras, and so on. Because they were often used in a contemptuous manner, and were associated with evil events, these terms are now often disliked. I hope that readers of this book will be able to adopt a more objective view, and see them for what they are—mere descriptive words. There is no logical reason, for instance, to perceive the word 'blacks' as any more objectionable than the word 'whites'.

Phrases used to describe rural 'stations' also need clarification. Where squatters leased areas of land and used them to graze stock, the names of their runs or stations are given, where known, in quotation marks. This serves to distinguish such stations from similar locality names, rivers, or townships situated nearby. The names of government Aboriginal Stations (such as Loddon River) are invariably capitalised, in order to distinguish them from squatters' stations in the same area.

The department of government known as the Aboriginal Protectorate was headed by a Chief Protector, always specified as such in this book. Under his direction were several Assistant Protectors. For the sake of brevity, these men were often referred to simply as Protectors, although their official classification always remained that of Assistants.

M.C.

PROLOGUE

PORTENTS

OF

DISASTER

To the white adventurers and settlers who flocked to the south-eastern corner of the vast Australian continent in the 1830s, the region seemed liked a paradise on earth, for here lay one of the fairest domains ever created by nature. Permanent life-giving rivers meandered through its extensive plains; lush grasslands and forests flourished on its rich soil. The white men could scarcely believe their luck, as they penetrated further into undulating pastures and negotiable bushlands.

This land, it seemed, *was not being used*. To be sure, there were a few Aboriginal tribes wandering over the ground, but they couldn't be seen as *using* it, could they? They planted no crops, grazed no animals: occasional possums, wallabies, fish and yams kept them alive as they meandered on, merging silently into the echoing emptiness. How could such primitive people, brutish in many of their known customs, present any lasting problem?

The white newcomers were determined that the whole continent of Australia should belong to them—the soil, the

1

beasts and birds, the rivers and fish, the minerals and trees. A dream of total possession had taken hold of normally stolid men. Such lust for new lands ran through the whole British race that monarch and lowliest labourer alike glowed with the glory of creating a new empire.

These enthusiastic settlers quickly demonstrated that much of Australia was suitable for rapid expansion of wool-growing. Flocks spread over all available grasslands. By the end of the 1840s, the then-amazing figure of 40 000 000 pounds of wool was being exported to Europe each year. The cash return supported the early growth of a squatter-dominated society, whose acquisitive ethos could scarcely be counter-balanced by all the forces of government, religion and humanitarianism.

If you, the reader, are white, try to change roles for a moment. Become one of the native people, the children of nature, who have trudged over these Australian lands for so many hundreds of generations that your origins have been lost in legends and dreamings.

How would you regard the pale-skinned creatures who appeared suddenly from huge boats borne on the deep salt water? Were the newcomers returned spirits, bringing magical possessions—iron axes, and strange mirrors in which you could see your own image—wearing colorful tight-fitting warm clothes; sporting peculiar smoke tubes in their mouths; carrying longer straight tubes which they pointed at distant animals to kill them in a thunderous blast?

No, they were mortal men all right, with their dank odours and all-too-human appetites. They brought food, even if it was a strange grey powder to be baked into mouth-watering 'damper'; and novel drinks, some sweetened with brown crystals, some which burned your throat raw, eased your aching muscles and induced powerful visions.

Of course they were men, for they wanted women at night, as all men did—but they wanted *your* women. What you didn't know at first was that they invisibly carried a range of exotic diseases, which would kill off most of your tribespeople in particularly disgusting ways, and rob you of the next generation.

None of this took long for you to get used to, for hardship was customary in the bush, and death a frequent companion. More surprising were the strange beasts brought by the whites, especially those small animals covered with a white springy coat. To you they were nothing less than portable meat, munching the grass placidly and ready for slaughter when you were hungry. The idea of growing wool for export was incomprehensible to meat-hungry people.

Every so often, in a quick ceremony, one of the white men would tumble an animal on its back, draw a razor-sharp blade across its throat and release its lifeblood into the soil. When the carcass was skinned, carved up, and hung for a while, you had the makings of a fine feast.

The newcomers brought a stern law as well. Anyone could stalk and spear kangaroos in the old manner, but only a white boss could order the killing of a sheep. No matter that these new flocks grazed and bred prolifically on the same grasses as the native animals you used to hunt, over what was so recently your tribe's exclusive hunting grounds and water sources. Grazing animals were the white man's private property. 'Property'—what was that? You soon learned. No matter how fiercely hunger gripped your belly, if you dared to break the white man's law, his face turned purple, his eyes bulged from their sockets, he shouted for horses and saddles, and he would ride you down and kill you stone dead with that long thunder-tube.

Very soon whites and blacks were leaping at each other's throats.

Aboriginals had long been used to defending their territories against other tribes. Armed combat between adult males was an age-old tradition. Many of the warriors, as the young squatter Tom Browne wrote, were 'grandly-formed specimens of humanity, dignified in manner, and possessing an intelligence by no means to be despised. Why should these proud men give ground peacefully to white settlers and their abominable convict servants?

So, during the 1840s, as squatters tightened their grip on the land, tribal leaders emerged to lead their warriors into battle against the white interlopers. They did not know that in the face of European technology and social organisation, their cause was hopeless. All they could do was to fight on blindly and die in defence of their native soil.

As the effects of colonisation on Aboriginal races became apparent to liberal statesmen in London, all kinds of palliative measures were attempted—everything, that is, but an enforceable prohibition on the Empire's seizure of hunting grounds, which lay at the root of all subsequent problems.

Sir George Gipps, Governor of New South Wales (of which Port Phillip was one district), arrived in Sydney early in 1838 with instructions to use the full force of British law in protecting the Aboriginal people. His most determined action, taken later in 1838, was to authorise the public execution of seven convict shepherds who had massacred nearly thirty black men, women and children in appalling circumstances at Myall Creek in northern New South Wales. The hangings provoked a furore in all settled parts of Australia, causing Gipps to be regarded forever as the squatters' enemy. Finding little public support, Gipps felt that he could never again be so adamant in defence of Aboriginal rights.

Tensions continued to increase in 1839, when 38-year-old C. J. La Trobe arrived to take up his post as first Superintendent (chief government officer) of the booming Port Phillip district. La Trobe was one of the bravest and gentlest men ever to head an Australian government. An expert mountaineer, an accomplished author, an indefatigable horseman, and a committed anti-slavery advocate, La Trobe at first sight seemed to be everything that was needed to solve the new district's racial problems.

Unfortunately, like Gipps, La Trobe became bogged down in the complexities of establishing authority over a wild land.

With few exceptions, he was surrounded by incompetent or self-seeking assistants. His police forces, when not actually corrupt, were heavily biased in favour of the squatting ascendancy. His judicial system was incapacitated by the fact that rural magistrates were either run-holders themselves, or inevitably allied to that system. Even the Supreme Court was made a laughing-stock by the antics of Judge John Willis, a sick and embittered reject from other British jurisdictions.

The newly-appointed Aboriginal Protectors, who were supposed to save the vanishing natives, were beset with a thousand barely understood problems. A major defect was that George Robinson, the lowly-born Chief Protector, was so ambitious to cut a figure in polite society that he did not often dare to run counter to its accepted ideas.

What hope was there for the well-intentioned La Trobe? More importantly, what hope was there for the thousands of Aboriginals, dying out of sight and out of mind, in sickness and sudden affrays reported and unreported, throughout the length and breadth of this fair land?

1

GALLANT PROTECTORS TO THE RESCUE: HOW THEY FUMBLED IT

At the same time that white immigrants were seizing the grasslands of Australia, the older civilisation 'at home' in Britain produced a group of progressive social leaders who were concerned with notions of human justice as well as economic advancement. Their first major success was the outlawing of the African slave trade. Their second was the virtual abolition of convict transportation to Australia. Their next concern was amelioration of the condition of native races in lands already colonised.

As squatting enterprises spread inexorably into the bush, frightful stories reached England about the treatment of Aboriginals by convict shepherds. With the new settlement at Port Phillip, reformers saw a chance to impose stricter controls before similar genocide could occur. This would take the form of a system of 'Protectors of Aborigines', employed by the government and armed with magisterial powers. Protectors, it was hoped, would not only prevent exploitation of the tribes, but would also gradually persuade them to emulate the white man's seemingly superior and Christian civilisation.

Life is never so simple. The Aboriginal Protectorate in Port Phillip began under chaotic conditions early in 1839, and never lost its aura of baffled crisis. At best the Protectors became rather like today's ambulance services, coming along after the damage is done and trying to patch up the survivors.

The government's original intention was that four Assistant Protectors should accompany the main tribes as they moved around the countryside, guiding them towards a more settled way of life. Under frontier conditions, the policy proved naive and hopeless.

The Chief Protector, 51-year-old George Robinson, enjoyed an excellent record for his efforts to save the remnants of tribes slaughtered in the notorious Black Wars in Van Diemen's Land. He was also the Protectorate's only experienced bushman. But in Port Phillip, he seemed reluctant or unable to give firm leadership, becoming instead the district's first exponent of the art of building up an almost useless central bureaucracy, while his subordinates in the field were expected to do the dirty work.

Robinson's assistants, mostly idealistic Londoners, were left without rational instructions for months on end. Even when they were sent into the bush, not enough bullocks were made available to haul their drays. When one of them tried to set off into the wilderness with a single bullock, he became bogged in a deep creek and had to return. It took La Trobe more than a year to persuade parsimonious Sydney authorities to allow each Protector a six-bullock team.

Finally a more realistic policy was laid down. The Protectors were instructed to establish semi-permanent Aboriginal stations as 'places of resort' for natives in their respective districts:

James Dredge to the Goulburn River Station,
William Thomas to Melbourne and Western Port Stations,
E. S. Parker to Sunbury and Loddon River Stations,
C. W. Sievwright to the Western District Station.

Of these men, James Dredge was competent, but soon

resigned in disgust; his replacement, William Le Souef, always seemed terrified of Aboriginals, and later lost his job as a result of misappropriating public funds. William Thomas was given the almost impossible task of controlling restless tribes near Melbourne. Edward Parker was modestly successful, despite constant criticism from his chief. C. W. Sievwright was renowned for gambling, immorality, and neglect of his family.

Under the circumstances, it is amazing that any amelioration of racial conflict was achieved.

Goulburn River Station

James Dredge, a 44-year-old former Wesleyan schoolmaster, was the first to give way to the strains of life as an Aboriginal Protector, after only a few months in the bush.

Early in 1840 he, his wife and three small children, sat outside their bark hut on the Goulburn River (near today's Mitchelton), hoping to catch a cool breeze from the river. They had no supplies left, while 200 hungry blacks carrying weapons were camped all around them.

'The brawling lubras commence their clamour and rattle their sticks', Dredge scribbled in his diary. Many, he wrote, were noticeably infected with syphilis. Moving towards one disturbance, Dredge found a woman 'weltering in her blood', while 'her angry lord' brandished his iron tomahawk—one of white civilisation's gifts—over her head.

Isolated and despairing, Dredge soon sent in his resignation, and fled with his family back to Melbourne. There someone stole the very saddle from his horse.

Superintendent La Trobe wrote to the Governor in Sydney that Dredge was 'the best fitted of the Assistant Protectors', and 'the only one of the Department who showed a disregard to his private convenience.' La Trobe asked Dredge to remain on duty until a suitable replacement could be found.

In July 1840 the Chief Protector, George Robinson, recommended William Le Souef, an immigrant newly arrived from Kent, for the position. Robinson requested immediate confirmation, so that Le Souef could get to the Goulburn in time for the crop-planting season. Two months later La Trobe expressed 'wonder and disappointment' at finding Le Souef still wasting time in Melbourne.

Meanwhile, the NSW government in Sydney approved the appointment of experienced overseers to manage agricultural operations at the Aboriginal Stations. Gipps cautioned that the establishment of these homesteads must not prevent Protectors from 'itinerating amongst the Tribes.' George Bertram won the appointment as overseer at Goulburn River Station, at £100 a year, plus a shilling per day for rations. In September 1840 he began the attempt to train local blacks in the arts of husbandry.

Le Souef finally ventured to the Station late that year, but was never able to win the natives' trust. A servant visiting Melbourne told Dredge that 'Le Souef is like a madman, as he is so afraid of the natives and keeps one of his men continually on guard to prevent the natives coming too close to his tent.' After one incident, Le Souef was alleged to have given blacksmith Michael Lynis a pistol 'and told him to shoot any black that molested him'.

After only a few weeks at Goulburn, Le Souef resigned, asking La Trobe to appoint him as a police magistrate instead. When this was refused, he agreed to remain as Protector.

At the end of April 1841 Le Souef reported that the 170 blacks living on the station were working hard, hoeing the ground and planting potatoes; this gave them 'good appetites', making increased rations a necessity. The station had now been laid out in a regular pattern. Charles Street, thirty feet wide, contained 'three excellent roomy huts' for the overseer, a constable, and convict servants. George Street contained three smaller huts for natives, but many more such shelters were needed. Le Souef even prepared a plan for development of a complete Aboriginal township, bordered by Charles, Sophia, Louis Philippe and Victoria Streets. The town, he slyly suggested, should be called 'La Trobe'.

Rebellious blacks were another matter. Le Souef reported in horror that on 29 July one of his 'tame' natives had been killed by two wild blacks, Larry and Charley, 'in order that they might get his [kidney] fat, which was torn out of him before he was actually dead.' Several explanations were given for the common practice of extracting an enemy's kidney fat. One was that if even a small piece were taken, the opponent had no chance of survival. Another belief was that if the fat were eaten the enemy's physical strength would be absorbed by the victor.

On one occasion an Aboriginal became convinced that an enemy had stolen his kidney fat, even though there was no mark on his body. He became extremely weak, and scarcely able to move. The cangkuar (native 'doctor') was summoned. At night, as the tribal elders formed a tight circle around a smouldering fire, the 'doctor' purported to 'fly' to a great distance. On his 'return', the old men chanted in unison, 'Come, bring back the kidney-fat—make haste.' The doctor rubbed the dying man violently, then announced the cure was complete. The whole camp burst into shouts of joy, and the man quickly returned to full health.

Progress continued on the Aboriginal Station. By the spring of 1841, 400 trees had been grubbed out, and 286 perches of temporary fencing erected. Planting included 53 acres of potatoes, nearly 4 acres of wheat, 2 acres of barley and oats, and a quarter acre of maize.

By now the health problems of Goulburn River blacks were desperate. Venereal disease spread rapidly among them and the whites, circulating freely between lubras, their husbands, white stockmen and mounted police. Peter Snodgrass of 'Doogallook' run wrote to La Trobe requesting action. Within a month La Trobe appointed Dr William Baylie as Resident Medical Officer, at £200 a year, plus an allowance of 2s. 6d. per day when called to treat patients at distant homesteads.

Dr Baylie reported that a great number of the Goulburn River Station's residents were suffering from ailments 'of the most painful character'. In the fashion of the day, he treated many cases of colic with purgatives; skin eruptions and granulations were cleaned up with caustic solutions. The skull of Charley's wife had been laid bare 'from blows given her by her husband'. Other blacks, both men and women, suffered 'sloughing of the parts about the organs of generation': some 'could hardly crawl about'. Dr Baylie claimed 'great success' in countering the effects of syphilis and gonorrhoea. The Aboriginals, he wrote, submitted quietly 'even to the most powerful treatment', such as the free use of mercury and caustic. These were not permanent cures, but doctors of the day did not admit it.

Six months after his appointment, Dr Baylie complained that his salary was too low for the arduous duties involved. Acting on a procedure recommended by Gipps, La Trobe promptly dismissed Baylie, appointing Dr Neil Campbell to take medical charge of both the Goulburn and Loddon River Stations, at a salary of only £120 a year. The change also meant the loss of Mrs Masters, a governess with Dr Baylie's family, who had taken it upon herself to teach sewing and dressmaking to the younger black girls.

A little while after these moves, it was discovered that overseer George Bertram had been profiting personally from the sale of possum skins collected by station blacks. George Gilbert, a constable in the convict-manned Border Police, deposed that, during Le Souef's absences, Bertram gave government flour to the natives in exchange for a large number of possum skins and cloaks. He then sold the goods to a Constable Purcell for £6. Bertram was dismissed after the enquiry.

Late in 1842 a Goulburn River 'chief' named Billy Hamilton, who had been released from Melbourne Gaol after Major Samuel Lettsom's roundup of warring blacks (chapter 2), returned to his tribal area. Gaol experience had done Billy Hamilton no good. After his return to the Goulburn, Le Souef complained, the black leader caused 'much trouble' in the district. He 'repeatedly incited the natives to acts of violence'. A shepherd named Peter Cummins was killed on the Goulburn in December 1842, possibly by Billy Hamilton, but few clues to the circumstances of this murder were ever found.

On the evening of 18 December 1842 Le Souef heard uproar in the native camp. When he ran out, Billy Hamilton fired a musket. Taking the doctor, overseer and constable with him, Le Souef demanded that Billy Hamilton give up the weapon. The native refused, was handcuffed after a violent struggle, and charged with attempted murder. Muskets were also removed from two other natives.

Superindendent La Trobe treated the affair with surprising lightness, writing later that Billy Hamilton was 'one of the most intelligent' blacks he had ever met, spoke good English, and often acted like a European. He felt that the native had merely played on Le Souef's 'nervous and anxious temperament' in order to 'amuse himself'. The result was that in February 1843 Billy Hamilton was bound over to keep the peace, and released after nearly three months' remand in gaol.

Melbourne and Western Port Stations

William Thomas, a 46-year-old former London schoolmaster, early in 1839 was made responsible for Aboriginals living along the still-forested Yarra bank near Melbourne.

A few months later Thomas set up his first permanent station near Arthur's Seat on the Mornington Peninsula. Here his wife Susannah dispensed medicines, when not suffering her frequent bouts of illness; and his eldest daughter showed tribeswomen how to sew dresses and make straw hats.

Thomas reported in January 1840 that he had gathered together about ninety blacks, who were camped in twenty-three mia-mias along a series of waterholes called Tubba-rubbabel. But when his cart arrived from Melbourne without rations, said Thomas, the Aboriginals felt 'deceived', and would not work at establishing a homestead. Thomas scarcely mentioned the semi-starvation suffered by his own family. In February the blacks moved to Tuerong, where an Aboriginal child was born. During that summer, food was hard to find.

The elders called a council, and agreed to divide into six smaller groups to scour the country from Mount Martha to Cape Schanck.

Following the instructions of Chief Protector Robinson, Thomas and his convict bullock-driver James Davis accompanied the largest party. 'I cannot describe to you Sir my feelings and the unpleasantness I have to endure,' Thomas wrote to Robinson, 'travelling with these people without supplies.' The blacks led the two starving white men 'through parts almost impassable for man or beast—My bullocks have been three times nearly smothered—Our yokes broken &c.' Near Robert Jamieson's run the infant born at Tuerong died. After struggling across four Western Port rivers, Thomas gave up and headed for Melbourne, where he was promptly told to return to his Station.

By the middle of 1840 Thomas had gained a fair command of the Mornington Peninsula dialect, and could communicate some European ideas to the natives. He tried to impress on their minds that 'should they meet any wild blackfellows (as they term strangers) not to kill them'.

Alas—when the last twenty men returned from their wanderings to the camp at Arthur's Seat, and were cross-examined by Thomas in their own language, they confessed tearfully that they had killed nine Gippsland blacks—one man, two lubras and six boys. They had eaten the kidney fat and flesh from thighs and arms to keep themselves alive. Two Gippsland children were cut into quarters and carried to eat during the trip home.

Thomas pressed on with plans for a permanent station where, he hoped, his blacks might be brought to a state of grace.

In June 1840, after much tribal consultation, the natives took Thomas to an isolated spot which they called 'Kullurk', on the western shores of Western Port Bay. (Today it is known as 'Coolart', a former squatter's homestead converted into a government-owned bird sanctuary and tourist attraction.) Thomas agreed that the swampy land, with patches of arable soil, would make a good Aboriginal Station. His recommendation was rejected.

During August Thomas's blacks trekked back to the Yarra River, camping on a hilly section of E. A. Walpole's run, 'Callitini' (part of today's Botanic Gardens). Robinson 'remonstrated with them on the impropriety of their coming without permission.' He instructed Thomas to remove them further up the Yarra to 'a lagoon called Bolin' (today's Bulleen). Thomas rejected this as a permanent site, because it was too close to white settlement at Heidelberg, and lacked game.

Robinson himself made an arduous journey along the Upper Yarra, 'having on several occasions had to travel without food, and at night to lay down without covering or fire.' He found several possible sites for a more distant station, where wild life was still abundant.

On Robinson's return, he was told that the natives had already agreed upon a site at Narre Warren, then a sheep run (between today's Dandenong and Beaconsfield). With La Trobe's approval, squatters were evicted from a five-mile radius of the site. Within a month Thomas took his family to Narre Warren, and began farming operations in a rather haphazard way.

More natives slowly gathered. In November 1840 Superintendent La Trobe authorised a special 1000 lbs flour ration, to be doled out only to blacks who proved their worth by attending Sabbath services.

White labourers, working under Thomas's direction, ran up five huts from the unsatisfactory scrub timber in the neighborhood. All the huts were mud-plastered and covered with bark, except the overseer's hut, which was thatched with grass.

Disaster struck just before Christmas 1840. Thomas complained to Police Magistrate James Simpson about the insolent behaviour of his two convict servants, James Davis and James Ross. Before constables could arrive to arrest them, the convicts persuaded 120 blacks under their leader Billibellary to abscond with them into the bush. Thomas was left with only three decrepit natives on the entire Station.

This mass desertion followed closely on Major Samuel Lettsom's brutal treatment of blacks in Melbourne. Thomas himself thought the vanished blacks 'expected had they remained that they would all have been killed' when the police arrived.

That summer about twenty of the missing blacks trickled back to Narre Warren, begging for rations. As soon as their wasted flesh had returned to normal, they announced their intention of returning to the bush. La Trobe instructed Thomas and schoolmaster James Wilson to accompany the blacks into the wilderness. Daily rations were then to be issued only to those who returned to the permanent Station. 'Let the rest learn', wrote La Trobe, 'that by leaving their district they forsake their comforts and advantages.' But by June 1841 there was 'not one black left' on the Station.

Some natives went to Thomas Ruffy's Cranbourne Inn. There, for some reason unknown, on 7 June they speared a young native boy named Little Jimmy. The innkeeper heard the boy's mother 'crying very much', and came out to find the lad with 'a dreadful wound' in his ribs—so bad that 'the fat was hanging out.' Henry Worth, staying at the inn, bound up the wound with adhesive plaster. That night someone removed the plaster, and next day the boy was dead.

The murderer was possibly a black man named Kurboro, who had spent much of the afternoon of 7 June beating his two lubras. The dead boy was his nephew. No white eyewitness evidence of the murder was available: under existing law no legal action could be taken.

As winter set in, many lubras and their children, and a few men, emerged from the bush to beg for food at Narre Warren. Thomas granted their request, on condition that the children attend school and the men work on the farm. By August forty boys and girls were at school each day, where Mrs Thomas entertained 'great hopes of the female children'. The men, meanwhile, built ninety yards of three-railed fencing around the wheat paddock.

The farm overseer, Daniel Taylor, was the next to cause trouble. Schoolmaster James Wilson reported in September 1841 that, during the Protector's absence, Taylor had become drunk in Melbourne and stayed that way for a week. He was also prone to use 'abusive and blasphemous language', which had 'a most bainful influence upon the minds of the poor blacks.' An inquiry by Thomas purported to clear Taylor, but a short time later the overseer absconded at night and was never seen again.

Drunkenness also began to spread among the station blacks. 'Some time back the generality of blacks feared taking liquors', Thomas wrote. 'I have known them after being pressed upon to drink and becoming intoxicated keep from the settlement for 3 & 4 days, fearing as they used to term it "the white man's bitters," but not so now.'

During the spring of 1841 an infectious fever, probably typhoid, ran through the school, killing two children and affecting many others. Thomas said the sickness was 'superstitiously attributed to their attending school', but in fact its spread may have been due to the unhygienic white practice of using open communal latrines and failing to wash before handling food. La Trobe's reaction was to authorise employment of a bush carpenter to build a 12 ft by 21 ft slab hospital, and to employ a 'medical dispenser' named Henry Jones.

The blacks followed their traditional custom of leaving an area where deaths had occurred. They took refuge on the Reverend James Clow's adjoining sheep run. Dispenser Jones followed them there, treating forty-six blacks for a variety of complaints, including a good deal of diarrhoea and other bowel problems. One tribal leader, the 40-year-old rebel Billibellary, was treated for catarrh. His nephew Beruke (Gellibrand) was one of many described as suffering from 'pseudo-syphilis'.

Most natives eventually returned to the Protectorate Station. During 1842 two acres of potatoes and an acre of melons and pumpkins were planted, but little else was achieved.

Henry Dana, commandant of the new force of Native

Police recruited among fit young Aboriginals, reported in February 1842 that Dandenong Creek had dried up, causing a dangerous shortage of drinking water. He shifted his men from the nearby Police Paddock to permanent water on Merri Creek, north of Melbourne, recommending that Thomas do the same. The Protector retorted that his blacks had dug three water holes near the station, and were now self-sufficient. Nevertheless, most of the natives accompanied the Native Police to Merri Creek.

Further criticism of the Narre Warren site followed. In August Governor Gipps wrote that it appeared 'very doubtful whether any Aboriginal Station should be established so near to Melbourne.' Even if continued, he said, expenditure should be drastically reduced.

Thomas strongly defended the station. 'If Narre Warren is broken up,' he wrote, 'where are the Aborigines of that District to go to?' He pointed out that 'They are still an injured people: their lands are disposed of without reference to the Protectorate.' More money had been raised by the sale of land in the Melbourne district 'than the whole of the remainder of Australia Felix.' Yet 'the blacks of the Yarra, Western Port and Port Phillip are the only tribes who have not suffered their land to be stain'd with white man's blood: they have peaceably given way to our intrusion', said Thomas.

The debate was pointless. Since most of the blacks preferred other places, Thomas's arguments were fruitless. In 1843–44 the Narre Warren site was handed over completely to the returning Native Police. Thomas, himself, was forced to follow his charges to Merri Creek.

Sunbury and Loddon River Stations

Edward Parker, a 37-year-old printer and Methodist preacher from London, established his first Aboriginal Station in a wattle-and-daub hut at Jackson's Creek, Sunbury, in 1839. He lived there with his wife Mary and their young family, and rode all over the locality to gather information and settle tribal disputes.

Parker did not enjoy Robinson's confidence. The Chief Protector called his subordinate 'very indolent and loitering; a gossip, but little good to the blacks and no energy . . . little good will be done by him.' Yet there is evidence that Parker soon knew at least as much about his charges as did Robinson. Parker's report of April 1840 convincingly laid out the real basis of the Aboriginal problem: 'the rapid occupation of the entire country by settlers, and the consequent attempts made to deprive the Aborigines of the natural products of the country, and even to exclude them from their native soil.'

Robinson continued to snipe at Parker, calling his Sunbury site 'the worst that could have been selected . . . thickly surrounded by settlers.' Early in 1840 the two Protectors rode around much of the area north-east of Gisborne. Finally they selected a fresh site on Far or Fourteen-Mile Creek (now Bet Bet Creek), alongside Henry Dutton and Henry Darlot's run (north-west of today's Maryborough).

Governor Gipps approved the site in April. An inner reserve of one square mile was allowed for the Station, with the Protector's homestead to be kept 'especially remote from the great lines of communication'. An 'outer reserve' of five miles radius was also allowed as hunting grounds, but as the blacks succeeded in taking up agriculture, this was gradually to be diminished.

About fifty local Aboriginals visited Parker's new camp. 'They appear to welcome my arrival in their country with great warmth,' he wrote, 'saluting me as "Marmingorak" or Father.' By December their numbers had increased to ninety adults and eighty children. All had been ordered by the squatters 'away from places where they have been accustomed most frequently to look for food.'

Establishment of Parker's new station brought protests from nearby settlers, who agreed that the Aboriginals should be helped, but not at white men's expense. Henry Darlot, for instance, tried to persuade Parker to move, at the same time as his men were enticing native women to their huts. One of his convict shepherds, Patrick Clark, was notorious among the tribes under the nickname 'Fuckemall'.

Early in February 1841 two blacks named Abraham and Tommy were wounded by gunfire. Tommy later died, and his body was found wrapped in an opossum cloak, eight feet up in a hollow tree. Parker committed five convict shepherds for trial: Edward Collins, Robert Morrison, John Remington, William Martin and William Jenkins. All were released in May due to lack of independent white evidence. 'There is no chance of justice being obtained,' Parker concluded bitterly. Meanwhile, however, two relatives of the dead man went roaming the country seeking revenge. On the property of David and Ebenezer Oliphant near the Pyrenees mountains they found an isolated shepherd, speared him to death, and robbed his hut.

Parker had concluded during the summer of 1841 that the site on Bet Bet Creek was not suitable for intensive agriculture. The alluvial areas, which looked so promising in spring, dried up completely in January's heat.

La Trobe sent Crown Commissioner Powlett and Chief Protector Robinson to investigate. They agreed that Parker's station should be shifted to Jim Crow Hill, one of A. F. Mollison's out-stations on the upper reaches of the Loddon River (near today's town of Franklinford). Powlett instructed Mollison to move his sheep from a five-mile radius of Jim Crow.

Once this new camp was established, Parker's first task was to treat diseases rampant among the Loddon tribes. He caused a sensation in October 1841 when the young son of a tribal leader fell ill with inflammation of the lungs. Normally the boy would have been treated by the cangkuar, who according to legend gained his power by being changed, while sleeping, into a swan, flying to an immense distance, and there receiving extraordinary gifts of healing. The tribal women 'clamorously demanded' that their 'doctor' should 'take the evil' out of the boy. This was to be achieved by massaging 'as if to bring the evil to a given point, and then pretending to take it away in his hands, and either bury it in the ground, or put it on a stone, and cause it to "fly away".'

Parker decided to 'show the people the utter absurdity of their notions.' He challenged the doctor to cure the boy immediately, or be shown up as 'a great deceiver'. The doctor paused a few minutes, then slunk away. Parker tried white man's magic: he bled the boy, and dosed him with tartarised antimony. Fortunately the patient 'so far recovered in a few days as to be able to run about.'

With other cases, using only a few popular medical works to guide him, Parker was forced to appeal for professional assistance. The main problem was 'the rapid and extensive spread of syphilitic infections' (called 'wombi' by the natives), owing to constant promiscuous intercourse between Dutton and Darlot's men and the native women. One shepherd had recently died from 'this filthy disease'. More than half the black women were infected. Perhaps there was some kind of rough justice in the fact that a short time later, 'the younger Mr Darlot' and 'a person named Elliman' presented themselves to Parker for treatment, both being 'severely afflicted with syphilis'.

Parker found himself with 'upwards of 100' patients, including cases of dysentery and ophthalmia. Dr Henry Baylie, sent to report on Loddon River, agreed that the blacks were in 'a most painful condition', but were suffering mainly from 'excrescence, improperly called venereal by the whites, a disease almost peculiar to themselves, and gonorrhoea.'

Richard Tobin was appointed as permanent medical dispenser at Loddon River at three shillings a day. Dr Baylie left him instructions on how to treat the sick. Before breakfast he should parade those able to walk, enter details on the medical register, and apply external or internal medicines. 'Let your treatment be simple,' warned Baylie, 'avoiding bleeding or the use of calomel [mercurous chloride, a purgative] except in cases of necessity.' Then he should attempt to treat the bedridden. Babies were still being born to infected mothers, added Baylie, but within a few days 'the poor children become covered with a syphilitic eruption, and speedily perish.'

La Trobe himself visited Loddon River Station in September 1841. He granted £55 for erection of buildings, and allotted two convicts to assist overseer William Beasley in commencing farming operations. Parker found their conduct excellent. On Christmas Day a double ration of meat and sugar was authorised for all residents.

By 1842 quite a village had arisen. It comprised the Protector's cottage of six rooms with detached kitchen, the overseer's four-room cottage, a constable's large hut used as a temporary schoolroom, smaller huts for convict labourers, a smithy, and a storeroom. Native attendances at the Station often totalled well over one hundred men, women and children.

In March 1842 La Trobe gave Parker the task of investigating the spearing to death of Alexander Moffatt Allan, a 26-year-old squatter on the Loddon River. Parker replied that on the day of the murder, 13 March, practically all Loddon blacks were attending divine service at the station. He had no doubt that Allan had been killed by aggressive Mallee (Mallegoondeet) tribesmen from the arid north. Parker was later told by friendly blacks that two men named Kolkoulburrar and Terimburum had speared Allan, but he could not discover 'a particle of evidence' admissable in court.

During the winter of 1842 whites and blacks all worked hard on completing a substantial 1100 square foot timber church, which could also be used as a schoolroom. Several black youths learned how to split timber into slabs, demonstrating 'some eagerness to work'. Parker paid them with tokens supplied by the Chief Protector as a form of coinage, which could be exchanged at the store for food. The use of native labour was not achieved without opposition. Two older blacks told Parker he was 'stealing their children, by taking them away to live in huts, and work, and "read in book" like white fellows.' They invited the Protector to return to 'woorer woorer' (up in the sky) whence he had come.

Parker suffered a heavy blow in October when his wife Mary died. (Of that heroic woman we know little, except that during the voyage to Australia she had been pursued, if not seduced, by Protector Sievwright.) She had just presented Parker with their first daughter to add to their quiver-full of six healthy sons. The young family urgently needed a mother: in December 1843 Parker married Hannah Edwards of Richmond, by whom he had several more children.

Western District Stations

Charles Sievwright, a 38-year-old former army officer of mixed reputation, was posted as Protector to the Western District in 1839. At first he established headquarters at Geelong, but from there was unable to control or even investigate many horrific events occurring at distant points in the district.

In mid-July 1840 a small group of natives attacked John Thomson's 'Keilambete' run north of Terang. They killed a shepherd named Thomas Hayes, and badly wounded another. Reporting the affray to Chief Protector Robinson, Sievwright proposed that he should evict the squatter and form an Aboriginal Station on the shores of salty Lake Keilambete.

Robinson agreed, but neglected to seek higher approval. Sievwright moved to the lake with stores and friendly natives in March 1841. Squatter Thomson protested to Superintendent La Trobe, who told Robinson that approval from himself, the Governor and Crown Commissioner was essential. 'Mr Sievwright's conduct cannot be justified', wrote La Trobe. Yet when Robinson arrived on tour, he allowed Sievwright to remain. The Chief Protector noted in passing that 'The native women offered their persons to my men. They are a lascivious lot.'

Thomson complained to La Trobe that the Protector's men continued 'to fall [sic] the trees close to my hut, plough the ground in front of my door, and to collect natives about my establishment without any supplies.' The result was constant slaughter of sheep and 'minor pilferings every day'.

La Trobe wrote direct to Sievwright with peremptory instructions to move from 'Keilambete'. Sievwright grudgingly shifted three miles from the homestead. Here his group of blacks ate government rations by day, and mischievously speared stock by night, according to local squatters.

In August 1841 Captain James Webster, JP, of nearby Mount Shadwell, complained of 'dreadful depredations'. Webster noted in a protest to La Trobe that 'up to the time that the Protector of Aborigines settled in the neighborhood, I never lost a sheep.' Now they were being slaughtered in hundreds.

Sievwright was finally persuaded to move his establishment to Mount Rouse, a site (just south-east of today's Penshurst) selected by Robinson in February 1842. Mount Rouse was 'the richest and best fattening run in a rich fattening district', according to Thomas Browne, who would later describe events under the pseudonym of 'Rolf Boldrewood'.

The move meant the eviction of squatter John Cox, pioneer storekeeper at Port Fairy. Wrote Foster Fyans:

> As Commissioner of Crown Lands, I was compelled to order one of my best friends in life off. He remonstrated with me on the hardship. However, he could not blame me; I had to act according to my instructions from Government.

For years Cox fought for recompense. When forced to move to Mount Napier, he had left behind a slab hut with hinged doors and windows, a log stockyard, and more than 2000 cut posts and rails, which he valued at £500.

Later in the decade, when it seemed likely that Mount Rouse Aboriginal Station would be closed, Cox unsuccessfully demanded its return to him.

The desire of some white men to cohabit with black women continued to inflame racial relations throughout the 1840s.

Protector Sievwright reported in 1842 that one of his convict servants, James Evans, had contracted venereal disease 'from improper connection with native women' at the Aboriginal Station. The following year, Dr Watton wrote from Mount Rouse requesting urgent supplies of 'mercurial pills' to help combat syphilis on the station.

In the virtual absence of white women, even respectable settlers sometimes turned to tribeswomen for their sexual needs. Charles M. Gray, son of a major in the Royal Marines, settled in 1840 on 'Nareeb Nareeb', near Darlington. A young lubra claimed him as her dead husband come back to life in the guise of a white man. Over the years she presented him with several half-caste piccaninnies.

Serious allegations against Sievwright's moral character began to concern the authorities early in his career as a Protector.

In June 1839 Mrs Christina Sievwright and her eldest daughter Frances Anna, 17, complained in writing to Police Magistrate William Lonsdale that the father had attempted to seduce the daughter. While at Geelong, Mrs Sievwright insisted on living with the daughter in a separate tent, where Sievwright left them 'in want of many necessaries of life both in food and clothing.'

The two women borrowed a small sum from a convict servant, fled to Melbourne, and threw themselves on the government's mercy. The Lonsdale family took them in: they learned 'many things which were most disreputable and abominable.'

Lonsdale summoned Sievwright to Melbourne. The Protector refused to attend, claiming falsely that one of his other six children was sick.

After a few days Christina and Frances agreed to return to Geelong. Local Police Magistrate Foster Fyans visited them in their 'very dirty and miserable tent'. With solicitor William Meek, he attempted to reunite the family. Sievwright's reaction was to call his wife 'an old maniac woman', and to flourish unpaid bills in her face. He said he would agree to a legal separation and pay an allowance only if she left all the children behind.

'You vile creature,' screamed his wife, 'you well know your conduct, and the indecent liberties which you have taken with my poor child.'

Fyans immediately left the tent, 'never wishing to see such people again.' Solicitor Meek thought 'the meanest laborer must have felt ashamed and disgraced to have seen his wife in such a state of poverty and wretchedness, whilst he himself was revelling in comforts and luxuries.'

A slight improvement in the family's circumstances came in 1841, when they moved to Fyansford, into a bare hut which did not even possess a fireplace.

In an undated letter to Foster Fyans, probably written in August 1842, Mrs Sievwright said she had 'attempted to submit quietly to all Mr Sievwright's degrading and coercive treatment', but that his conduct had again become unbearably tyrannical.

In a further confidential despatch early in August 1842, La Trobe renewed charges that Sievwright had conducted 'an improper intercourse' with Protector Parker's wife Mary during the voyage to Melbourne four years earlier. Full details of this allegation did not become available until years after Mrs Parker's death, when Sievwright's legal tactics made it necessary for La Trobe to obtain further evidence from Parker.

Parker replied that his first wife had once known only the secluded life of a clergyman's daughter. During the voyage, Sievwright had confided in her that his own wife's 'loose conduct' made it impossible for him to love her. He had then 'endeavoured by every means in his power to effect her [Mrs Parker's] seduction.' When that failed, Sievwright threatened to kill Parker if she told him what had occurred. Not until their landing in Melbourne did the terrorised Mrs Parker inform her husband.

Parker wrote to Sievwright forbidding all future contact. Sievwright wrote back maliciously threatening 'public exposure'. That seemed to be the end of the matter in 1839.

Suddenly, in September 1842, the whole situation turned upside-down. Both Mrs Sievwright and her daughter Frances, now living again with Sievwright, wrote to La Trobe withdrawing all their earlier allegations. These letters, formal in character, bore indications of being dictated by Sievwright himself. Mrs Sievwright said she was aware of her husband's friendship with Mrs Parker, and that it was 'not improper'. As regards the 'foulest accusations' (of incest), Sievwright was 'wholly incapable' of such debasement. The daughter's letter, dictated on the same day, said she was prepared to deny on oath these 'strange and incomprehensible charges'.

But the stream of their allegations, reported La Trobe to Gipps, 'cast an air of ridicule' over Sievwright's activities as Protector and Magistrate. Gipps felt he had no alternative but to dismiss Sievwright. La Trobe passed the Governor's instructions to Robinson, who agreed the reports were 'well founded' (even though he had never taken any action over them).

When the documents reached England, Lord Stanley replied that he wanted the case hushed up, 'as it is not of a character fit for public investigation'. The further actions of Sievwright himself made that impossible. He fought against his dismissal, both publicly and privately, for several years, submitting 'indignant denial' of the truth of each and all of the charges.

Again he returned temporarily to live with his family, paying the tradesman's bills so that they at least had enough to eat.

When that ploy failed, Sievwright yet again abandoned his wife and children. They tried to get work, but although mother and daughter were 'highly accomplished' in French and music, no one seemed willing to employ them. In May 1843 Geelong Police Magistrate Nicholas Fenwick found the family 'in the greatest state of destitution'—'how they manage to get their daily bread nobody can tell, and their children are in rags.'

Following an appeal to Sydney, Gipps replied that he was unable to grant any official aid. Privately he sent £10 from his own pocket to the family, instructing La Trobe that they must not know 'whence it comes'. In addition, ten shillings a week was deducted from Sievwright's account and sent direct to Mrs Sievwright for twenty-four weeks. She wrote a heart-rending letter of thanks to La Trobe, begging him to 'understand my actions'.

By 1845 the whole family was apparently reconciled again, and had even obtained money from sources unknown. Later Sievwright set sail for England to lay his case before the Secretary of State. When Mrs Sievwright asked La Trobe for a written assurance that her husband's dismissal was not due to her evidence, La Trobe refused.

In 1847 Mrs Sievwright wrote again to La Trobe, saying she wished to purchase land in her husband's name, and inquiring about a possible remission due to her husband's former military service; La Trobe replied that this was outside his power.

In London Sievwright had no better luck; he blamed most of his problems on 'some secret enemy' and on Robinson's 'supineness'.

La Trobe's lengthy rejoinder of December 1847 traversed the whole case, concluding with his conviction that Sievwright 'lay under a moral disability which never could be removed.'

At the end of August 1842 La Trobe appointed Dr John Watton to take over Mount Rouse Station from Sievwright. 'Rolf Boldrewood' described the new Protector as 'good old Dr Watton, a genial, cultured English gentleman [who] lived a peaceful, patriarchal kind of life at Mount Rouse.'

Acheson French, visiting at the end of 1842, found that up to 200 natives were living there happily. Their 'erratic habits', he thought, could be overcome by more generous supplies of flour and rice. That was the simplistic reaction of even well-educated whites towards the race whose way of life they had so casually shattered.

2

ARMED ABORIGINALS LAUNCH GUERRILLA RAIDS ON WHITE SETTLERS

How did tribesmen get the guns? Who taught them to load powder and shot? As armed bands of Aboriginals launched vengeful raids against the white invaders, most settlers looked in vain for any effective remedies beyond direct retaliation.

Training of Aboriginals in the use of firearms apparently began when Melbourne merchants employed them to shoot lyre-birds, for the tail feathers which were to be exported. Some natives kept the muskets and ammunition, returning proudly to tribal areas to demonstrate their phenomenal power of being able to kill at a distance.

In July 1839 Chief Protector Robinson instructed his assistants to remove the weapons. That was easier said than done. A native with a gun in his hand felt at least equal to a white man. After wreaking vengeance on enemy tribes or Europeans, he could melt into the bush with ease and live off the land.

Reports of tribal slaughter began to reach Melbourne in 1839. According to Robinson, a group of Yarra musketeers, led by the Aboriginal heroes Derrimut and Billy Lonsdale, massacred numbers of the Lake Colac tribe. Nothing was ever proven or even investigated, for Robinson's strangely assorted crew of Protectors were too busy trying to establish stations which could care for any black refugees.

The next outbreak occurred early in 1840, when a large group of armed Melbourne blacks, led by Jackie Jackie, descended on the Upper Yarra property of James Anderson. The squatter accused the blacks of stealing potatoes from his paddock. 'Several of them stood up and seized their musquets', Anderson deposed. Shots were fired, and he 'heard the balls whiz past me into the scrub.'

Henry Gisborne, Commissioner of Crown Lands, rushed from Melbourne with a detachment of his newly recruited Border Police. On 15 January 1840 he reported to La Trobe that the marauders had moved upstream to the Ryrie brothers' run at Yering (opposite today's Yarra Glen).

Troopers and squatters enticed the natives to the Ryries' station by slaughtering a bullock. Three police crept up behind Jackie Jackie, seized and handcuffed him, and took him to the homestead. The other natives retreated to the bush to get their guns. A running battle with the troopers followed. In the confusion Jackie Jackie managed to free himself and escape.

Reporting the clash to Sydney, Superintendent La Trobe scoffed at suggestions that natives needed arms for protection against white settlers. The 'terror of the law', he thought, had surely taught 'patience and caution' to 'the scattered white population of every class'. La Trobe blamed the Aboriginal Protectors for not moving more energetically to seize guns from the tribes. He asked for a law to prohibit natives from handling firearms. This was passed by the NSW Legislative Council in August 1840.

The following month La Trobe advised his police magistrates that, under the new law, 'any constable or free person whatsoever' could take firearms from natives or half-castes, 'provided that no personal violence be used in so doing, further than may be absolutely necessary.' The only exceptions were cases in which JPs gave written permission for trusted Aboriginals to bear arms.

Meanwhile Jackie Jackie and his guerrilla group infiltrated the Goulburn River region and stirred the tribes there into rebellion.

Henry Monro, son of the Anatomy Professor at Edinburgh University, who had squatted on the Campaspe River and been severely wounded by a spear in 1839, reported to La Trobe late in January 1840 that Jackie Jackie's men were roving the countryside making violent threats. They had stripped one of his shepherds naked, stolen his warm clothes, threatened to kill and eat him, and driven away about 1500 sheep.

La Trobe despatched a force of Mounted Police to Monro's aid. Before they could get there, the squatter took the law into his own hands. On 25 January Monro set out on horseback with six other squatters, pursued a group of Aboriginals, and watched while two blacks were shot dead. Others were wounded, but escaped with the tribe.

Crown Prosecutor James Croke felt that the available evidence was 'of a very serious nature'. He wanted to charge Monro and the other six squatters* with murder, but no independent white eyewitnesses legally able to testify could be found.

The survivors of Jackie Jackie's band proceeded to Peter Snodgrass's run on Muddy Creek (now called Yea River). In March 1840 they sent word that they would kill Sam Dayton, one of Snodgrass's shepherds whom they particularly hated.

On 17 March a group of thirty men led by Jackie Jackie, Windberry, Puckemal, Mister John, William and Billy, trapped Sam Dayton and other whites in a hut. They 'pushed their guns at my breast and threw me on my back', Dayton deposed. The shepherd begged Windberry to protect him. The

---

* Identified only as Messrs Pollock, Arthur Lloyd, Hamilton, Carter, Brownfield and Murray.

black leader replied that he was 'no good', but persuaded the others to spare his life. The blacks contented themselves with stripping the hut of all possessions.

Snodgrass told La Trobe that his own life had also been threatened. 'My station is now in a dreadful state of confusion', he wrote. 'My men refuse to take the sheep out to feed.' He was sure that if the blacks' guns could be seized, they would 'again become quiet and tractable'.

La Trobe instructed Protectors Robinson and Dredge to hire horses, take two steady men from the Border Police, and ride up to 'tranquilize the district'.

Even if the Protectors could have retrieved the guns, they arrived too late. In May 1840 the guerrilla band reappeared on the Yarra River, several miles upstream from Melbourne. Armyne Bolden, a settler at 'Banyule' in Heidelberg, reported to La Trobe that more than two hundred blacks, armed with about thirty guns, were 'shooting in every direction', and threatening to burn down his huts.

By the time the regular Mounted Police rode up from Melbourne the blacks had again disappeared. They were tracked by several troopers, led by Lieutenant F. B. Russell. About forty miles upstream the blacks had concealed themselves in dense scrub by a ford. With muskets ready, they successfully ambushed the whites as they attempted to cross, wounding three and forcing them all to retreat.

La Trobe was at his wit's end. Protectors and police alike had failed him. The only solution he could envisage was to keep all Aboriginals away from townships. 'The time is come when the periodical visits of the blacks to Melbourne must be put a stop to at all hazards', he wrote to the Sydney authorities. Any civilising advantage they received was 'counterbalanced by the increase of disease and depravity among them.'

In August 1840 La Trobe instructed the Mounted Police to patrol the outskirts of Melbourne and prevent any Aboriginals from entering the town. Black women in particular must be stopped from sneaking in 'to purchase powder and shot.' Severe penalties were proposed for any shopkeeper who supplied them.

Under government instructions, Protector Thomas continued efforts to persuade even peaceful blacks to move from the Yarra, but found the task 'utterly impossible'. He rejected coercive measures as 'incompatible' with his original instructions, writing plaintively to Robinson: 'How has the Gold become dim!'

The main scene of action shifted to northern districts. On 25 August a group of Aboriginals, led by Woomdalla, Buckley and Tom, stole two guns and bedding from an out-station of the Stieglitz brothers, north of today's Ballan.

Later that day, the same group encountered two splitters named William Turner and Alexander Robb, working in the bush about five miles from John Campbell and Dr D. H. Wilsone's run 'Ingliston' (south-east of Ballan). The blacks demanded damper and tea. When refused, they grappled with the whites, running off only when one picked up a gun to fire.

Next day, 26 August, the same blacks appeared on Kenneth Clarke's Werribee River run. They stole a blanket, a greatcoat and a gun from a hutkeeper.

In mid-September the group appeared on C. F. Mackinnon's run. Now armed with five guns, they pursued a convict shepherd named James Rogers back to his head station. Returning later to his hut, Rogers found everything gone, including his 'moleskin trowsers, plush waistcoat, two shirts, and a new bedtick.'

As whites reacted with violence, blacks living at Protector Parker's camp at Sunbury warned that they too would 'by and bye take to the mountains, and try to drive the "white fellows" from their country'.

La Trobe's alarm at these developments echoed in Sydney. Governor Gipps despatched Major Lettsom of the 80th Regiment to Port Phillip with a strong contingent of soldiers and Mounted Police, bearing orders to arrest any blacks found carrying arms. La Trobe circulated a list of the most wanted men:

Jackie Jackie, a stout man with a mole on the left side of his nose, and a scar on his forehead; often wears a band. Windberry, alias Larry or Yarry, lame in one leg.

Merriman. Harlequin. Tom.

La Trobe cautioned Major Lettsom that, 'wherever the first fault may have been', the natives were becoming 'more and more decidedly hostile' and able to 'set our power almost at defiance.' But they had to be taught a lesson, 'for their own ultimate good'. Lettsom and his force of nearly sixty troopers should try to 'overawe' any opposition, arrest the ringleaders, and remove their guns without shedding blood.

Faced with these fine sentiments, Major Lettsom planned his moves shrewdly. First he neutralised the Protectors by demanding their co-operation as magistrates in 'facilitating the ends of justice'. His notion of justice was to take 'hostages from each tribe as guarantee for the behaviour of the whole.'

Protector Thomas replied angrily that his duty was 'as a Protector to the liberties of the Aborigines'. If he complied with Lettsom's demand, it could 'bring this fair Province into perhaps a far greater theatre of carnage.'

Major Lettsom awaited his opportunity. On a Saturday night, 10 October 1840, Goulburn blacks visiting Melbourne exhausted themselves in one of their regular corroborees with the Yarra tribe.

Very early on Sunday morning Lettsom's men surrounded the blacks' camp. First they bludgeoned or stabbed all the dogs. When Protector Parker arrived a little later, he reported: 'Great numbers of the dogs belonging to the Aborigines were lying about dead or miserably dying.'

The black leader, Windberry, heard the commotion, leapt up and grabbed his weapons. As he raised his waddy to club Lieutenant F. D. Vignolles, he was shot dead by Sergeant Denis Leary. Inquiring later into the circumstances, Protectors Robinson and Parker concluded that as Windberry was resisting arrest for a felony, 'his death must be regarded as a justifiable homicide'.

The remaining 300 or so blacks were rounded up at bayonet point in the early dawn light and marched into the township, the men shouting and groaning, women and children keening and weeping. As they milled around inside the gaol stockade, they cried to Parker: 'Are we going to be shot?—to be sent in a big ship to Sydney?'

Next day most Yarra Aboriginals were identified and released, but more than thirty visiting Goulburn blacks were locked into the basement of the newly erected Commissariat store. This did not yet have a door, so a strong timber palisade was nailed into place.

That night, 12 October, some of the Goulburn warriors dug a tunnel under the store's foundations, while others broke a hole in the palisade. James Rattenbury, Clerk of Works, who lived next door, heard a noise at 2 a.m.; he looked through his window, and saw several blacks escaping. He ran to alert the guards.

Constable William Hallard fired one shot after the escapers, then fired another shot through the gap in the palisade. Later it was found that his second shot had hit the black named Tom, who was still inside the store.

Corporal Samuel Jennings and two privates next arrived on the scene. Because of the confusion it was not clear exactly what happened, but when Dr Patrick Cussen came to examine Tom's body next morning, he found extensive fresh sabre wounds on the man's upper side. The soldiers denied that any sabres had been used.

Chief Protector Robinson came to the conclusion that Tom's death was 'unjustifiable and illegal'. La Trobe referred the question to Crown Prosecutor Croke. This officer felt he could not 'pronounce a decided opinion'. Everything depended on the extent of Major Lettsom's authority. If the natives had been 'illegally put into the store, they were guilty of no offence in endeavouring to escape'. There the matter seems to have rested forever, with no investigation of Lettsom's activities.

Major Lettsom returned to Sydney on 23 October reporting direct to the Governor. Gipps then warned La Trobe in a personal letter that 'utmost circumspection' would be needed in neutralising any reports sent home by the Protectors:

> Their representations we know in England will be credited (I do not mean by the Govt.—but by Persons perhaps more powerful than the Govt.) whilst the reports of all persons filling official stations here will be received with suspicion—or entirely disbelieved.

The blacks remaining in Melbourne Gaol were clamped in irons while attempts were made to gather evidence of their depredations on the Goulburn River. On 16 November the magistrates found no case against twenty men, but committed the remaining ten for trial. One fell ill with 'gaol fever', and died. All the Goulburn men still in gaol were found guilty of theft and sentenced to ten years' transportation. This involved shipping them to Sydney to serve their sentences with white 'lifers' on Cockatoo Island.

On 14 January 1841 the convicted blacks, still in irons, were placed on a barge to travel down the Yarra to the shipping point at Williamstown. 'At a signal,' wrote La Trobe, 'they jumped overboard ... eight of the nine disappeared under water, or in the thick tea-tree scrub lining the banks.' The ninth man, Turratt Mullin, was shot in the hand and recaptured.

Brought before Melbourne's first Supreme Court judge, J. W. Willis, the wounded man was set free on the ground that the earlier trial was invalid since the accused could not comprehend the proceedings. For the same reason, no immediate pursuit was made of the other escapers.

The blacks at large made their way through the bush back to the Ryries' station on the Upper Yarra, where their presence was reported by Protector Thomas. One native was suffering from a severe gunshot wound, but all had somehow freed themselves from their leg-irons. Because of Judge Willis's ruling, La Trobe instructed Crown Commissioner Powlett not to attempt to recapture them.

The Goulburn blacks could not forget nor forgive what had happened to them in Melbourne. 'Tame' natives on Parker's station warned him that the Goulburns were 'seeking to revenge themselves for the death of the men who were shot, by bringing the "myndie",* and practising the "wooreet"† upon all the black fellows who are in amity with the whites.'

Three months after their escape, the determined Goulburns again threw their tribal lands into uproar.

On 14 April 32-year-old Richard Grice, who had squatted at Mount Alexander, saw a group of armed blacks approaching his hut. As he ran for the door, three spears caught him—on the side of his head, his shoulder and back. A shepherd, John Shottley, followed him in; a spear had penetrated right through his arm. Another shepherd, John Ashurst, who had been wounded in three places, later reported that 1000 sheep had been slaughtered or stolen. In spite of their injuries the men managed to seize their guns, drive off the blacks, and recover some of the stock.

Later that month the same blacks attacked Henry Bennett's run on the Campaspe River, knocking out the eye of a shepherd named Dickens, and then killing him with seven spears.

Early in June 1841 a group of about sixty Goulburn River blacks took sheep from the run of George Benson, a squatter who professed Quaker beliefs. Benson and his men kept close watch, and on 3 June tried to arrest several blacks as they were crossing the river. A volley of spears flew from the far side. Benson's men shot one named Charley, wounding him in the left hip, and probably killed another, Coomurthegee, alias Mister White.

La Trobe referred the evidence to the Crown Prosecutor, whose opinion was that Benson was 'justified in firing in self-defence'.

---

* The destroying spirit, which took the form of a great snake. See also Smyth, *The Aborigines of Victoria* (1876), vol. 1, pp. 444-6.
† Death spell.

During November the rampaging Goulburn River blacks settled in at Arthur Sergeantson's run on the Plenty River. He fed them for three days, but then had to go to Melbourne on business. 'They immediately killed three imported sheep and one lamb', Sergeantson complained. 'Since then they have robbed three stations and attempted to spear Mr A. Kemmis's stockman.'

Even more worrying was that the blacks had now accumulated 'two dozen stand of fire arms'. La Trobe ordered Protector Thomas to seize the weapons and take the blacks into his camp. But they simply melted back into the bush, ready to fight another day.

In December a few of the Goulburn River natives appeared on Robert Whitehead's station near Heidelberg. That night they killed a friendly Adelaide black named Jemmy, slashing open his belly below the navel and extracting his kidney fat. At the back of the legs, above the knee joints, they removed only the skin.

The attackers fled. Full details of the attack were given to Protector Thomas by a native constable, Beruke.

Precise information on Major Lettsom's actions in Melbourne, which were the immediate cause of the subsequent events, never reached the authorities in London.

Happily unaware of the true situation, Secretary of State Lord Russell instructed Governor Gipps, in August 1841, simply

> to send an Assistant Protector to the Aborigines, and require them to deliver up for trial any one or more of their number who might be identified by a Settler, complaining of an attack or loss of property.
>
> Should they refuse to give up the offenders, they will then render themselves liable to such proceedings as those adopted by Major Lettsom . . .

It was beautiful, it was British, and it was totally unreal on the pastoral frontier.

3

FURTHER AFFRAYS
ON THE
NORTHERN RIVERS
IN 1840

North of Melbourne several rivers flow from high land to help feed the mighty Murray. These north-tending streams include the Campaspe, Goulburn, Broken and Ovens Rivers. They water some of Victoria's most fertile land—and they run close to the main routes from Melbourne to Sydney.

Ever since the frightful Faithfull massacre of 1838, when seven convict servants were speared to death on the Broken River near today's Benalla, government officers had closely watched events in this area. Establishment of military posts along the main road helped to reduce violence. In 1840, however, native attacks on white settlers again erupted.

Captain Charles Hutton, one of the original settlers on the Campaspe Plains, thought that the Campaspe warriors numbered only about forty able-bodied men. He added:

They were rather fine men, but very mischievous, and did much damage . . . No doubt, there was blame on both sides, and had the whites not been over-familiar with them, for the sole purpose of getting their women, many of the outrages then perpetrated might have been avoided.

In even franker vein, Hutton told Chief Protector Robin-son in January 1840 that

it was never intended that a few miserable savages were to have this fine country . . . the only way to govern the blacks was by fear . . . no good would be done with them until they are served as the Murray blacks are, one half destroyed.

So even an educated squatter like Hutton, able to see both sides of the question, had been converted into an apologist for racial murder.

Late in April two wood-splitters, Anthony Byrne and Jeremiah Martin, employed by Charles Cropper on 'Laceby' station on the King River (south of today's Wangaratta), returned to their hut after the day's work. They found all its contents had been stolen, and the convict hutkeeper Richard Thomson nowhere to be seen. The two splitters fled immediately to J. W. Chisholm's neighbouring station to get help. Next day a search party found the hutkeeper's body lying in a water hole. The body had been cut open to extract the kidney fat.

On 27 May a band of armed Aboriginals, led by Harlequin and Merriman, attacked 29-year-old Dr G. E. Mackay's run at Whorouly Creek (south of today's Beechworth). That day they speared two horses and robbed a shepherd's hut. Next morning they returned, tied another horse to a tree, and threw heavy sticks at it until it died. They besieged Dr Mackay's brother John at the head station, then found a hutkeeper who was said to have raped black women, hacking him to death with tomahawks.

The attackers drove off nearly 3000 head of cattle, killing about 200 as they travelled. Dr Mackay wrote:

The rest were recovered at such an expenditure of money and of personal energy, as have left me an invalid for life, and to this day comparatively a poor man . . . My demand for compensation was treated with contempt . . .

The same tribe continued to David Lindsay Waugh's station on the Devil's River, Delatite, killed two of his shepherds, and drove away his sheep. Waugh was ruined financially by the attack, and later tried unsuccessfully to sue the Crown for failure to protect him.

'Oh, for the good old days when the settlers could take the law in their own hands', sighed Alexander Hunter, another settler in the area. What frightful unknown deeds did that statement recall?

On 5 July natives attacked the station of Daniel Jennings and Dr George Playne on the Campaspe River, about thirty miles north of Mount Macedon. They began to drive a whole flock of sheep across the river. When shepherd Alexander McKenzie interfered, the blacks hacked him to death and tore out his entrails. He was said to be the third shepherd killed in this way on the station.

Late in October squatter James Watson reported that one of his shepherds had been murdered in the Mount Battery area (north-east of Mansfield). He suspected the group of Goulburn River blacks led by Harlequin and Merriman.

The tribe retreated into Watson and Hunter's mountain run, but was pursued by a party of Mounted Police, accompanied by Dr George Mackay and some of his stockmen. The whites 'scoured the whole of that immense country as though it were a small saucepan', Richard Howitt recalled. Passing through 48-year-old Reverend Joseph Docker's run, 'Bontherambo', in December, the police handcuffed and 'necktied' several local blacks to take them away for questioning.

Docker employed fourteen Aboriginals as the sole guardians of his 6000 sheep: he complained that if police continued such 'unnecessarily rough usage', he would have to abandon the experiment of using native labourers, even though he had found them 'excellent shepherds, faithful and honest'. Docker especially resented the arrest of Joe, an 'intelligent and well-behaved' young Ovens River black, by a drunken trooper and one of Mackay's stockmen. 'I dread the visits of the Police more than I should those of the wildest savages', wrote Docker. On the sole evidence of Mackay's stockman, Joe was necktied and dragged away on foot to Melbourne. Docker wrote to Robinson asking him to do what he could for Joe.

Meanwhile, the police had also captured eleven of the Goulburn River tribe, and brought them back to Dr Mackay's head station. All managed to escape at night.

John Mackay deposed that he had been sworn in as a special constable for the renewed pursuit. His group had located two of the absconders, Mickey and Larry, and tried to take them to the Broken River police barracks. En route they were attacked by a strong party of blacks. In the confusion Mickey tried to escape, whereupon John Mackay shot him dead.

At about the same time, another police party arrested the leaders, Harlequin and Merriman. They were chained around the neck, and 'in this manner had been compelled to walk or run by the side of the troopers' horses—and this in the hottest season of the year.' The group covered about 220 miles in seven days.

On arrival in Melbourne the two Aboriginals were thrown into gaol without committal proceedings. Two days later Harlequin died 'of violent fever'. No legal evidence existed against Merriman, and he was released.

Gipps instructed La Trobe in January 1841 to send Chief Protector Robinson to the district to make a first-hand investigation. One result was that early in February three more blacks taken at Dr Mackay's urging were released, 'there being no evidence against them'. These blacks were Larry, Simon, and Joe, the latter described by the Reverend Docker as 'a true and intimate friend of mine'.

Robinson outfitted each man with 'a suit of slops and a

blanket', and sent them back to their tribe.

When accounts of these proceedings reached London, Secretary of State Lord Stanley felt that the killing of Mickey 'from Mr Mackay's own account appears to have been utterly indefensible'. He insisted on a further investigation.

In Melbourne Crown Prosecutor James Croke pointed out that Mackay's own evidence was not admissible, as a man could not be allowed to incriminate himself for murder. Other first-hand European evidence was needed. Robinson, in his capacity as a magistrate, sought such evidence from John Keefe, one of George Faithfull's assigned servants. Keefe, however, deposed that Mickey had pulled John Mackay off his horse and held him under water in an attempt to drown him, before the settler managed to shoot him dead. Robinson added his opinion: that, in the circumstances, 'no proceedings with justice could be instituted against Mr Mackay.'

Croke's final word was that he did not consider Mackay had a satisfactory excuse 'to act with the precipitancy with which he seems to have acted.' But what white jury would convict? The matter remained unresolved forever.

4

RACIAL MURDERS

IN THE

WESTERN DISTRICT,

1840-41

As squatters moved rapidly to occupy the best of western grazing lands, confrontations with the Aboriginal population increased markedly. Many conflicts were never reported to the authorities. There seems no trace in the official records, for instance, of early affrays which horrified that strict Presbyterian, John G. Robertson of 'Wando Vale' (north-east of today's Casterton).

Robertson wrote in later years of a friendly Aboriginal named Yarra, who was persuaded to help identify a warrior who had speared a shepherd. When Yarra tried to run away, a wood-splitter shot him dead. Robertson continued:

After this there was a constant war kept up between the natives and the two stations—Bell's and Gibson's—and, I regret to say, a fearful loss of life to the poor natives by two young heartless vagabonds Gibson and Bell had as overseers when they left.

Gibson can be identified as Matthew Gibson, who leased 'Kenilworth' on the Wannon River in 1840–41. Bell was probably Edward Bell, an overlander of 1839, who later became La Trobe's private secretary, and denied any knowledge of trouble on his 'Englefield' station on the Glenelg River. No other information regarding affrays on their particular runs seems to have survived. Enough cases of outright murder can be established to show that taming of the land by white pioneers was an unmitigated disaster for Western District blacks.

One day in February 1840 a native named Woolangong was sitting in a shepherd's hut on John Henty's Glenelg River station. He was chatting quietly to the hutkeeper, William Manuel. In came a shepherd named Blood, who cried to the native, 'Come here you bugger or I'll shoot you.' Woolangong escaped through the doorway and ran for his life. Blood fired, hitting him in both legs. The hutkeeper took the wounded native by bullock cart to the Henty's house about a mile away, while Blood absconded from the station.

Woolangong's left leg turned gangrenous. John Henty called in a doctor, who said that only immediate amputation could save the man's life. Woolangong refused to submit to the operation, and died soon afterwards.

That same month Superintendent La Trobe visited Geelong. A mounted policeman rode in from the Western District and reported to him that five natives had been killed on the Winter brothers' run, 'Murndal', on the Wannon River. La Trobe ordered the nearest Aboriginal Protector, C. W. Sievwright, to investigate. The squatters told Sievwright that a party of natives had attacked their station. Only after five blacks were shot dead did the remainder retreat into the bush.

When Crown Prosecutor James Croke studied documents in the case, he concluded that 'the Messrs Winter make a strong case of homicide against themselves (on their own admission too).' The depositions were sent to the Attorney-General in Sydney; he promptly passed them back to Sievwright, claiming they were not complete enough to proceed. There the matter seems to have rested.

La Trobe complained at the end of 1840 that 'in no single instance has a settler been brought before a proper tribunal'.

When Chief Protector Robinson arrived at the Winters' station in June 1841, he found it was now 'a complete armoury of small arms'. In addition, they had mounted a large swivel gun in front of 'Murndal' homestead: 'intended, they say, to be used against the blacks if necessary.'

Early in March 1840 Aboriginals raided the Whyte brothers' run near Coleraine, taking more than 100 sheep. In retaliation, the Whytes and their men admitted, they killed more than thirty blacks in a two-hour battle. Protector Sievwright was sent to investigate. He was prevented from laying charges when Crown Prosecutor Croke gave his opinion that 'the natives were the aggressors', and that the white men had only used their guns in self-defence.

James Blair, Police Magistrate at Portland and a grazier on his own account, was informed of many such affrays during 1840. In later years his memory became curiously selective. 'Messrs Whyte Brothers were the only settlers I heard of being annoyed by the aborigines as early as 1840', Blair wrote in 1853. 'They . . . harassed them in every way—setting fire to the grass round them, throwing spears at their shepherds, and stealing their sheep.'

Another squatter, John G. Robertson of 'Wando Vale', was franker in his reminiscences. The natives on Whytes' run, he wrote, had taken shelter in a clump of tea-tree:

> Fifty-one men were killed, and the bones of the men and sheep lay mingled together bleaching in the sun at the Fighting Hills. It must have been a great relief to me and most of this part, for the females were mostly chased by men up the Glenelg, and the children followed them.

The sole male survivor of the massacre, a native named Lanky Bill, fled to Francis Henty's run, 'Merino Downs', on the Wannon River. Here he found a shepherd named George MacNamara alone in his hut, and 'clasped him in his arms'.

MacNamara shouted for assistance: two other convict servants, named Winnicott and Cagley, rushed to his rescue.
MacNamara then shot Lanky Bill dead. The shepherds
reported the incident to both Francis and Stephen Henty. The
brothers failed to advise Protector Sievwright, even though he
had interviewed both men on other matters about that time.
Before Sievwright discovered the facts, all three shepherds absconded from Francis Henty's run, and were never seen again.

Later that year 22-year-old Gloucestershire farmer W. J.
Purbrick arrived, and took over part of the Whytes' run,
naming it 'Koroite'.

Chief Protector Robinson happened to be in the area in
June 1841, and saw several natives weeping. An English-
speaking lubra told him she had escaped from 'Koroite', where
two other lubras and one boy (Mary, Kitty and Piccaninny
Jemmy) had been shot dead by half a dozen white employees.
Robinson reached the scene three days later, attempted to take
sworn evidence, but gave up. 'I felt indignation at this murder
by my countrymen,' he wrote, 'but could not act, as the
evidence of the blacks was not admissible.'

Once again for legalistic reasons a series of fearful crimes
went unpunished.

John G. Robertson added to his reminiscences that another
Glenelg River squatter, whom he failed to name, 'kept a harem
for himself and his men. The consequence was, he, like many
more, had to sell out. All the men and masters got fearfully diseased from these poor creatures.'

Robertson estimated that whites had shot more than 500
blacks in the district, but that those who were 'murderers of
these poor creatures' rarely survived as successful squatters. Did
he mean that God was just, and that retribution came to the
unjust in this world as well as the next?

The Wedge brothers' station near the Grange (today's Hamilton) was constantly attacked during 1840. Over several months
they lost hundreds of sheep and a horse.

On one occasion a group of natives tried to seize the storeroom, throwing thirty to forty spears at the whites. Charles Wedge fired at them with 'a small swivel gun loaded with musket balls', forcing a retreat.

In a later affray on Wedges' station during August 1840 five natives were killed. Charles Wedge wrote later that 'depredations did not cease till many lives were sacrificed, and, I may say, many thousands of sheep destroyed.'

Asked for his opinion, Crown Prosecutor Croke thought that the blacks 'ought, if possible, to be brought to punishment': 'Taking possession of a flock of sheep amounting to 1290 is no trifling offence.' As to the homicidal part of the case, he felt impelled to ask the Attorney-General in Sydney for his advice—which meant that nothing was ever done.

The same party of blacks which attacked the Wedges proceeded to Augustine Barton's station nearby, and began driving away his sheep. When the whites gathered all available men, horses and guns, the blacks 'placed themselves in battle array' and began hurling spears. In the skirmish which followed, 'several natives have been killed, and a great many wounded', Protector Sievwright reported.

Sievwright asked James Croke for guidance. The Crown Prosecutor replied that since 'hostilities were commenced by the natives', no case lay against the whites. From Sydney, Attorney-General Plunkett advised once again that the whites could not be prosecuted on the sole basis of their own sworn statements.

During a further battle on the Wedges' run, an employee named Edwards was thought to have been speared and carried off to be eaten. In August 1841, however, Edwards was seen leading the same group of natives across S. G. Henty's station near Portland. Apparently he had saved his life by agreeing to lead the blacks against the whites. Police Magistrate James Blair described Edwards as a runaway convict, but was unable to apprehend him. Nothing further seems to be known of his fate. We are left with the curious picture of a rogue white trying to use the blacks to win vengeance against his own race.

The Wedges' bookkeeper, Patrick Codd, was known to Crown Commissioner Foster Fyans as 'a very respectable gentleman'. Others claimed he was 'too free with black lubras', and had 'ill-used many of them'.

Following the series of attacks on the Wedges' station, Codd resigned and went to work for John Cox at Mount Rouse run (near today's Penshurst).

On 19 May 1840 Codd and the station superintendent, James Brock, were standing near their camp fire. Brock was blowing calls on his bugle. Eighteen natives appeared and asked for food, and Brock shared a large damper between them. A station worker named Patrick Rooney took some of the natives into the scrub to gather firewood in return for more food.

Suddenly the blacks attacked all three whites. Codd was hacked to death. Rooney was clubbed on the head, and his jaw and right arm broken. Brock received severe contusions, but managed to run to the hut and secure a loaded gun, scaring the natives away.

When Foster Fyans arrived on the scene, he found Codd's body 'dreadfully decomposed, almost torn to pieces by wild dogs.' The wounded man Rooney was 'a dreadful object'. Fyans and Brock went to work on him, 'cleaning the jaw well, removing all the broken bone and teeth, laying on strong plasters.' The stockman lived for three years, although barely able to talk.

Leader of the attack was said to be Roger—'a fine noble looking person, of great intelligence,' wrote Fyans, 'and only for his malpractices might have been a most useful man.'

Fyans pursued Roger intermittently for nearly two years. In April 1842 information came to him that the Aboriginal was lying low at Protector Sievwright's new Station on the Mount Rouse run.

At dawn on 20 April Fyans's troopers surrounded the huts. Fyans demanded that Roger be brought out. Sievwright replied, 'The man is innocent, and your apprehending him on the Station will destroy it.' Finally Sievwright agreed to send

Roger 'to Mr Burchett's for mutton in two hours', so he could be arrested away from the Aboriginal Station. Fyans agreed. Later that morning his troopers surrounded Roger's cart 'at full gallop'. Within a few seconds they 'had two pair of handcuffs on the savage'.

In a separate report Sievwright affirmed his belief in Roger's innocence. Other natives told him that at the time of Codd's murder, Roger 'was unable to move from a loathsome disease' (syphilis).

Brought to trial later in 1842, Roger was found guilty by a white jury in Melbourne. After sentencing the native to death 'on the clearest evidence', Judge Willis recommended that he should be hanged at Mount Rouse Station, as an example to others. La Trobe agreed with the principle, at first suggesting the execution should take place on the actual site of the murder. After talking to Chief Protector Robinson and the Reverend Benjamin Hurst, La Trobe withdrew his remarks.

La Trobe then wrote personally to Gipps stating that he did not wish to see Roger executed after all:

Even if Roger be the murderer of Mr. Codd—(a fact of which I cannot help feeling some doubt in spite of judge & jury)—I should hesitate in backing the implied recommendation of the judge that he should be executed, because I fear from what came to my knowledge in the P. [Portland] Bay dist. last year, that the murder of Mr. Codd, however lamentable, was far from being an unprovoked one. If my information was really to be relied on, Mr. Codd's conduct towards the natives had been criminal in the highest possible degree . . .

Gipps did not feel he could exercise the prerogative of mercy in this case. On 5 September, after a breakfast of mutton chops, Roger was hanged, to the cheers of white spectators in a boisterous public ceremony outside Melbourne Gaol. Residents walked away congratulating themselves that at last the barbarians of the bush had been taught a salutary lesson.

A couple of years later John Cox, original holder of the

run on which Patrick Codd was killed, told 'Rolf Boldrewood' how they had pursued some natives who had killed their sheep:

> It was the first time I had ever levelled a gun at my fellow man. I did so without regret or hesitation in this instance. I never remember having the feeling that I could not miss so strong in me—except in snipe shooting. I distinctly remember knocking over *three* blacks, two men and a boy, with one discharge of my double barrel. Sou'wester [a station black] had a good innings that day, which he thoroughly enjoyed. He fired right and left, raging like a demoniac. One huge black, wounded to death, hastened his own end by dragging out his entrails, meanwhile praising up the weapons of the white man as opposed to those of the black. Sou'wester cut short his death-song by blowing out his brains with the horse-pistol of the period.

Arthur Lloyd, a pioneer of the Colac district, returned from Geelong on 21 August 1840 to find that, during his absence, natives had driven about 100 sheep off his station.

Lloyd heard that Peter Manifold had lost nearly as much stock. Joining forces, the squatters pursued the natives, and rode down on a group of forty or fifty. Lloyd told Geelong Police Court: 'They presented their spears and showed signs of resistance, upon which we fired on them. I have no doubt some of them were wounded.' No further inquiry was made or charges laid. White settlers could do no wrong.

A prominent squatter, W. J. T. Clarke, made much of his money by taking out £10 squatting licences in different districts and placing expert managers in charge. In 1840 John C. Francis was one of these managers, and he superintended Clarke's 184 000-acre property, 'Woodlands', on the Wimmera River (north-west of the present-day town of Crowlands).

After about 100 sheep were killed by local tribesmen led by Billy Billy, the station hands began to carry loaded weapons at all times. In September 1840 Francis surprised a native bending over a sheep in the stockyard, and shot the native through the top of the head.

Francis and two companions (one a convicted horse-thief) claimed that on 21 December they found themselves surrounded in a creek bed by a group of blacks with spears poised ready for battle. Francis fired and one man fell dead. Spears were then thrown, the whites fired again, and three more blacks were killed. The remainder fled. The manager reported the affray by letter to La Trobe next day, claiming self-defence.

La Trobe sent Protector Parker to the scene. The blacks told Parker a rather different story:

> The natives were sitting down near the creek, when three men on horseback suddenly rode among them—they were much frightened, and "manned" their spears—the three men then fired at them several times.

Parker concluded that Francis had acted 'with a cruel and reckless disregard of human life', but that there was not enough evidence to charge him.

When Robinson arrived at the scene in July 1841, Francis readily admitted to killing four blacks: 'No enquiry had been made and he supposed none would be made.' Robinson refused the squatter's hospitality, even when Francis offered to play him 'a tune on the fiddle'.

In his later reminiscences, W. J. T. Clarke wrote simply: 'When my people found it necessary to defend themselves, a number of the blacks, I am sorry to say, was shot.'

Francis's violent career continued until September 1842 when he was murdered by one of his own shepherds, John Connolly ('Mad Jack'), who was sentenced to life transportation for the offence.

In addition to sending troopers and Aboriginal Protectors to the scene of known outrages, the government made futile attempts to do something about the basic cause—the rapid expansion of squatting into areas beyond official surveillance.

In September 1840 Governor Gipps instructed each of the Crown Commissioners to refuse squatting licences 'for stations which he is unable to protect'. But most squatters already possessed licences, and continued to demand protection.

La Trobe told the Sydney authorities that Crown Commissioners, even with full complements of ten Border Police each, could not supervise all remote districts, where native attacks were 'seldom to be anticipated even by the parties on the spot'.

On 3 October 1840 Robert Jamieson's run, 'Tobin Yallock' on the Lang Lang River in Western Port, was attacked and pillaged by a large group of blacks.

To investigate the attack on Jamieson's run, La Trobe borrowed some of Major Lettsom's visiting troopers. He also instructed Protector Thomas to take two black-trackers from Narre Warren and to attempt to follow the marauders.

Thomas and his men were forced to abandon their supplies and to swim across four flooded creeks to get to Jamieson's station. They found its glazed windows smashed, saddles cut up, flour mill and plough broken, and most domestic utensils stolen. Among the victims were immigrant farm hands just arrived from Scotland, who lost everything they owned. The attackers had also attempted 'to make off with Mrs Houlston', but 'gave her up after pulling out her earrings.'

Following the raiders deeper into Gippsland, Thomas recovered a volume of Dwight's *Theology*, part of a mirror, and other oddments, but his trackers refused to go any further into such unfamiliar territory. The marauding tribe was never satisfactorily identified.

One of the most beautiful of the Henty family's properties was 'Sandford', located at the junction of the Glenelg and Wannon Rivers. But dark deeds were alleged to have taken place on its grassy plains.

In November 1840 an agitated gentleman-squatter, Augustine Barton, sent some gruesome evidence to La Trobe. An Aboriginal had told Barton that about sixteen kinsfolk, 'principally women and children, had died in the greatest agony, immediately after eating a damper which had been divided amongst them.' Barton named the alleged poisoner as Thomas Connell, an overseer for the Hentys.

La Trobe instructed Robinson to visit the scene. The Chief Protector took his time, not reporting on these events until January 1842. He told La Trobe he had been unable to discover bones of those allegedly poisoned, or any informants among the surviving blacks. Robinson said he had ordered Sievwright to conduct similar inquiries during 1841, but was 'astonished to find he had neglected that duty' for five months.

Sievwright's report from the Wannon River finally appeared. He located the alleged poisoner Thomas Connell at another Henty station, 'Merino Downs'. There Connell swore on oath that 'no such circumstance regarding the poisoning of natives took place.' However, when Sievwright proceeded to Samuel Winter's station, 'Murndal', he interviewed a native who gave him the names of three men, four women and a child whom he had seen die 'in much pain accompanied by retching' after eating damper at 'Sandford'. Although every white employee and squatter denied knowledge of the event, Sievwright concluded that a 'diabolical act' had been committed.

Stephen Henty entered the argument. In March 1842 he said he was 'perfectly satisfied' that Connell was 'innocent of such a revolting crime'. The overseer was of the Wesleyan persuasion, and possessed 'a most quiet and orderly nature'. There, in lieu of any independent white evidence, the matter rested, with 'no satisfactory result'.

In later years, the theory spread among whites that if any blacks were ever poisoned, it was because they had eaten dead mutton poisoned as bait, or live sheep carrying arsenical dressing to cure scab. No 'brave pioneer' would commit such an act as premeditated mass poisoning!

More lethal than occasional poisonings, if they ever occurred, was the practice of supplying blacks with liquor. In rural areas nothing much was done to prevent it.

On 24 February 1841 two constables saw the publican Andrew Smith sell liquor to an Aboriginal, and watched him drink it. Smith was arrested, but told the court next day that 'it was nothing but porter'. Magistrates Fenwick and Fyans dismissed the charge.

Although people today may find it hard to believe, cannibalism was a normal way of life among some Aboriginal tribes in the early nineteenth century.

Protector Sievwright left a graphic eyewitness account of one orgy at Lake Terang in 1841. A young native woman was severely wounded in a tribal clash near the Protector's tent. As soon as she died, an old man eviscerated the body with a sharp flint. Sievwright continued:

> From the impatience of some of the women to get at the liver, a general scramble took place ... it was snatched in pieces, and without the slightest process of cooking, was devoured with an eagerness and avidity, and keen fiendish expression of impatience for more ...
>
> The kidnies and heart were in like manner immediately consumed ... A quantity of blood and serum which had collected in the cavity of the chest was eagerly collected in handsful and drunk by the old man who had dissected the body ...
>
> The flesh was then entirely cut off the ribs and back, the arms and legs were wrenched and twisted from the shoulder and hip joints ... doubled up and put aside in their baskets.

Sievwright and two of his sons were given the feet 'and some half picked bones' as their share.

Not possessing white man's metal-smelting technology, Aboriginals usually used sharp flints or split reeds to cut strips of flesh. In the Portland Bay district early in 1841 the blacks took a reed about twelve inches long and split it with their teeth, making what G. A. Robinson described as 'a truly primitive knife'.

'The sharp edge of the reed is the saw with which they cut

their meat,' Robinson wrote, 'and it was surprizing with what expedition it was accomplished.'

One day in May 1841 a new-chum Englishman called Francis Morton set out with his convict servant, William Lawrence, and a party of black men and women to cut bark and slabs for their huts on the Glenelg River.

Two days later the females returned alone to the station. This excited some suspicion, for on previous occasions the women had always stayed with the party. After a three-day search, stockmen found the bodies of both whites, presenting 'a most horrifying spectacle'. Lawrence's body was 'stretched on its back with the arms and legs extended and secured in that position by wooden pegs driven through the hands and feet.' The cheeks and ears had been sliced off. Morton's body, nearby, had 'the head almost severed from the body by some edged instrument.' Both men's flesh had been 'cut off in long strips . . . before life was extinct.' The blacks, thought Police Magistrate James Blair, had 'then feasted on their remains.'

Chief Protector Robinson was not far away, camping at Portland, when news of the outrage was received. He did nothing about it, simply noting in his journal the opinion of James Blair and Edward Henty that the tribe should either deliver up the culprits or face extermination.

Edward Henty thought there would be little difficulty in making arrests: the blacks 'had only the river to fly to', and armed men 'could soon flush them out from among the rocks.' But Robinson stayed well away from the area, leaving investigation to local squatters—none of whom reported what, if any, further action they had taken.

By 15 August 1841 Robinson was back in Melbourne. He reported coolly to La Trobe that his expedition had 'proved to the fullest extent successful', he had obtained much useful 'statistical information', the government's humane intentions had been 'fully made known'; and his tour had 'tended materially to produce tranquility'. Generally he found the natives 'pacific', needing only more government handouts to 'render them a quiet and useful community'.

A few months later, when a group of Portland settlers complained to La Trobe of continued uproar in the district, Robinson pooh-poohed them as mostly young men, 'inexperienced in colonial matters'.

One of the few white men tried in Port Phillip for killing Aboriginals was 22-year-old Sandford George Bolden.

At their home in Lancashire the Boldens were renowned Shorthorn cattle breeders. Sandford and three brothers emigrated to Australia in 1838. By 1840 they held much pastoral land along the Hopkins River (south of today's Hexham).

A younger brother, Lemuel Bolden, pioneered the famous 'Banyule' property on the Yarra River at Heidelberg. In March 1841 he complained that Protector Thomas's blacks, camped over the river, often crossed 'under pretence of fishing in the lagoons', but actually to steal turkeys, pigs and farm goods. One of them, Billy Hamilton, 'threatened to kill Mrs Bolden and her children' if they interfered.

Seven months later, on 27 October 1841, Sandford Bolden saw on his Hopkins River station a native named Totkiere, accompanied by his lubra and son. Cattle had previously been killed; and Totkiere was armed with spear and waddy. Bolden ordered him off the run, allegedly using his whip. The black man tried to club Bolden's horse, then levelled a spear at him. Bolden swerved, drew his pistol, and killed Totkiere with two shots.

Meanwhile, the lubra was knocked down by a stockman's horse, and injured so badly that she later died. Only the boy escaped to tell Protector Sievwright what had happened.

Sievwright managed to get the case to court, but was ridiculed by Judge Willis. After a strong charge to the jury on the nature of trespass and self-defence, Bolden was acquitted to unrestrained cheers in the courtroom.

La Trobe was perturbed by the verdict. In a long despatch to Gipps, he pointed out that squatters now had a legal precedent to forcibly expel all 'trespassers', including blacks, from their runs. There would be, wrote La Trobe, 'manifest inhumanity' in pursuing such a course. La Trobe asked Gipps to include in squatting licences a provision that Aboriginals must not be excluded from traditional hunting grounds. Gipps, already at odds with landholders in his Legislative Council, refused to act in Bolden's case.

Fate instead dealt with Bolden. In 1843 he severely injured himself in falling from his horse, and died in agony. Two months later his 26-year-old brother Armyne died of apoplexy.

In 1841 Reverend John Skevington, a Wesleyan minister employed at Buntingdale Aboriginal Mission near today's Birregurra, shivered with horror as he listened to the squatter's tale. He was talking to Robert Tulloh, son of the Laird of Kenzie Castle in Scotland, who had settled on 'Bochara' station at the junction of Grangeburn Creek and Wannon River. The 22-year-old squatter had a perverse sense of humour. Yes, he said, he frequently rode out on the sabbath to hunt down blacks and shoot them like kangaroos. Yes, one of his men had kicked an Aboriginal child into a camp fire, and watched it burn to death.

Reverend Skevington did not know that Tulloh was a notorious teller of tall tales—'So much so that an extraordinary story is always called a Tulloh', wrote an acquaintance, David Edgar of Lake Condah.

Skevington reported Tulloh's conversation to his superior, the Reverend Benjamin Hurst. Hurst in turn sent the allegations to La Trobe, who instituted a formal investigation. Hurst, however, could not contain himself. He gave the full catalogue of alleged horrors to a public meeting in Launceston. After that they gained wide currency. La Trobe then criticised Hurst with some heat; the missionary, he said, should not have repeated 'the most palpable fiction' until the magisterial investigation was complete.

Under oath at the inquiry, Tulloh and other local squatters

all vigorously denied the allegations.*

David Edgar admitted that about a year earlier he had accompanied Tulloh in a hunt for blacks who had taken sheep. Tulloh was armed with pistols and 'the blade of a sheep shears lashed to a long pole'. However, when they chased the blacks into a swamp, Tulloh had succeeded only in wounding his own horse with the shears. Edgar believed that most homicides were committed by the blacks themselves: 'I have seen pieces of blacks, generally feet or fingers, in the baskets of the gins.' They had recently killed a child at Emu Creek 'for crying for something to eat'.

Thomas Norris in his evidence thought that, due to immigration, shepherds had changed from 'a debauched, drunken, good-for-nothing set' into an 'amenable' class who would not attack blacks. George Winter said he had just dismissed a man 'for kicking a black'.

John Henty deposed that several natives had been killed in clashes on Henty properties in earlier years, but none recently. When a white employee shot himself accidentally, 'the blacks asked me for his body to eat it.'

Stephen Henty gave additional details of these early clashes, but said that none had taken place on his stations recently.

Robert Savage said he and his men had killed a black about nineteen months earlier when blacks had attacked them with spears during a sheep-stealing episode.

So much anger was caused in the Portland area by Hurst's allegations that La Trobe was forced to issue a general denial 'when applied to the present time and present inhabitants'. Privately, however, La Trobe requested police magistrates to exercise 'the utmost vigilance'. Where material interests of landholders were affected, wrote La Trobe, 'The passions of men . . . are easily excited.' Although the district had been

---

* James Blair, PM, conducted the investigation from 30 December 1841 to 15 January 1842. Those who gave evidence included Arthur Pilleau, James Allison, T. W. McCulloch, Edward Barnett, C. P. Cooke and William McDowell.

quiet for some months, real-life atrocities were still possible.

La Trobe also decided that young Tulloh must be punished for his stupidity. He recommended to the Governor that the squatter's licence be cancelled. Tulloh sent a pathetic plea to La Trobe, stating that he was 'of good family', had 'never been accused of doing a dishonourable action', had never even met the Reverend Hurst, and had been given no chance 'of proving myself honourably not guilty'. Now he faced ruin. La Trobe replied fairly sympathetically, granting Tulloh four months to dispose of his sheep. After that, the young man seems to have left the district.

Protector Edward Parker, who toured the Western District in 1841, was told by blacks of several alleged killings by whites.

That year the overlander C. B. Hall had squatted on Mount William Creek; Hall's Gap in the Grampians was named after him. The squatter found relations between the races full of violence and reprisals, 'in which the superior arms and energy of the settlers ... told with fatal effect upon the native race.' Parker claimed that two blacks named Charley and Billy were shot on Hall's run in 1841 by an American Creole named John Williams, 'because they would not give him their women'. Parker could find neither bodies nor legal evidence. Crown Prosecutor James Croke recommended withdrawal of squatters' licences where 'moral suspicion of guilt' existed, but nothing was done.

Another squatter near Mount William was Horatio Wills, 30-year-old son of a Sydney emancipist merchant. Wills married Elizabeth McGuire, and travelled overland in 1839 with his wife and their baby Thomas, naming Mount Ararat on the way.

Late in 1840 a native named Cockatoo Jack murdered one of their hutkeepers at Mount William and stole a calf.*

---

* A stockman on Captain R. H. Bunbury's neighboring run, known as Bill the Native, allegedly killed Cockatoo Jack in 1841—but Parker could get no evidence except from the dead man's widow.

Perhaps the attacker tried to do more. When Chief Protector Robinson arrived at Mount William in July 1841, he noted in his journal: 'Informed that the natives attempted to have connection with [i.e. rape] Mrs Wills and take her away.'

Robinson found Mrs Wills 'living with her child (boy) in a small tent.' She was reluctant to emerge, and abruptly turned him away.

The third lot of unprovable alleged killings reported by Parker occurred on William Kirk's station 'Burrumbeep', on the Hopkins River. In the winter of 1841, said Parker, three convict wood-splitters, named Bill, Mather and Darby, killed three black men and a girl. However, all of Kirk's assigned convicts had since been withdrawn and replaced by immigrants, so Parker could obtain no further evidence, even from blacks, mainly because of their 'well-known reluctance . . . to speak of their deceased relatives, especially by name.'

On 5 December a shepherd, Christopher Priest, disappeared into the bush on Thomas Woolley's run at Mount Sturgeon (north of today's Dunkeld). Only some of his clothes and an axe were ever found: it was presumed he had been killed by blacks. As with many similar cases, Priest's disappearance simply became another of the dark mysteries of pioneering life.

5

ABORIGINALS CLUSTER AROUND MELBOURNE AND GEELONG

To the Aboriginal inhabitants of Port Phillip the white invaders were both a scourge and the godlike bearers of astonishing gifts like baked bread and woven blankets. When aggressive settlers began to drive the blacks from their ancient hunting grounds, and the survivors found government officials and missionaries in the towns who treated them more humanely, the tribes naturally began to congregate near populated centres. Yet to whites striving for orderly development, the existence of tattered native remnants was itself an affront: a constant reminder on their doorsteps of what was being done to the original inhabitants.

The attitude of townspeople varied greatly. Edmund Finn wrote that in the 1840s

At almost every turn one met with the Aborigines, in twos, and threes, and half-dozens—coolies, lubras, gins, and piccaninnies— the most wretched-looking and repulsive specimens of humanity that could be well found. The men half-naked, with a tattered 'possum rug, or dirty blanket, thrown over them, as far as it would go; and the women just as nude, except when an odd one decked herself out in some cast-away petticoat, or ragged old gown.

Young George McCrae, however, recalled that 'Of the women, some of the younger were well favoured and really pretty.' Certainly some of the lonely white men of early Melbourne found them so.

The Aboriginal Protectors, from the time of their arrival early in 1839, continually tried to persuade the tribes to leave the south bank of the Yarra and return to the bush.

In April 1840 La Trobe banned any further Yarra bank corroborees on Sunday evenings. He wrote to Protector Thomas: 'I need scarcely point out to you the disorders and scandal to which they give rise from the attendance of large bodies of the townspeople.'

At the same time La Trobe prohibited Yarra punts from plying after 6 p.m. on Sundays. As a result, the blacks decided to move across the river and camp on the north side near the town buildings. La Trobe instructed Thomas to tell them this was 'decidedly against my orders and can under no pretext be permitted.'

A few days later the emigrant ship *Glen Huntly* arrived at Williamstown with typhus fever raging on board. Eleven passengers had already died. La Trobe used this event to give a 'positive order' that the Aboriginal camp must be broken up and each tribe returned to its own district. 'There must be no exception', he wrote.

By June 1840, however, many tribespeople had drifted back to the Yarra. La Trobe so far softened his attitude as to write to Chief Protector Robinson:

I am much gratified by finding that Mr. Assistant Protector Thomas has induced the blacks in his vicinity to bring him various small trifles to be remitted to Melbourne for sale, such as baskets, squirrel and other skins, and I think it will be proper to give to him and the parties furnishing them every encouragement.

The Protectors were to sell the goods, and return the value in 'provisions or useful articles'—not cash which could be spent on guns and alcohol.

At his Sunbury Station Protector Parker fixed a regular scale of exchange:

1 kangaroo skin	=	2 lb flour
2 ” skins	=	1 shirt
2 opossum skins	=	1 lb flour
8 ” skins	=	1 shirt
1 basket, small	=	2 lb flour
1 ” large	=	6 lb flour

George Lilly, a Melbourne auctioneer, agreed to sell the items without fee, and credit the proceeds to the Protectorate. Settlers sent many such artefacts home 'to England as curiosities'—relics of a vanishing race.

Once they knew they could make something worth trading, the blacks increasingly flocked to the towns. During July 1840 the Barrabools had to be forcibly driven away from Geelong streets by order of Police Magistrate Nicholas Fenwick. When the Protectors protested to La Trobe, he replied: 'The native obtains a little food and a little clothing either through pity or as a reward, and he carries away with him vice, disease and the means of injury both to himself and his neighbours.' It was in their own interests that they should be banished.

Early the following year, the Reverend Francis Tuckfield reported to Protector Sievwright that a Barrabool black named Mumbourin had murdered one of the station blacks at Buntingdale Mission near Birregurra. He was also believed to have killed a Goulburn River black in Melbourne. Police Magistrate Fenwick issued a warrant for Mumbourin's arrest and the native was taken into custody at Geelong. When the Barrabools heard the news, they formed a war party and tried to rescue him. Fenwick reported in March 1841 that the tribe attempted to force open the watch-house and threatened to 'murder all the white inhabitants in the town' unless Mumbourin was released. Fenwick hastily shipped the prisoner in the cutter *Governor La Trobe* to Melbourne.

Later in 1841 Crown Commissioner Addis reported that the 150 remaining blacks of the Barrabool tribe had settled down in excellent order outside Geelong. They were peaceable, in good health, 'and certainly improving in their social habits—particularly the young men, who are now more disposed to make themselves useful.' These blacks were wearing European clothes, bringing in stray stock, cutting wood, delivering parcels, and exchanging birds and skins for rations. Addis concluded they were 'but little inferior in intellect to the uneducated peasantry of Europe'.

In the spring of 1840 large numbers of native men, women and children re-entered Melbourne. The Protectors, using every argument they knew, could not persuade them to leave.

There followed the forcible rounding-up and imprisonment of Aboriginals by Major Lettsom's troopers on 10–11 October 1840, when two black men were shot dead (chapter 2). This terrible lesson of white supremacy and ruthlessness, performed under cover of legal power, kept the Aboriginals out of Melbourne for a time.

Some white men made every effort to save the lives of sick or wounded natives. In May 1841, when squatter Thomas Thorneloe was searching for clues to the murder of shepherd Luke Slattery on Henry Bennett's run on the Campaspe River, he came across a wounded Aboriginal named Jack, hiding in a hollow stump.

Thorneloe sent the man to Melbourne for treatment. Government surgeon Patrick Cussen found he had a compound fracture of the right thigh bone and knee joint, caused by two bullets. Inflammation had set in, and amputation of the leg was necessary.

Helped by three other doctors, Cussen removed Jack's leg on 11 May 1841. As the patient recovered, however, he continually tore off each fresh dressing. Gangrene set in, and he died eight days later.

In July Protector Thomas found 170 Goulburn River natives camped on the Upper Yarra, near today's Warburton. He tried to persuade them to return to the Goulburn River Protectorate, but they refused, claiming that the Broken River tribe would come down and kill them. Several of the Goulburns walked to Merri Creek, a few miles north of Melbourne, camping near the hut of a stockholder named Edward McGuigen.

After a corroboree on the night of 17 December, four Goulburn warriors attacked a Yarra black named Jimmy, a servant of overlander James MacFarlane. The Goulburns knocked Jimmy down with a waddy, split his head with a tomahawk, removed his kidney fat, and skin from buttocks and hips, and fled from the area. No trace of the murderers was ever found.

By March 1842 other outcast blacks had crept back as far as Turruk [Toorak], a few miles up the Yarra, where Thomas again attempted to cater to their needs. Having learned some of the white man's strange ways, the blacks humbly asked the Protector to give them written passes to visit Melbourne. Convict servants were often given such passes—why couldn't black men have them too? Thomas was bound to refuse.

Another year passed. By February 1843 the Yarra and Western Port tribes felt safe enough in camping opposite Melbourne again, on the site of today's Sidney Myer Music Bowl.

On 23 February the tribesmen told Thomas that they must conduct their traditional mock battle: 'only a small one, throw a few spears and then all over.'

As they were conferring, a large body of daubed warriors armed with spears came up from the river in battle formation. They included twenty men of the Native Police, led by Billibellary, and wearing war paint instead of uniforms. Thomas cried out to them to 'show an example' and 'leave off such dirty wild habits'.

The warriors ignored the Protector's pleas. Vigorous clashes began and continued for some hours, until eight men were speared, the Western Port chief seriously wounded, and 'a young man's face awfully lacerated'.

In 1844 the Melbourne Town Council complained to Chief Protector Robinson that 'large numbers of dogs following in the train of the natives' were an unacceptable nuisance in the township. Robinson promised to inform all blacks near Melbourne that unregistered dogs would be destroyed forthwith.

During the following year Aboriginal beggars were again becoming 'a great evil' in Melbourne. According to mayor Henry Moor, they were 'prowling into every back yard', and using 'abusive and threatening language' to obtain food and grog. Allowing them to beg, said Moor, was fostering 'an inveterate mendacity, predatory disposition, and imitation of the worst examples of European manners'.

After applying to Sydney for instructions, Superintendent La Trobe was again told 'to discourage by every possible means consistent with law and humanity' the visits of Aboriginals. La Trobe passed the message to the Chief Protector. Robinson replied that the whites 'have only themselves to blame'. Just a few days before, he had visited a native camp on the Richmond road, and found 'twenty-five large baker's loaves, a quantity of biscuit and meat, besides tea, sugar and tobacco'—all given by the excessively charitable citizens of Melbourne.

In fact the morale of the Yarra tribes had been shattered for ever. By 1846 the blacks had practically abandoned their traditional meeting grounds south of the river. When small groups of visiting blacks gathered there in June 1846, got drunk, and attempted to force the door of a brickmaker's hut, Sergeant Henry Rose and a couple of troopers had no difficulty in dispersing them.

As the white population tightened its ownership of freehold land near the towns and began to build fences, wandering

Aboriginals became regarded as illegal trespassers on what had only a few years before been their own land.

In February 1846 Edward Curr senior called on La Trobe to have blacks removed from his enclosed property on Heidelberg Road, about four miles from Melbourne. His property, said Curr, was 'in peril from their fires'.

Protector Thomas was sent to move them, and found the task 'most unpleasant'. The Aboriginals, visiting from the Goulburn, Loddon and Devil's Rivers, were determined to remain on this part of the Yarra. When Thomas insisted, they simply 'crossed the river with their baggage—which they do as easily as ducks', and waited for the Protector to leave.

The following month Police Magistrate James Simpson complained that blacks had twice 'plundered' his vegetable garden at Yarra Grange, near Richmond. Simpson wrote that leniency shown by the courts on earlier occasions had done no good. He demanded that the Protectorate 'remove these nuisances from the neighbourhood'.

Again Thomas was sent to do the job. Examining bare-foot tracks, he concluded that truants from Merri Creek school for Aboriginal children had stolen the magistrate's vegetables. He lay in wait on the Yarra bank for three days without success, then visited the school and 'severely cautioned' the black youths against stealing. 'They appeared much frightened', he reported.

Major Charles Newman, of 'Pontville', at Heidelberg, complained early in 1849 that the blacks were 'not only very troublesome, but daring, entering in and making fires in enclosed paddocks'. Thomas again went out to move them from the locality, but wrote, 'It is really distressing; I know not what to do with them.'

Samuel Ramsden, a prominent Melbourne builder, was walking home on the night of 17 September 1849 past St Peter's Church in East Melbourne. An Aboriginal named Mister Lowe rushed out from behind a tree and attempted to throw a blanket over his head, with the intention of robbing him. Ramsden managed to break free. Mister Lowe raised a tomahawk to strike him, but was prevented by two other white men who ran up and seized the black.

Mister Lowe spent a month in gaol on remand. Judge à Beckett told him 'he might go home but never again to molest the whites by raising a tomahawk.'

6

THE TRAGEDY

OF

ROBINSON'S

BLACK IMMIGRANTS

The attractive 28-year-old Trucanini felt she had been abandoned by her best friend. George Robinson, Chief Protector, no longer depended on her for assistance in dealing with mainland Aboriginals. Besides, she was now a social impediment. It was very different from the old days in Van Diemen's Land, where they had worked together since 1830 in Robinson's untiring efforts to save the few remaining blacks from the effects of white settlement. Possibly Robinson and Trucanini were occasional lovers during those years, although the evidence is inconclusive.

Now, in 1840, Robinson was a highly-paid official, preoccupied with building a bureaucratic department and a respectable domestic life. He rarely took Trucanini or her relatives on field trips. He could do nothing for them when Crown Commissioner Henry Gisborne's Border Police, acting on a general Government order, confiscated their most valued possession, the firearms which made them feel able to deal with emergencies.

Disgusted with restrictions on life in Melbourne, the Tasmanian blacks continually 'absconded' from Robinson's camp. In July 1840 Trucanini and her friend Charlotte were found cohabiting with white shepherds near Point Nepean.

Superintendent La Trobe demanded that Robinson find a solution to the problem of his wandering black immigrants. In August 1840 Robinson felt they might as well 'be returned to the care of the Van Diemen's Land Government at Flinders Island.' The following January he decided to retain four individuals in his private service.

La Trobe instructed that the other thirteen should dwell at Protector Thomas's new Aboriginal Station at Narre Warren until their future was decided. They continued to go walk-about, causing trouble wherever they went.

Early in October 1841 five of the absconders, including Trucanini, stole two guns and ammunition from Sam Anderson and Robert Massie's hut at Bass River. On 6 October they encountered at Cape Paterson a party of whalers walking to Melbourne. For reasons never clearly explained, the blacks shot two of the white men dead. One whaler was 'beaten about the head with sticks' to finish him off.

Crown Commissioner Powlett soon arrived at the scene. He swore in several special constables, pursuing the blacks for some weeks without much success. After several incidents, on 30 October the fugitives raided James Allan's station at Western Port and escaped with a large quantity of ammunition.

La Trobe ordered the Chief Protector to join the hunt. Robinson prevaricated, sending Protector Thomas instead with six black-trackers. Powlett was joined by a strong force of nine Border Police, several mounted troopers and eight soldiers of the 28th Regiment.

At last, in the early hours of 20 November, Powlett managed to find and surround the blacks' camp near Cape Paterson, capturing them after several shots were fired.

The five Aboriginals were tried at the Supreme Court from 20 to 22 December 1841. Robinson vigorously defended the three women (Trucanini, Martha and Matilda), pointing out that they lived 'in entire subjection to the men'. The jury took pity and acquitted them. The two men, commonly known as Bob and Jack, were found guilty of murder. Judge Willis's trial notes showed that he regarded the case as one of 'great atrocity'. He disregarded the jury's recommendation to mercy, and sentenced the men to hang. Forwarding the documents to Sydney, La Trobe added 'regret that I am not able to advance anything' in favour of a lesser sentence. Governor Gipps agreed.

Melbourne's first scaffold was accordingly erected outside the new gaol site in Russell Street. Here, on 20 January 1842, before a crowd of avid spectators, convict executioner John Davies placed nooses around the terrified Aboriginals' necks. His assistant jerked away a temporary platform, the blacks fell, and slowly strangled to death, writhing convulsively 'in a manner that horrified even the most hardened'.

After these shocking events, the remainder of Robinson's black immigrants including Trucanini were repatriated to Flinders Island in July 1842.

As late as 1846 La Trobe was still pondering the murderers' motives. 'No reason could be adduced', he wrote. 'They had a knowledge of the principles of religion, and knew right from wrong.' Yet they had killed two men, wounded four others, and robbed seven stations in their doomed rebellion against white domination. Sheer despair might well have been their true motivation.

7

WHAT DOES
BRITISH LAW SAY
WHEN ONE BLACK
HARMS ANOTHER?

'The natives of the Colony have an equal right with the people of European origin to the protection and assistance of the Law of England.' This was the noble sentiment with which Governor Gipps announced new appointments in 1839 of Commissioners of Crown Lands, to exercise extraordinary powers in enforcing the rule of law over remote squatting districts.

In practice it was not so easy to dominate the Australian frontier with legalistic ideals. For a start, natives could rarely understand the meaning of white men's law. Unless they could speak reasonably good English, their evidence normally could not be accepted in court. Was it right anyhow to use British law to overturn native traditions, even where these involved cruel and unusual punishments?

These problems came to the fore in September 1841, when the first attempt was made in Port Phillip to try an Aboriginal on a charge of murdering one of his own race.

A young Aboriginal named Bon Jon served for several years as a jack-of-all-trades in Commissioner Fyans's Border Police. 'He was a stout lad, very civil and useful', Fyans noted.

One night in July 1841, near Colac, nine Aboriginals armed with spears and covered with white paint—a death warning—came to Fyans's hut and demanded Bon Jon's kidney fat, as revenge for the killing of a Colac native at Geelong. Bon Jon challenged them all with sabre and loaded pistol, forcing them to retreat. Some time later he picked up his carbine and followed a black named Yamowing, making no secret of the fact that he coveted the man's lubra, a charmer called Mary.

No witness saw what followed, but Yamowing's body was found a few days later with a bullet wound in the back of the head. Far from denying the killing, Bon Jon confessed to Reverend Francis Tuckfield in native dialect that 'he had shot Yamowing because he wished to get his wife.'

The case seemed clear enough. But when it came before a jury at Geelong, Tuckfield claimed that Bon Jon could not plead guilty or not guilty, 'as murder is not always so among the Aborigines'. Another defence witness, government surgeon Dr John Clerke, claimed that Bon Jon was 'totally unable' to form any idea of legal responsibility. Judge Willis added his strong opinion that Aboriginals were not amenable to British law, but should be 'governed among themselves by their own rude laws and customs.' He remanded Bon Jon while the legal position was considered.

In Sydney Chief Justice Sir James Dowling told Gipps that such questions had already been judicially determined in April 1836, when Jack Murral was tried for murdering another black; and in May 1838, when Long Jack was convicted of murdering a black woman.

Gipps issued fresh instructions in April 1842 that 'all Magistrates should proceed as they would do if the parties were white men.' By this time Willis had discharged Bon Jon from custody, so that he escaped scot-free from punishment, although undoubtedly guilty in white eyes of premeditated murder.

Until his forced removal from the bench, Willis continued to defend the view that illiterate Aboriginals should not be tried in normal courts. In a letter to Superintendent La Trobe at the end of May, Willis pleaded that 'in these our days of boasted humanity and philanthropy', natives should be left unmolested.

After his release, Bon Jon returned to serve with Commissioner Fyans in the Portland district. Duty with the Border Police 'on many occasions tried the courage of this savage boy', wrote Fyans. Finally Bon Jon left the service, and was killed 'in a scurry with some natives at a corroboree', apparently about 1843 or 1844.

The frequent impotence of British justice in resolving tribal affairs was again demonstrated early in 1842.

Protector Sievwright reported from Lake Terang in the Western District that on 8 January 1842 a woman named Elingapooterneen refused to carry water from the lake for a man of her tribe named One-Beeturon. That night the black man approached her while she slept, and slew her with a spear thrust through the heart.

Sievwright pleaded for legal action, as otherwise the natives 'must imagine that such practices are tolerated'. La Trobe referred the matter to James Croke, Crown Prosecutor. Croke's view was that 'there is no evidence but native evidence (and that is no evidence at all).' Sievwright should realise, wrote Croke, that 'the evidence of an Infidel who has no notion of a future state of rewards or punishments is not an admissible witness.'

La Trobe again wrote to Sydney for guidance. 'My own opinion', he said, 'is that unless we assume power to interfere to prevent or at least punish murders of the natives among themselves, we shall never teach them to respect European life.'

The same answer came back as in the Bon Jon case—that
'in all cases of murder and other very heinous offences occurring among the Blacks, the Protector and all Magistrates should
proceed as they would do if the parties were white men.'

During the early months of 1842 Commissioner Fyans
rounded up many Aboriginals suspected of being implicated in
attacks on squatters and their flocks in the Portland Bay
district.

Among them was a warrior named Tagara. When his
arrest became known on 23 April, his tribe at Mount Rouse
Aboriginal Station fell into 'a paroxysm of lamentation'. His
brother, Kalkin-wherdon, seized his spears 'and slew the first
person who came in his way', a mission boy named Waw-
allow-bron. Kalkin-wherdon freely admitted to Protector
Sievwright that he had killed the boy, but no official action
seems to have followed.

By 1844 the law had been regularised to the point where
interpreters of Aboriginal dialects were accepted in court,
enabling almost any native charged with a serious crime to be
tried. An opportunity was soon to arise.

On 20 January 1844 a Merri River settler, James Cos-
grove, and his wife were driving cattle from one of the
Manifolds' out-stations near Fyansford. At the Wardy Yallock
Inn they were joined by a native boy named Little Tommy.

A group of local blacks recognised the lad as one of the
Port Fairy tribe, against whom they had sworn revenge for the
killing of one of their number (Tom Brown, who had accompanied G. A. Robinson on his tours). The Cosgroves told
Little Tommy to mount a mule and try to outrun his attackers.
But the blacks managed to catch him, plunged eight spears into
his body, and 'blew out his brains' with a gun. The whites
and their cattle were left unmolested. So was a Sydney native
named Bill, a servant of the Cosgroves.

At the preliminary court hearing, Bill was sworn in with
the words 'I know that it is wicked to tell a lie; I will tell the

truth.' He then identified Jacky Jacky as one of those who speared Little Tommy, and Long Bill as the man who had shot him.

Gipps told La Trobe that the case seemed 'to offer a fair opportunity of proving to the natives that they are answerable.' Fyans was sent in pursuit. The Commissioner advised that 'some time must elapse, to make it appear to them that all is forgotten.' With these tactics, Fyans eventually succeeded in arresting the ringleader, Jacky Jacky, who was brought to trial before Judge Jeffcott in Melbourne on 15 May 1844. Reverend Tuckfield was sworn in as interpreter. On being called to plead, Jacky Jacky replied, 'Another one black fellow killed him.' This was taken as a plea of not guilty, and as showing sufficient mental capacity to be tried.

Jacky Jacky was found guilty and sentenced to death, later commuted to transportation to Van Diemen's Land for life.

Booby was a 'useful native' who worked for a squatter in the Pyrenee Ranges (west of today's Avoca). In November 1844 his master sent him to help two white men bringing drayloads of supplies from Melbourne. Not far from town, Booby was set upon by a group of tribal enemies and speared almost to death.

Four natives were arrested. The dying man appeared to identify an English-speaking native constable named John Bull as the ringleader. White witnesses supported this identification in court. Protector Thomas had his doubts, mainly because the spears used belonged to a different tribe. Due to the Protector's evidence, John Bull was acquitted in March 1845.

Aboriginals around Melbourne unanimously believed that Woomdalla, a native of the Buninyong tribe, had committed the murder. After a long chase, Woomdalla was captured near Buninyong by Sergeant-Major Peter Bennett and Native Constable Buckup.

'The prisoner cried upon being taken,' wrote La Trobe, 'saying that the white fellows would hang him for spearing Booby; and made no secret as to his being the murderer.'

Each evening the police handcuffed Woomdalla and

fastened him to a tree with a tether rope. One night he managed to gnaw through the rope, break the handcuffs, and escape. Apparently he was never recaptured.

By the mid-1840s deep enmity had developed between Aboriginals who tried to co-operate with settlers, and those who continued to resist the white invasion.

Black guerrilla fighters had learned that it was extremely dangerous to launch direct attacks on whites. Instead, they often turned their wrath on natives living peacefully on white man's terms.

Early in 1845 warriors from the Grampians attacked the blacks' camp only thirty yards from D. C. Simson's homestead on the Loddon River. They killed four lubras and severely wounded three: the penalty for cohabitation with whites.

In February 1845 a native named Harry was killed by a person or persons unknown at Fyansford, just outside Geelong. Harry was possibly the man who had led the kidnappers of Abraham Ward's three-year-old daughter in 1843 (see chapter 10).

When the native's body was fished out of Major Mercer's well, it was found that Harry's kidney fat had been extracted in the traditional manner.

Later that year, in October, three native constables, John Bull, Nerribinyak, and Banol, vanished from Melbourne and reverted to wild life in the bush. Joining the chief Bungerring and another man, the five journeyed to the Joyce brothers' run 'Plaistow', on the headwaters of the Loddon River. There, on 23 October, they murdered a friendly native named Robinson, apparently in retaliation for the killing of two of Bungerring's family by Loddon blacks.

In 1847 a Western Port black named Nerreninnin abducted the lubra of tribal chief Ben Benger from Arthur's Seat. Ben Benger tracked down the pair, but the abductor was armed with a gun, and shot Ben Benger dead near George Smith's cattle station at Tootgarook.

Protector Thomas later reported that several young Gippsland blacks armed with guns, purporting to hunt lyrebirds for Melbourne merchants, were actually seeking 'to seduce or barter for young lubras'.

A few months later two of these blacks, named Tommy and Bonnie-laddie, were charged with attempting to murder an Indian stockman, 19-year-old William Robinson, on Robert Allan's Western Port run on 15 December 1847.

William Robinson told the Supreme Court he was tailing his master's cattle when the two blacks seized him by the throat and attempted to strangle him. He managed to break free and flee. Justice William à Beckett sentenced the two men to twenty-four hours in gaol, a mild enough sentence for attempted murder.

In 1849 a peaceful encampment of Yarra blacks at today's Studley Park was suddenly attacked by a group of Goulburn River blacks. 'Four glass-barbed spears were thrown, three effectual, one lubra was severely wounded, and two males', Thomas wrote. No legal action seems to have followed.

Early in 1851 Hector MacDonald, a squatter on the Crawford River in western Victoria, reported that his station blacks 'rushed to me for protection' against armed marauders. Outside his homestead, 'One of the blacks was cut to pieces, another lays in the last agonies of death, also a lubra dangerously wounded.'

MacDonald named the gunmen as Big Peter, Dick and Jacky. He asked Portland Police Magistrate James Blair for prompt action, adding the warning: 'If not, Sir, I must proceed to other extremities with them, as it causes both me and family great alarm.'

So even while Victoria was on the verge of independence and the gold rush, the pastoral frontier could still sometimes erupt into murderous activity.

8

Race War

in the

Western District,

1842

As a veneer of white civilisation spread outwards from
Melbourne and Geelong, racial atrocities near those centres
lessened. But the pastoral frontier itself in many areas continued to be stained by bloody confrontations.

A few runs remained peaceful. When 27-year-old Scottish
pastoralist Thomas Chirnside occupied a property at Mount
William in April 1842, neighbours told him it would be
essential to place two shepherds with double-barrelled guns
over every flock. Chirnside made it clear to the Aboriginals
that 'if they did not steal, they should be at liberty to roam
about as usual'. He claimed to have experienced very little
trouble after that. At his out-station on the Wannon River, he
was the first local man to employ natives successfully on
pastoral work.

The blacks' struggle against white incursions was ulti-
mately doomed to failure. In the meantime, however, those
who had been treated harshly continued to use every device
within their knowledge to slow down the invasion. The harder

they fought, the more the whites regarded them as 'barbarous savages'. Severe reprisals, many of which we can never know about, took place. In the end, most squatters would stop at nothing to win sole title to the land and its riches.

Even magistrates participated in an unspoken conspiracy to suppress information on racial confrontations. Edward Bell, a Wannon River squatter who sat with Acheson French on the bench at Hamilton, and later became a Crown Commissioner, confessed that 'The collisions with the blacks, which I had heard of on almost every station after my arrival in the Western District, if they took place at all, were kept very quiet.'

Here then are the surviving fragments of this part of the story, for the crucial year 1842.

Early in January James Guthrie, overseer at Hunter, Hoskin and Davidson's run, 'Eumerella West', went searching along the Glenelg River for a horse supposed to be stolen.

He returned to the station on 3 January, but could see nobody there. As he approached the main hut, an Aboriginal named Jacky came out and seized him by the arm. Another black emerged with a leanguil (a heavy club with a sharp beak) raised as though to strike. Guthrie managed to break free, seized his gun, and shot the second Aboriginal dead. The white man jumped on his horse and galloped to Furlonge's dairy station nearby. Returning with assistance, he found the hut stripped, but no other damage.

On 8 January blacks, using spears fitted with tips of broken glass, attacked John Hunter's run at Mount Napier (south-east of present-day Hamilton). They destroyed all the property, 'even the fowls', killing and eating two horses. The attackers were identified as Jupiter, head of a tribe which hid in nearby caves; and Cocknose, 'a restless, malevolent savage' named by the settlers 'from the highly unclassical shape' of his nose.

Commissioner Fyans sent two of his Border Police to investigate. As soon as they arrived, the blacks attacked again.

'A heavy blow from a leanguil smashed the sabre of one of the troopers', wrote Fyans. 'A native aimed another at the head, which floored the poor fellow, fracturing the skull.' This man, Private Francis McCarthy, died of his wounds some months later. The other trooper, wielding his sabre, managed to clear the hut. Two blacks suffered deep cuts, but escaped.

Police Magistrate Acheson French immediately swore in six special constables from among local squatters, and set off in pursuit. But when the posse reached Hunter's station, they found it abandoned. No trace of the blacks could be found.

Two medical men, Dr James Kilgour and Dr William Bernard, set up a squatting enterprise in 1840 at a spot twelve miles north of Port Fairy. Hundreds of Aboriginals used to gather there each autumn for the eeling season. They called it 'Tarrgon'. The doctors changed the name to 'Tarrone', and took out a pastoral licence for 47 000 acres.

Towards the end of January 1842 Portland Police Magistrate James Blair reported that the station's overseer, a highlander named Robertson, 'had been rushed and speared in both sides' while supervising milking at 5.30 a.m. His attackers took away three horses.

The blacks returned on 1 February, creeping up behind a stockman and pinioning his arms, while shouting 'White fellows no good, must kill 'em.' Other employees came to the rescue, but not before a musket had been stolen and two more horses driven off. Next day, searchers found the horses' bones by the blacks' camp-fire.

Under these circumstances, complained Dr Bernard, 'the whole property is going to ruin.' He himself had been bailed up by a party of blacks on the Port Fairy road, and escaped only by brandishing a loaded pistol. The blacks' usual reply to protests, said Dr Bernard, was, 'You touch black fellow, Mr Sievwright hang you.'

Superintendent La Trobe then instructed Chief Protector Robinson to visit the area. Robinson had been there a year before, when the blacks told him 'it was their country and white men steal it.' Now they were going hungry.

Robinson believed that the two doctors had been unwise in their choice of employees: 'A more depraved set of servants I never met with.' His opinion was borne out by a probable mass poisoning of blacks on the run later that year.

La Trobe agreed that part of the blame for thefts of sheep should be placed on squatters who left daily operations to indifferent employees. Fyans pointed out that both John Hunter and Dr Kilgour were absent during all the months he was patrolling the district.

La Trobe wrote of his 'exceedingly strong suspicions' that many outrages resulted from 'the careless and reckless manner in which large herds are committed to the care of improper characters.' In June 1842 he instructed Crown Commissioners to refuse licences to any squatters whose 'lax conduct and mismanagement' may have led to 'the commission of outrages by the natives.' Under this order, John Hunter's licence was not renewed.

Dr Kilgour's licence became the subject of anxious correspondence between La Trobe and Gipps. La Trobe proposed on 23 August 1842 that the licence should not be renewed. Gipps replied in a personal letter that there was 'a growing disposition on the part of the Squatters to try their strength against the Government.' Nothing would suit their purpose better 'than to be able to get up a plausible case of hardship inflicted on a Squatter'.

La Trobe took the hint, and left Dr Kilgour's licence in force until his abandonment of squatting three years later.

Native attacks intensified during the summer of 1842. On 6 February an aged hutkeeper, Thomas Bird, was speared to death on John Ritchie's station, 'Urangaranga', on the coast between Port Fairy and Yambuk. When found by other shepherds later that day, Bird had one spear wound in his forehead, another through his eye, and four in his chest. His killers had taken all the food stores, clothing, bedding, a musket, and ammunition.

The attackers were claimed to be Mister Murray,* Puckemal and Charley.

Chief Protector Robinson departed from his principle of non-intervention on this occasion. He identified the group as the same men who had speared Kilgour and Bernard's overseer. In addition, Mister Murray was 'the same man that fired at Loughnan, and was the leader in sheep-stealing.' La Trobe offered a substantial reward for capture of the men.

Commissioner Fyans, now a hardbitten, hard-riding, 52-year-old veteran of many campaigns, swept through the district with his fourteen troopers. On 10 April, traversing stony ground between Mount Napier and the Eumerella River, the whites saw one of the suspects, Charley. They pursued him through the scrub: he threw three spears at Fyans, but missed each time. Fyans charged at the black with sabre drawn. Charley parried most of the cuts with his shield, and managed to cripple Fyans's horse by spearing it through a nostril. He then escaped, perhaps to proceed to the murder of squatter Donald McKenzie and his hut-keeper.

Another of the wanted men, Puckemal, was arrested near Portland in May by District Constable John Allsworth. Police Magistrate James Blair attempted to obtain evidence from white eyewitnesses: when this failed he was forced to release the native.

A full nine years after these events the whites won their revenge on Mister Murray. A shepherd named William Hick-ling, employed on Peter Hutcheson and James Kidd's 'Bushy Creek' run on the Hopkins River, came into conflict with the ageing native on the evening of 1 May 1851.

Little is known of the precise circumstances, for Hickling

---

* Mister Murray had previously spent three months on remand in Melbourne Gaol late in 1840 on a charge of felony near the township. He was discharged when no witnesses appeared against him, but he could not forget or forgive the privations of imprisonment in a foul gaol.

refused to make any statement in court. One of his fellow-labourers, Alexander Dunlop, said that on the night of 1 May, he heard a disturbance in the blacks' camp. Hickling came running into the hut, secured the door, and said that during a fight he had struck a black man with a stick. Other natives surrounded the hut, throwing spears and shouting that Hickling had killed Mister Murray.

Another labourer, John Webster, said that he found Mister Murray lying in his mia-mia with severe wounds on the back of his head. Although tended by Ann Edwards, a white woman from the homestead, Mister Murray died two days later.

As no white man had seen Hickling strike the fatal blow, and black evidence was still inadmissible in such circumstances, a jury at Geelong Circuit Court on 20 October unhesitatingly declared Hickling not guilty.

Black women were generally regarded as fair game for white settlers and their employees.

On 12 February 1842, at about 7.30 p.m., Constable Thomas Smith saw a man named Robert Sugden having 'connexion with an Aboriginal female' in Gawler Street, Portland. 'The woman was lying on her back in the street and he was on top of her with his trousers down', said the constable. Smith 'seized the defendant by the collar and dragged him off the woman.'

Sugden was sentenced to one month's imprisonment with hard labour.

A fearful outrage against the Aboriginals occurred late in February, when four black women and a child were shot dead at the station of Thomas Osbrey and Sydney Smith at Muston's Creek (near today's Caramut).

All squatters and employees in the neighbourhood had been on the alert for bands of marauding blacks. Where any doubt existed, they were liable to shoot first. R. W. Sutton, manager of Robert Whitehead's run near Port Fairy, told

G. A. Robinson how such men threw a cloak of legality over their actions:

> Under pretence of being after sheep, ride furiously up to them, and in a threatening attitude, when the natives would be terrified into an offensive position, which would be the signal for an attack as they would be able to swear the natives made the first attack.

On 23 February, a hut-keeper on Osbrey and Smith's Station, Joseph Betts, asked another station hand, George Arabin, to lend him a gun loaded with ball 'to shoot kangaroos'. Betts proceeded to the homestead, and told owner Thomas Osbrey that 'there was a mob of blackfellows at hand'. Three other gentlemen were present: Robert Whitehead, and two visitors named Boursiquot and Smith. One of Whitehead's own shepherds had recently been speared and 'left for dead, three spears in him'.

The visitors jumped up and took their guns to accompany Betts. Two other employees went along: Henry Beswicke, and a 'colonial experiencer' named Richard Guinness Hill, nephew of Sir Richard Guinness, of Hillthorp Brewery in Dublin.

All mounted horses and rode nearly a mile down the creek. They came to a clump of trees, fired several shots, and returned home within an hour.

Next day Protector Sievwright heard of the shooting, and rode over from Mount Rouse. On 25 February he found three black women and a male child lying dead in the scrub. One of the dead women was 'big with child'. Another whom he knew as Coonea had been killed by shots to the abdomen and left arm. Obviously she had died an agonisingly slow death.

Sievwright took away a fourth woman; she had been wounded with a gunshot in the back, and had hidden in the bush for two days. She died later at Mount Rouse.

As soon as La Trobe heard of the affair, he offered a reward of £50 for information. Gipps increased the reward to £100, and offered a free pardon to any convict witness who did not actually fire shots. La Trobe also sent two Mounted Police to

Portland to reinforce two already at Hamilton. He ordered all government officers to give 'prompt attention to the duty of detecting the perpetrators of this detestable crime'.

A special note was added for Commissioner Fyans: if he did not receive 'the fullest aid and assistance from the settlers', he had authority 'to order the removal of every station within thirty miles of the spot.'

Local squatters sent a memorial to La Trobe protesting that they were under severe permanent threat from native attacks. They claimed that the women killed were attached to a marauding party, and asked for extra police protection. La Trobe replied with one of his rare emotional outbursts:

> The evils you complain of are those which have everywhere accompanied the occupation of a new country inhabited by savage tribes ... Whatever augmentation of the present means of protection be practicable, it will never fully meet the difficulties of your position ... But gentlemen, however harsh, a plain truth must be told ... the feelings of abhorrence which one act of savage retaliation or cruelty on your part will arouse, must weaken if not altogether obliterate every other ... Will not the commission of such crimes call down the wrath of God?

La Trobe requested the squatters, as their 'first duty', to tell all they knew of the massacre. Innocent settlers were incensed by the imputations, and told La Trobe so. In a further reply the Superintendent repeated that detection of the murderers was 'a common duty', and was the only way of removing stains on the district's reputation.

When nothing had been achieved by June, La Trobe appointed a special commission of three magistrates to search anew for evidence. Its members were Foster Fyans, F. A. Powlett, and Charles Griffith. Three weeks later the commission reported that, although the perpetrators must be locals, 'no clues to their persons however faint has been gained.'

Nearly a year passed. Guilty consciences, offers of rewards and pardons, finally had an effect. In May 1843 two employees on Osbrey's station confessed to G. A. Robinson what they knew. Christopher McGuinness, an expiree-convict and bush carpenter, said that on the day of the massacre he saw the men ride away from the homestead, followed them on foot, saw them fire into the trees, and saw black figures fall. Another station hand, George Arabin, corroborated much of the carpenter's evidence.

Both men repeated their evidence and were cross-examined before Melbourne Police Magistrate Major St John on 5 June 1843. McGuinness now testified that on the day of the murders, the squatters 'rode off in great glee'. He had heard six shots fired, and seen the whites returning with native weapons in their hands. Betts told him that night that they had killed lubras. Next day McGuinness went to the spot and saw three natives 'apparently lying dead'. Arabin's contribution was to testify that Betts had told him the same night they had been 'shooting blacks' and that his gun had 'carried well'. Arabin had not spoken up earlier because of fear of consequences.

Two of the visiting 'gentlemen', Boursiquot and Smith, fled back to England during the investigation. The remaining five alleged participants were charged with murder. George Arabin was charged with concealment of a felony, but released.

The two main squatters involved, Thomas Osbrey and Robert Whitehead, were brought up before the Melbourne Magistrates' Court on 14 June, but discharged on the ground of insufficient evidence.

Osbrey blamed the killings on the three station hands— Betts, Hill and Beswicke. These three men were committed for the murder of the woman Coonea.

On the first day of the Supreme Court hearing, Judge Willis vented his usual spleen. He claimed the Police Magistrate, Major St John, had improperly allowed hearsay evidence in the depositions. 'The Police Magistrate, I presume,' said Willis, 'knows more about putting a regiment of soldiers through their evolutions than he does of law.' La Trobe protested to Gipps that these remarks, widely reported in the press, were 'greatly calculated to prejudice the case'.

As the trial proceeded, the defence attacked the two prosecution witnesses as 'wretches, steeped to the lips in crime, self-convicted perjurers seeking to earn the price of blood'— that is, the £100 reward.

The trial had not even concluded when the jury announced they were unanimous on a verdict of 'not guilty'. Judge Jeffcott thought the jury was 'justified in not giving credence to the principal witness for the Crown.' The prisoners were immediately discharged.

J. C. Byrne, in Melbourne at the time, later claimed he was told by a member of the jury that 'if they had shot double the number he would not have found the prisoners guilty.' Another jury-member, the squatter John Hawdon, said that 'he would have eaten his boots' before agreeing to a verdict of guilty.

The main Crown witnesses, McGuinness and Arabin, were secretly paid £50 each to enable them to leave Port Phillip and find employment out of reach of private vengeance. Thomas Osbrey surrendered his run to Alexander Sprot, and left the district for parts unknown.

La Trobe remained convinced of the guilt of the acquitted men. In a confidential despatch to Gipps, he said it was obvious that 'Hill and Betts and the other parties named by Mr Osbrey were concerned with that atrocious affair.' Gipps replied in a personal letter that had he been on the jury, he would probably have found Hill and Betts guilty. Gipps also wrote to Lord Stanley that it had been 'established beyond any rational doubt' that those charged were the murderers.

If that was so, British justice had again failed on the frontier.

An extraordinary epilogue to this case followed nearly twenty years later. One of the accused men, Richard Guinness Hill, returned to London and married a 16-year-old heiress, Amy Georgina Burdett, who enjoyed an income of £14 000 a year. Hill persuaded his wife to bequeath all her property to him in the event that she did not have any children.

In January 1859 a son was born to the couple. Hill registered the child's birth under a false name, and persuaded his wife to put him out to a wet-nurse. He took the baby to 'a loathsome den' near Drury Lane, where he was 'suckled and fed among thieves, prostitutes, and beggars'. For nearly three years afterwards, the mother could obtain no information on the child's whereabouts. Her husband told her various tales, one that the boy had been kidnapped and taken to Australia, another that he had died.

The desperate mother finally engaged private detectives, who tracked down the child to a slum dwelling 'reeking with filth and stench'. The boy was covered with 'vermin, sores and wounds'. Police were brought in, who seized the child, and found one of Mrs Hill's shawls still in the foster-mother's possession.

Hill was arrested, committed by Rugby court on 27 September 1861, and tried at the Assizes in March 1862. The judge held that the evidence was insufficient to convict, and Hill was freed. Nothing about his alleged part in the Muston's Creek massacre was disclosed until Australian newspapers picked up the fact that this was the same man who had been tried and acquitted in Melbourne in 1843.

On 15 February 1842 at Alexander Irvine's 'Junction' run, near the site of today's Elmhurst on the Wimmera River, a shepherd named Andrew Walker offered an Aboriginal man, Keemoondannar, a bag of rations in return for sexual access to his lubra. Walker took the services, then refused to hand over the rations.

The black man speared the shepherd in the back and beat him severely with a waddy. A hutkeeper, John Griffiths, came to the rescue, receiving two spear wounds before driving off the blacks with his gun.

Towards the end of February Charles Smith, a settler at Spring Creek, south-west of today's Caramut, was fired at by an unknown native. He managed to escape on horseback.

A few months later, Smith surrendered his run to Robert Whitehead and departed from the district.

Early in March Henry Loughnan's property, 'Green Hills', west of Caramut, was besieged by a roving tribe. His men's ammunition ran out: as they cowered in their hut, the blacks drove all the sheep away and slaughtered them. But they spared the lives of their white enemies.

Near the end of March the Henty brothers' overseer and men were driven off their run at Mount Eckersley, north of Portland. The attacking blacks displayed great 'disposition for mischief—beating down a building with large stones—breaking a plough, and destroying as much property as they could.'

Police Magistrate Blair sent a party of three soldiers from the 80th Regiment to retake and hold the run until the marauders moved on.

During March squatter Horatio Wills reported from Mount William in the Grampians that 'strong parties from distant tribes' had appeared in the area. Wills's station had already been the scene of a murder and possible attempted rape by blacks in 1840 (chapter 4). This time his shepherds were 'rushed by the natives, and threats of bloodshed held out to them.'

Wills said he was 'willing to concede the right of their hunting grounds to the original possessors', but destruction of stock and promise of murder 'place them beyond the pale of the law.'

One night Wills and a stockman set out to 'take into custody' a tribesman who had threatened to kill a shepherd. The white men were attacked at their camp-fire, whereupon Wills's employee shot and wounded the wanted man. The remaining blacks fled.

La Trobe sent Wills's lengthy report to the Governor. Gipps replied that Wills had been 'extremely imprudent' in going out at night with only one man. Had the wounded native died, said Gipps, 'both you and your attendant must have been brought forward for murder.' As it was, the Governor did not see 'how you can escape for firing with intention to commit murder.' No further legal steps seem to have been taken.

Seething with rage, Wills abandoned his furthest run, and settled on 'Lexington' station (closer to today's Ararat). Within two years, the past had been so far forgotten that Commissioner Fyans recommended Wills for appointment as a magistrate.

Wills sold his station early in the gold rush for £35 000, and entered the Victorian Legislative Council. He later took up land in Queensland, but was killed by blacks in the Cullinlaringo massacre of 1861. His wife lived on to the age of ninety-one. When she died in 1907, practically the last direct link with pioneering days was broken.

Rampages through the Portland district continued through March and April 1842. A settlers' petition at the end of March claimed that in two months four shepherds had been killed and seven wounded.

Fyans's itinerary, unfortunately not carefully dated, showed that the Burchett brothers' run (near today's Penshurst) was attacked, the shepherd stripped naked, and the legs of 270 sheep broken as revenge against the white invaders.

A shepherd employed by the Hutcheson brothers was speared dead on their Hopkins River run. Another unnamed shepherd was shot by natives near Port Fairy. Dr James Robertson received two spear wounds in his left arm and side. When his attacker tried to seize his gun, Robertson shot him dead.

After squatter John Cox was evicted from Mount Rouse to make way for Protector Sievwright's new Aboriginal Station, he moved to 'Weerangourt' (five miles north-west of today's Macarthur). Here two of his horses were speared and eaten, and a shepherd killed, 'one spear through his chest, one through his lungs and passing through his stomach'.

From Alexander Cameron's run at Mount Sturgeon (north of today's Dunkeld) blacks drove his flock of 450 sheep to Sievwright's hut at Mount Rouse, killing and eating them at their leisure.

On J. M. Woolley's run the hutkeeper was speared to death and his cattle driven away into the bush.

On J. D. Bromfield's run, wrote Fyans, natives from Mount Rouse killed three quiet, harmless station blacks, 'cutting them open, extracting kidney fat, and eating some parts; also killing two women, extracting the kidney fat, left one living, with her entrails on the ground.'

Faced with this catalogue of disasters, La Trobe was forced to take strong action. At first he reinforced Portland with troops of the 80th Regiment. When these had to be withdrawn, he allocated additional troopers to Fyans's Border Police, and instructed the Commissioner to pursue any lawbreakers with vigour.

Proceeding towards the station of John and James Hunter on the Eumerella River, Fyans found two wanted Aboriginals 'in a forest about three miles from the house'. The first man, Jupiter, was handcuffed after a scuffle. The second, Jacky, an extremely strong man, managed to break loose. He was pursued for about four miles, eventually dropping dead from loss of blood caused by sabre slashes.

The Hunter brothers had left Richard Manifold in charge at 'Eumerella' while away on business. On 16 April overseer William Duncan informed Manifold that the wanted blacks were camped near Protectors Robinson and Sievwright, some miles away. All fifteen men on the station, said Manifold, were 'willing to do their duty' and 'take the blacks', as they felt their lives were in danger.

Manifold approached the Protectors, who refused to assist, believing their influence with the tribes would be lost if they became regarded as just another branch of the white man's law. After the first attacks on 'Eumerella', Sievwright had even told the station's stock-keeper he would be hanged for murder 'if he discharged firearms' at the blacks. Manifold's men retired.

Some days later, probably on 18 April, Fyans's troopers surprised the wanted blacks in a hut on 'Eumerella'. 'We thought it impossible for any to escape,' Fyans wrote later, 'but these wild savages, bounding through the hut from room to room, roaring piteously, giving the loud war coohey for assistance, the hut appeared almost to move with its contents!' Several blacks escaped through the chimney and thatched roof. Inside remained Cocknose, Bumblefoot and 'Doctor', the tribe's expert at kidney removal. After a severe struggle Cocknose was taken. 'Doctor' fought until he was shot: he died of the wound some time later.

Even after Fyans and his men had risked their lives in arresting the blacks, the two Protectors 'declined their services as magistrates' in committing for trial. The accused men instead were brought before Acheson French at Hamilton, committed, and sent by boat from Portland to Melbourne via Van Diemen's Land.

Several weeks later, in June, Redmond Barry, as Standing Counsel for Aborigines, demanded to know how much longer the blacks would be kept in gaol before being tried.

Crown Prosecutor James Croke admitted serious flaws in the deposition of Jemima Parnell, housekeeper at 'Eumerella'. Her dates for various events, and amounts of food taken by the blacks, were contradictory. The evidence of her husband, John Parnell, was also inconsistent. In view of this, Croke now doubted whether it was worth bringing witnesses 200 miles to Melbourne for a trial. The three Aboriginals were released early in July and shipped back to Portland.

A short time later they were again on the rampage. Early in August the manager at 'Eumerella', Samuel MacGregor, reported that about twenty blacks led by Jupiter and Cocknose had thrown spears at his shepherds, and driven off 1000 sheep towards their hideout in the rocks near Mount Eeles.

'Ever since Capt. Fyans took the said Jubiter [sic] there was not a Native to be seen', MacGregor concluded. 'But now as he has returned to his old Quarters the consequence is much to be dreaded unless we get Help.' Most of the sheep were recovered on this occasion.

Three days later, on 10 August, Jupiter returned with a force of 150 warriors. 'The shepherds behaved so nobly . . . that the aggressors were again defeated', MacGregor reported.

Jupiter returned to the attack on 18 August with an even larger band. This time the blacks managed to kill or carry off more than 500 sheep. MacGregor claimed that no blacks had been shot, but James Hunter admitted later that three were killed and several wounded when the whites were recovering some of the sheep.

La Trobe wrote to question Hunter on the behaviour of his employees. Hunter replied that his manager, Samuel MacGregor, was 'a highly respectable young man from Perthshire, in Scotland'. He was assisted by his uncle, Samuel Gorrie, an overseer 'of equally respectable character'. Originally the station employed twenty-five men and women, said Hunter, but many had absconded and forfeited their wages 'rather than expose their lives to the attacks of the blacks.'

La Trobe reported to Sydney his 'great regret' at 'the continued outrages of the natives upon the settlers . . . 'I am really inclined to fear at times that this state of things is without remedy.'

Nevertheless, La Trobe instructed Fyans to try to recapture the black leaders and bring them to trial again. Fyans was reinforced with temporary command of a Native Police detachment. He stationed them in a hut close to Mount Eeles (now known as Mount Eccles), while taking his own Border Police on an extensive tour of runs in the district.

This technique seems to have worked: nothing further was heard of raids by Jupiter and Cocknose.

On 15 May a settler, Donald McKenzie, and his hutkeeper, Frederick Edinge, were speared to death on a run at Emu Creek (near today's Hotspur). The raiders stripped the hut of everything useful, driving off several hundred sheep, and breaking their legs to make them useless to the squatters.

There seemed ample evidence to convict the blacks responsible. The main suspect was an ageing tribal leader, Koort Kirrup, who was believed by police to have taken part in the cannibalistic murder of Francis Morton and his shepherd in May 1841 (chapter 4).

According to Chief Protector Robinson, Koort Kirrup's camps at that time were 'little better than common brothels'. Since then, however, the black chief had dwelt peacefully on Donald McKenzie's run, living with his wife and children in a hut about 200 yards from the homestead, and drawing rations each day in return for labour.

Joseph Lillycrop Wheatley, a sheep-washer who worked with him, said that Koort Kirrup was 'perfectly domesticated' and 'in fact he did as much as a white man,' putting up yards and shepherding sheep. The black 'understood everything that was said to him and could express himself sufficiently [in English] to make himself understood', Wheatley added.

Early in May Donald McKenzie went to Portland for a few days. During his absence the atmosphere on the run changed for the worse. Koort Kirrup left his work and went into the bush, where 'plenty of black fellows' were camping. Wheatley began to feel 'a sense of danger'—so much so that he decided to forfeit his pay, and quit.

On his last Sunday, 15 May, Wheatley was sent out to round up straying sheep. When he was about a quarter of a mile from the homestead, a gunshot sounded and he 'heard Mr McKenzie's voice shout "murder".' Wheatley ran back towards the huts. From a distance he saw Koort Kirrup beating 'something black' on the ground with a waddy. Other natives threw spears at Wheatley, and he hid behind a tree.

'Come on you bloody wretch', Koort Kirrup called out. Wheatley asked the black 'what for he had killed Mr McKenzie.' In reply, Koort Kirrup threw two spears, but missed.

Other natives meanwhile tried to surround Wheatley. Using his double-barrelled gun, he wounded one in the left side, and killed another as they drove the sheep away. Wheatley succeeded in escaping across the creek, fleeing to the nearest neighbour, Daniel O'Neil, licensee of the Crawford Inn on Smoky River.

Next day O'Neil and two of Henty's men accompanied Wheatley back to the scene. First they found the body of hut-keeper Frederick Edinge, bearing wounds in the right side and back, and 'severely beaten about the head'. Then they found McKenzie's body. In addition to spear and waddy wounds, 'he had been dreadfully beaten about the private parts which were frightfully swollen and almost shapeless.'

Police Magistrate Acheson French mobilised what force he could at Hamilton and went in pursuit, but with no success.

White settlers were incensed by these murders, for McKenzie, said French, had been noted for 'the greatest kindness to the natives'. Daniel O'Neil, the publican, said he had 'several times cautioned McKenzie on reposing so much confidence' in Koort Kirrup, but he always replied, 'Poor fellow, there is no harm in him.' In addition, said O'Neil, 'I never knew a black who could better understand what was said to him.'

After the murders Thomas Snodgrass, brother of Peter Snodgrass, occupied the deserted run. When G. A. Robinson visited there later that year, he found the remaining natives 'remarkably peaceable' and trustworthy.

Koort Kirrup disappeared from the area for about two years, hiding out with a tribe at the mouth of the Glenelg River (near today's Nelson).

In March 1844 he led a raiding party on Stephen Henty's Mount Gambier run, stealing 320 sheep and driving them back to the Glenelg. Six men under a Henty overseer tried to recover the sheep, but were forced to flee when attacked.

The Native Police were given the job of arresting the black leader. Sergeant Peter Bennett and four black constables disguised themselves as itinerant workers. Finally early in August they found Koort Kirrup's deserted camp on a tributary of Emu Creek. One constable sat in the mia-mia, occasionally singing Aboriginal songs and beating sticks together. The other men concealed themselves in the scrub nearby.

At about 1 a.m. on 8 August Koort Kirrup returned to his camp, was rushed by the hidden men, and seized 'after a considerable resistance'.

Committal proceedings took place in Portland over several weeks between August and November. After Joseph Wheatley had given his eyewitness evidence about the 1842 murders, Police Magistrate Blair noted on his deposition: 'The prisoner asks no questions but states that he "very much cried when Mr McKenzie was killed".'

Corporal Henry Graham of the Mounted Police gave evidence that he too had disguised himself in attempts to find Koort Kirrup. On Graham's deposition the magistrate wrote: 'The defendant declines asking any questions, but states that Charley, Jemmy and Larry, Pickaninny Bill and Big Yarra Yarra did it.' From what we know of Charley's movements after the murder of Thomas Bird, this scenario seems at least a possibility.

Blair committed Koort Kirrup for trial at the Supreme Court in Melbourne. He was brought up before Judge Jeffcott on 16 January 1845, but Crown Prosecutor Croke said he was not ready to proceed, as all witnesses had not arrived.

When the prisoner appeared again on 19 February, Croke said that one vital witness still had not answered his subpoena. Redmond Barry, as Standing Counsel for the Aborigines, protested that Koort Kirrup had already been 'a long time in gaol'.

By the sitting of 14 March Judge Therry had taken over as Resident Judge. He tried to get the case moving, and asked whether an interpreter was present. Told no, he directed that one had to be found. Protector Thomas was instructed 'to use his best endeavours to communicate with the prisoner'.

Koort Kirrup's reactions to these legal delays can only be inferred. He refused any co-operation, seemingly losing all knowledge of English overnight. Edmund Finn often saw him in court, and wrote: 'In the dock the man seemed the incarnation of stupidity, and he looked around with as much unconcern as an old bullock.'

In the May sessions Barry demanded a discharge under the 7th section of the Habeas Corpus Act. Instead, Therry directed a jury to decide 'whether the prisoner were of sufficient mental capacity to understand that nature of the proceedings.' The jury said no. Instead of releasing Koort Kirrup, Therry decided he should remain in prison temporarily, to give the government a chance to resolve the legal dilemma.

Further remands took place every month from June 1845 to January 1846. Some witnesses travelled up to 2000 miles, back and forth between Portland and Melbourne, to be available in case the hearing went ahead.

Month after month the prisoner was brought up, Protector Thomas claiming he had found it 'utterly impossible' to communicate with him, teach him any English, learn his dialect, or convey the meaning of a legal trial. By September 1845, however, Thomas was able to report that he had 'made him acquainted with much of the English language; he can talk as readily as many of my own blacks.' G. A. Robinson's view, sent privately to La Trobe, was that 'Koort Kirrup is remarkably intelligent, indeed a more shrewd Aborigine I have seldom met with.'

During this period, the case was submitted to legal authorities in Sydney. Attorney-General Plunkett felt that 'the prisoner should be tried without further delay, but with every kind of reasonable caution that humanity can dictate.'

Had Plunkett's advice been followed, there is little doubt that Koort Kirrup would have been found guilty by a white jury. Plunkett canvassed this prospect, saying that the final penalty (i.e. hanging) should be determined in Sydney. However, Therry had also sent the matter as a 'Special Case' to the Sydney judges. They decided simply that 'the prisoner cannot be put upon his trial'.

By November Protector Thomas felt that a great injustice was in the making. He considered it 'by no means a strong case'. To keep Koort Kirrup in custody for twelve months formed 'a precedent that will strike at the root of Aboriginal liberty'. Thomas concluded that 'no court short of an Inquisition could deal so with an unfortunate fellow creature.'

In February 1846, when Koort Kirrup had been in gaol for fifteen months, William à Beckett took over as Resident Judge. One of his first tasks was to decide what to do with the native, who had returned to his non-co-operative demeanour.

At a hearing on 12 March à Beckett decided that 'it was necessary to draw the line somewhere . . . He must, although reluctantly, turn him out.' Koort Kirrup was thereupon discharged.

La Trobe's next problem was to decide what to do with the released native. He refused to allow him a free passage back to Portland. Instead, Koort Kirrup lived with Protector Thomas at Merri Creek for three months. On the night of 9 June the native disappeared, 'taking with him nothing but what belonged to him.'

For some time it was thought that Koort Kirrup had finally reached his own tribe and died there about 1847. However, in 1849 Dr Watton reported from Mount Rouse that the old 'incorrigible' had led an attack on Richard Lewis's run at Emu Creek, and attempted to carry off a lubra. He was foiled only by the prompt action of Lewis's stockman. Koort Kirrup's final fate remains unknown.

With Border Police and Native Police constantly patrolling the Portland district, the ferocity of attacks diminished during the remainder of 1842. Nevertheless, some deadly encounters occurred.

One day early in May, drays loaded with flour and wheat consigned to John Tulloch, a Portland storekeeper, were being slowly drawn by bullocks past Mount Eckersley. A party of blacks attacked with spears. Their leader, named Cold Morning, cried out, 'Bloody rogue, you Tiger, plenty spear for you.' The driver of the first dray, who went under the nickname of Tiger, fired several shots and managed to escape. The blacks seized the second dray and drove it into the scrub, where they began using the flour to cook damper. Police from Portland later found six sacks of flour and several half-baked dampers at the deserted camp.

Some days later, Cold Morning was identified at the Portland 'convincing ground' (long notorious as a spot where local Aboriginals had been murdered) by a whaler named John Robson. After a scuffle the black was arrested, and shipped to Melbourne.

When Cold Morning was brought before the Supreme Court in July, the jury decided that he was not sufficiently aware of the nature of the proceedings to stand trial.

Protector Robinson was instructed to educate Cold Morning, but no interpreter could be found. Crown Prosecutor Croke decided not to proceed, and the native was discharged at the August sittings.

When he got back to his district, Cold Morning and his tribe coolly plundered a dray en route from Portland containing Police Magistrate Acheson French's own supplies. The infuriated official wrote to La Trobe that 'this is but the commencement of a system which, if not immediately put down, will reach to an alarming height.' But no further complaints were heard about Cold Morning. Protector Thomas made inquiries at Portland in 1845, and was assured that the native and his tribe were altered characters, who 'had now become favorites of the whites'.

A native named Bob led attacks in July and August on Glenelg River stations between today's Balmoral and Harrow.

The first affray occurred on Thomas Ricketts's station, 'Clunie', early in July 1842. Investigators feared that a shepherd called Foreman had been taken away with his sheep to be eaten. The man turned up some weeks later with another missing shepherd, both barefoot and ragged, having lost their way in the bush. But the sheep failed to return.

The next attack occurred late in July further south on John Thomson's 'Keilambete' run. One of his shepherds was speared, and the sheep driven off to the stony rises south-west of Mount Napier. Police Magistrate French and his men tracked them for forty miles. They found about 200 dead sheep, but were unable to capture the marauders.

Late in August, back on the Glenelg River, Bob's tribe attacked Ricketts's neighbour, Francis Desailly, on 'Fulham' station, killing one of his shepherds. Police Magistrate Blair found the body on an open plain, stripped of clothing and covered with spear and tomahawk wounds. The blacks proceeded to drive sheep from the property of another neighbour, Thomas Norris of 'Kout Narrin' on the Glenelg. Norris and his wife Jane abandoned the property a short time later.

Sixteen-year-old Trevor Winter was one of the first settlers on the Wannon River, taking stock in 1838 with his brother Samuel to form the famous 'Murndal' station.

Five blacks were shot dead there in 1840, but no official action was taken (chapter 4). About two years later, one dark night early in August 1842, Trevor Winter heard the sheep 'rush' within their hurdles. Next morning he discovered that nearly 200 were missing. In the scrub, he and two other men saw the station blacks—'whom he had been feeding for the last two years'—feasting on barbecued lamb.

One black said to Winter, 'What for you sulky, sheep no belong you—Come on, me no frighten, by-by plenty spear you.' As the black raised his spear to strike, Winter levelled his gun and shot him dead. The whites retreated hastily before they could be surrounded.

Three days later, Winter took five men to search for any sheep still living. They found eighty 'with their legs twisted out of the sockets'.

The whites separated to ride around a swamp. The blacks ambushed two of them, throwing spears. Winter galloped from the other side of the swamp, fired his gun, and wounded one black. The remainder fled.

On the night of 15 September some of Captain James Webster's sheep were taken from his run at Mount Shadwell, on the Hopkins River (near today's Mortlake).

Next day Webster recruited a posse of squatters. They found a group of blacks 'roasting the sheep at their encampment'. The whites told the blacks to go to Mount Rouse Aboriginal Station for their food instead of stealing sheep.

When the blacks began to disperse, one called out to the others 'to stand and come on'. A shower of spears descended on the whites. 'We fired either two or three shots,' said one squatter, 'but did not see anyone fall.'

One of the natives subsequently died, leading to the taking of depositions by Police Magistrate Acheson French, but apparently no further action.

In December Dr John Watton, who had succeeded Sievwright as Protector at Mount Rouse, reported that his bullock driver had told him of a mass poisoning on Kilgour and Bernard's station, 'Tarrone', about six weeks earlier.

Two employees, John Lyons, and the overseer named Robertson who had been speared the previous January, allegedly sent a bag of flour laced with arsenic to natives in the bush. Upon eating it, the blacks were 'immediately seized with burning pains in the throat, excruciating pains in the stomach and vomiting.' By next morning, three men, three women and three children lay dead.

Their kinsfolk followed the local custom of burning the bodies, thus innocently destroying the evidence. One woman who survived to tell the tale was taken to Mount Rouse.

The white men involved fled in the direction of Melbourne, but apparently were never apprehended. La Trobe wrote some months later that 'every attempt to discover the parties has hitherto proved ineffectual ... it seems nearly impossible to obtain any legal proof.' Even if proof was available, what would a white jury have done to any of their own race brought to court, even on so abominable a charge as mass murder?

9

NATIVE POLICE ORGANISED TO CONTROL THEIR OWN PEOPLE

Many blacks longed to possess the power of whites. In October 1837, when Captain William Lonsdale arranged the first recruitment of a Native Police Corps, dozens of candidates gathered along the Yarra. They 'broke unsolicited their spears and other native weapons, and threw them into the river, saying they would no longer be black fellows', wrote Lonsdale.

This first attempt to control the black population through its own members broke down when the white commandant, a young South African bushman named C. L. J. De Villiers, failed to discipline his recruits in accordance with white standards.

Late in 1839, the half-trained black constables were placed under the Aboriginal Protectors. James Dredge and C. W. Sievwright each enlisted five new recruits from tribes in their vicinity. All were equipped with green artillery jackets, woollen shirts and duck trousers found in the Commissariat store.

This experiment also failed. Most of the Protectors were

gentle, tolerant men, unable to exercise the stern discipline necessary to convert young blacks into a cohesive body of police. Even the former military officer, Protector Sievwright, could not persuade his Barrabools to leave the relative safety of their own lands around Geelong for the perils of service in the far Western District.

During most of 1840 and 1841 the recruits simply squatted around the Protectors' stations, performing minor duties in return for rations. Protector William Le Souef reported from Goulburn River Station that his eight police spent their time 'Fishing for the use of the establishment and occasionally going to Mr Manton's station for a sheep.' That was all they did.

At Loddon River, Protector Parker one day found a constable with 'big tears rolling down his cheeks' after his wife's death from dysentery, and threatening wildly to 'kill a Goulburn black to whose machinations he attributed her illness.'

With the pastoral frontier in turmoil, Superintendent La Trobe decided he needed an effective native force to supplement the thinly stretched Mounted Police, Border Police, and military detachments.

Early in 1842 the Native Police were removed from the Protectors' care, and placed under the control of a young Englishman, Henry Pulteney Dana, whom La Trobe had known in London. The pastoralist Edward Curr, who met Dana early in his new career, left an amusing description of his 'jaunty ways', his 'preternaturally erect carriage', and his fondness for stroking his moustache with 'little caresses'. The squatter found Dana's habitual use of military phraseology for everyday actions to be 'extremely comical', but no doubt it impressed the recruits.

To expand Dana's force, La Trobe authorised fresh enrolment of twenty Aboriginals, and their training on military lines at Narre Warren. During the experimental stage, Dana was to be paid only £100 a year. Dana's assistant, his 17-year-old brother William, was allowed £40 a year.

'Captain' Dana, as he liked to be known, arrived at Narre Warren on 28 January 1842. He immediately despatched messengers 'to bring in all the young and able-bodied men' of the Yarra and Western Port tribes. Using Protector Thomas as his interpreter, Dana explained his plans, promising uniforms and rations 'the same as the Mounted Police'. Led by chief Billibellary ('has a great deal of influence'), and supported by his nephew Beruke ('obedient, cleanly and useful'), twenty-five men were soon sworn in, promising to obey all lawful commands and to uphold white law.

Discipline began instantly. During the first month, ten recruits were punished for misdemeanours ranging from dirtiness to insolence. After stoppage of rations, most saw the light. Several, described variously by Dana as 'perfectly useless', 'great scamp' or 'a great savage', were chained to trees or 'knocked down with the back of a sword'. The discipline, thought Dana, was good for them.

On 24 February the men who survived this initiation were issued with police jacket, trousers, belt, cap, shirt, blue work frock, and blankets. Dana was now drilling them twice each day, although during the heat of summer they were allowed to remove uniforms. An observer thought they were 'the drollest-looking set of recruits ever seen.' All were drilling naked, for when clothed, 'Him bery sore all ober.' Dana, however, was 'well satisfied with their progress and good conduct.'

The Commandant later expanded his ideas on the indoctrination of black troops into white ways. Fundamentally, he thought, they remained 'savages . . . unaccustomed to anything like discipline, order, or restraint.' In relation to whites, they were 'as children to adults', and hence 'should be treated with lenity and proper indulgence.' Nevertheless, the recruits needed 'firmness' to instil 'undeviating and prompt obedience to command.' Part of this training had to be 'a wholesome rigour of punishment . . . approaching to military law.' For minor offences, thought Dana, solitary confinement and semi-starvation would suffice. More serious cases of disobedience, insolence or flagrant neglect required a birching. Anything approaching violence to officers should be met 'by the lash and imprisonment'.

With water becoming scarce at Narre Warren, Dana shifted the unit on 28 March to Merri Creek, north of Melbourne. Here their headquarters remained for nearly two years. Instead of building mia-mias in tribal pattern, Dana ordered them to form straight military lines, pitching his own tent at the head.

Dana wisely allowed his recruits' wives and children to live with them at Merri Creek, preventing many tribal disputes over women. Rations were allowed for wives from 1 May, as long as their husbands' conduct continued to give satisfaction. If not, the families went hungry as well.

By June Dana had his police organised into two striking forces, each of a dozen men. He claimed they improved every day in cleanliness, discipline and orderly conduct. They were now fully equipped, except for cartridge boxes, and willing to follow their officers 'to any part of the District'.

As an experiment, La Trobe decided in August to detach four Native Police for field training by Crown Commissioner Powlett at Mount Macedon; and to send ten men under Dana to patrol the far Western District.

It will be recalled (chapter 8) that the entire area south of the Grampians, through Hamilton to Portland, was in a state of uproar throughout the early months of 1842. La Trobe instructed Dana to place himself and his men under the direction of Police Magistrate Acheson French, as 'useful auxiliaries to the more regular police'. He warned that 'great caution must be exercised' in these novel circumstances, and that all policing actions must be performed strictly according to law. These warnings seem to have had their effect. Dana's men were used on minor tasks for a few weeks, partly helping to track stolen sheep, partly supervising tribes being moved to Mount Rouse Aboriginal Station.

The only hint of serious trouble came when squatter Lauchlan Mackinnon complained, on hearsay evidence, that the Native Police had 'forcibly carried away' a male black servant from his station. Dana hotly denied the allegation.

Both Dana and French said they found the men 'ready and willing' on all occasions. Once, when Dana tried to swim across the flooded Wannon River, two of his troopers had 'gallantly rescued me from drowning'.

It appeared at this stage that white ingenuity had found a method of using blacks to convert their own people to new and better ways of life.

Unfortunately, Native Police proved just as vulnerable to alcohol as other Aboriginals. Any event such as the accession of a new recruit was worth celebrating, but, said Protector Thomas, they soon became 'like maniacs'.

In November 1845 a young black known as Lively was inducted into the Native Police. He and his friends got drunk at Philip Anderson's Commercial Inn, and began boasting 'Black fellows don't care white police come, black police soon drive them away—no gammon black police.' When the publican tried to interfere, Lively assaulted him. The native was gaoled by Melbourne Police Court for fourteen days.

'These convictions will tend much to break the blacks from drinking spirituous liquors', wrote Protector Thomas hopefully.

With their high reputation as trackers, the Native Police were usually called in when white children lost themselves in the bush—or, worse still, were thought to have been abducted by cannibal blacks.

In July 1842 Mrs Nathaniel Simpson, wife of the plough-man at Narre Warren Aboriginal Station, took her two small children for a walk and became lost in the bush for nine days. The Native Police immediately turned out, and despite heavy rain, tracked them to the nearby hills. They arrived just after James Dobie, the pioneer of Monbulk, found mother and children alive, although almost comatose from exhaustion.

In April 1846 the five-year-old son of squatter James Willoughby was allegedly taken away by Mornington Penin-sula blacks near Arthur's Seat. The body was later found near a

native camp-fire, but showed no marks of violence. Protector
Thomas believed the boy had died of starvation, and strenu-
ously defended native constable Nunuptune against rumours
that he was implicated in a kidnapping.

Later in 1846 a child of T. M. Atkinson, pound-keeper at
South Yarra, wandered from home. Native Police and Protector Thomas spent thirty-five days on horseback and twenty
days on foot searching for the child, apparently without
success.

At the end of December 1847, Mrs Ellen Riley, wife of a
stockholder at Dandenong, temporarily left her three children
with Mr and Mrs John Jones on a neighbouring property.
The youngest child, Catherine Riley, just over two years old,
wandered away from the homestead. She was missed within
a few minutes. Searching began immediately, but without
success. Even Henry Dana and his black troopers could not
trace her. Eventually, after five weeks, the child's remains were
found on open ground under a tree, on a neighbour's property
only a mile or so away. No explanation of this strange circumstance could be produced at the inquest.

In January 1849 the young son of rate collector James
Ballingall disappeared. The Native Police were again called in.
They searched closely at Brighton, where many blacks had
camped, but eventually the boy was found drowned in the
Yarra.

10

MORE CLASHES IN THE WESTERN DISTRICT, 1843

The massacres, revenge raids, and merciless policing activities of 1842 did not entirely quell racial violence in the Western District.

On 22 January 1843 a strong party of blacks near Mount Eckersley attacked drays carting supplies belonging to squatter Francis Henty. Although five white servants were with the drays, they carried only one gun between them: after firing one shot they fled. The attackers speared the bullocks to death and made off with the drays' contents. Mounted Police from Portland later recovered most goods, except for a bale of shirts.

After this encounter, Police Magistrate James Blair stationed two white troopers at Mount Eckersley until a Native Police squad arrived to relieve them.

In an incident near Geelong at the same time, a party of blacks set fire to dried-out grass on R. H. Kinnear's Moorabool River run. 'My sheep are now all but starving', the squatter complained.

The blacks returned to Kinnear's station on 6 February. 'I immediately shot one of their dogs', he wrote, adding that the same dogs had previously attacked his sheep. Revenge followed quickly. Next day the squatter found 'a valuable mare speared in several places and quite dead.' It had been foaling at the time.

Geelong Police Magistrate Nicholas Fenwick was uncertain whether the Dog Act should be enforced against Aboriginals. Crown Prosecutor Croke said this was legally possible, but advised against it on policy grounds.

Squatter John G. Robertson related an incident which did not get into the official records: 'the only outrage I have known of', wrote Robertson, 'where the whites were not the first aggressors.'

A white bullock-driver named George had forcibly taken a lubra from a black man. When the black tried to get her back, George threw a pot of scalding tea in his face. News of the event spread rapidly among the tribes. One day in 1843 a different white man named George Lewis was gathering mushrooms on the Corney brothers' run, 'Wando Vale B'.

A native appeared and asked his name. 'George', he replied. Another native behind him immediately speared 'George' through the shoulder, then fled.

Squatter Robertson was able to extract the spear-head with a pair of pliers. Afterwards, 'George' often used to scream out in his sleep that he was being killed and eaten. We don't usually learn much about the sufferings of such innocent white men caught up in the war between the races.

Reports of more serious clashes again began to come from the far Western District. In March James M. Hamilton, overseer at 'Ledcourt', one of Benjamin Boyd's stations east of the Grampians, reported 'depredations' by natives on the sheep.

Commissioner Fyans sent Trooper Charles Lamont of the Border Police to investigate. Lamont testified that when he arrived, James Hamilton seemed 'determined to destroy' the blacks. 'He wanted me to go out with him and give the natives a good scouring', the trooper reported. Hamilton was alleged to have added that 'there would be no quietness from the natives 'till some of them were put on one side; and that he should do his best to shoot them, if he could not take them alive.'

Trooper Lamont felt it was sufficient to capture the tribe's leader, old Billy Billy. This he achieved on 29 April. According to rumour, Billy Billy was 'kept chained to a tree with an insufficient supply of food for several weeks', as a lesson to the remainder of his tribe.

These reports were never proven, but the dates fit. Foster Fyans found Billy Billy in Hamilton lockup on 31 May, transferring him to Portland three days later. The aged native was committed to stand trial at the Supreme Court, but kept in East Melbourne watch-house instead of gaol, because of his 'serious state of depression and debility'.

Meanwhile, Chief Robinson sent Protector Parker to investigate conditions on Boyd's station. Parker reported in August that when the station was first established by Captain Robert Briggs, the tribe continued to live there happily. Since Hamilton's employment, however, 'a painful change' had occurred, with 'decided hostility' developing between the races.

Parker discovered that the 'Mr Hamilton' behind the trouble was actually G. D. Hamilton, formerly a squatter at Woolsthorpe, who was looking after 'Ledcourt' during J. M. Hamilton's absence. The illiterate Trooper Lamont had blamed the wrong Mr Hamilton: when his report, signed with a cross, is examined, it is easy to see how a mistake could have arisen. J. M. Hamilton complained bitterly that the error 'seriously injured my character and prospects', and caused his dismissal by entrepreneur Benjamin Boyd at the Governor's behest.

Ill-feeling at 'Ledcourt' continued. On 2 September shepherd Thomas Donelly saw a native stealing blankets from his hut. As the thief ran towards a group of other Aboriginals,

Donelly fired his gun and wounded him. All fled into the bush.

In Melbourne old Billy Billy was twice brought before Judge Jeffcott. On the first occasion, a jury decided he was unable to understand the proceedings.

Protector Parker was ordered to instruct the old chief. Parker, however, believed that incarceration had 'brought him to a state of terror and excitement nearly akin to insanity.' He felt it 'utterly hopeless' to explain British law under these circumstances. In a private letter to La Trobe, Judge Jeffcott stated that if Billy Billy 'cannot be so instructed, I never will consent that he shall be tried before me.'

Crown Prosecutor Croke believed that one more attempt should be made. When Billy Billy was brought up again in November, a fresh jury reached the same verdict, and he was discharged.

Several promotions and additions reinforced the Native Police during 1843. William Dana's salary as assistant to his brother was more than doubled, to £100 a year. Peter Bennett was promoted to Sergeant-Major, and Samuel Windridge of the 28th Regiment took Bennett's place as Sergeant.

The most promising natives too were promoted. Buckup, described by Protector Thomas as 'a fine intelligent young man', was made corporal and put on the payroll for the first time.*

Another promotion to corporal was that of Yuptun, whose father, mother and brother had been killed by whites during a sheep robbery north of Melbourne in the early days of settlement. According to Thomas, no other black could equal Yuptun for patience, perseverance, courage and loyalty on long journeys. Unfortunately he was dangerous when drunk. After one gaol sentence, Yuptun took Thomas's advice and went to live with the remote Devil's River tribe.

In July Sergeant-Major Bennett was instructed to remain behind at Merri Creek to continue training fourteen Native

---

* After an injury, Buckup's leg had to be amputated. He survived one of Melbourne's first operations using ether, but died on 2 September 1848.

Police recruits. He was enjoined to work them hard to 'keep them out of mischief'. La Trobe sent the remaining thirteen black troopers under 'Captain' Dana to the far Western District, charged with 'protecting the property of the settlers and preserving the peace of the district during the winter months.'

Dana divided his force into two groups, one based at Hamilton and the other at Mount Eckersley.

'Rolf Boldrewood' described amusingly how one patrol rode to 'Squattlesea Mere' in 'regular cavalry style'. They were led by Corporal Buckup, who saluted the young squatter: 'We been sent up by Mr Dana, sir, to stop at this station a bit. Believe the blacks been very bad about here.' Coming from a black trooper, this struck Boldrewood as 'altogether lovely and delicious'. He answered gravely that raids had indeed been very bad lately. 'They only want a good scouring, sir', quoth Buckup.

Dana viewed his men much more seriously than did Boldrewood. 'An Australian Aborigine can do things as well as any other man, when he is made to do so, and feels that he must', wrote Dana. He felt that expansion of the Native Police Corps, its members controlled by rigid martial law, 'would do more to civilize them than any system that has as yet been tried.'

Exactly what 'a scouring' meant was shown in August, when blacks attacked Henry Dwyer's run in the Victoria Valley, south-west of the Grampians, driving off more than 100 sheep.

Dana and four troopers tracked the missing sheep forty miles through mountains to the headwaters of the Glenelg River. There, in dense bush, they found a proper sheepyard, with the stock being guarded (and occasionally eaten) by about thirty blacks.

The troopers attacked. The defence put up 'a very strong resistance', which included rolling boulders down the mountain side on to the troopers. In the mêlée, reported Dana, 'several of the natives were killed'. About seventy sheep were recovered.

While Dana was engaged in the Victoria Range, a group of blacks at Branxholme kidnapped the three-year-old daughter of Abraham Ward, licensee of the Traveller's Rest Hotel. The kidnappers were led by a black named Harry, who had once lived on the Whyte brothers' station 'Konongwootong' (near today's Coleraine).

Sergeant Samuel Windridge took three native constables to track the group through the stony area between Mount Napier and the coast. The kidnappers showed 'such a determined opposition' that Windridge was forced to return empty-handed.

Dana led a second party in search of the little girl, but no trace of her was ever found. Blacks near Mount Eeles told Dana she had been killed.

While Dana was engaged on this search, word came that an unarmed settler named Christopher Bassett had been brutally murdered on 31 August 1843 at his Crawford River run (near present-day Hotspur). Dana hastened to the scene, and found Bassett naked on the ground, speared through the heart, with pegs driven into his eyes. About 200 sheep had been driven off.

Dana organised a search for the murderers, accompanied by several troopers and David Edgar, a local publican/squatter and discoverer of Lake Condah two years before.

Early in September the party came across a number of blacks breaking the legs of sheep at the edge of a swamp. The troopers pursued them into thick reeds, where several spears were thrown. When one native stood up to spear David Edgar at close range, the publican shot him dead.

On an island in the middle of the swamp, the troopers found 'a great number of dead sheep', Christopher Bassett's coat, and a cache of forty muskets. No doubt these had been stolen from local squatters, but were now useless from long exposure to damp.

During the night, the natives returned to the swamp and attempted to carry off some of the sheep. Dana mustered his men for a dawn attack. 'Spears, waddies and tomahawks were thrown at us from all directions', he reported. The troopers behaved 'uncommonly well and steady', and succeeded in shooting 'eight or nine' natives.

Dana believed that the same tribe was responsible for killing Donald McKenzie in 1842, kidnapping Abraham Ward's daughter, and killing Christopher Bassett, but this now seems unprovable.

Returning to their base, the Native Police called in at Samuel Pratt Winter's property, 'Murndal', on the Wannon River.

Winter asked Dana to 'remove a large number of natives from his home station, as they were constantly killing his calves and stealing sheep from the yards at night.' A day or two earlier Winter had caught two black boys driving away and killing his imported rams. Dana questioned the lads and their father. All admitted the incident: the father said, 'Very good beat them.'

Two old tribesmen held the lads in front of the whole tribe, while a black constable gave them 'four lashes each with a small whip'. Later the boys told Winter 'they would never steal sheep again.'

A few days after the flogging incident, on 16 September, another Wannon River squatter named George Duncan Lockhart was driving a loaded dray alone from Portland back to his station 'Kanawalla'. A group of blacks attacked, and seized all his stores, but let the squatter go unharmed.

Sergeant Windridge led five Native Police from Mount Eckersley in pursuit. They caught up with the blacks at nightfall, shot two dead, wounded another, and recovered most of the stores. One native constable, Tunmiel,* was severely speared in the affray. Large quantities of glass and flint from two spears were later extracted from his arm.

---

* 'A young steady, and faithful policeman', according to William Thomas. Tunmiel died at Narre Warren in 1850.

Sometimes the black police were useful in helping to arrest runaway convicts.

One such convict, Timothy Sullmein, escaped from irons in a government work gang near Portland on 17 March. He roamed the countryside, stealing a double-barrelled gun from Duncan McRae's 'Glenorchy' run. Wounded by blacks, he sought refuge at Dan O'Neil's inn on Smoky River, but was arrested there by the native constables on 11 October.

Although the Native Police were now blooded and keen for more, the district remained quiet for a few weeks.

Then, on 6 November, a group of blacks again appeared on Thomas Ricketts's station 'Clunie' on the Glenelg River, which had been plundered the previous year (chapter 8). This time more than 130 sheep were taken.

Ricketts did not wait for the police to arrive. He enlisted the aid of several neighbours, and tracked the sheep for three days. When the squatters found the missing mob, they rode down hard, guns ready. In the brief words of Police Magistrate Blair's report, 'The natives attacked them with spears and obliged them to fire in their own defence.'

Six blacks were shot dead. Strangely enough, no white man was injured. No proper investigation seems to have followed.

Late in 1843 the Native Police prepared to return to their headquarters at Merri Creek in time for Christmas.

Dana reported that they had travelled some 2500 miles, taking part in five more minor 'collisions', with stolen property being recovered each time. Apparently no further deaths or woundings occurred.

Two blacks were charged with stealing a few sheep from William Pettett's station in the Pyrenees in November, but these were sent to Melbourne by Protector Parker for trial.

Western District settlers now felt reasonably certain that if further clashes occurred, all the forces of government were arrayed for action on their side.

11

THE
PROTECTORATE
BEGINS
TO FALTER

The existence of Aboriginals proved a frightful nuisance to active white men, both government and private, who found themselves beset by every other kind of problem common in pioneering situations.

The Protectorate had been charged with the duty of reaching some reasonable accommodation with the original inhabitants—in other words, of humanely neutralising them as an obstacle to white settlement. Given the characteristics of both races, this was an almost impossible assignment. When events progressively proved this to be the case, it became only too easy to blame the Protectors for their individual failings, instead of examining the unrealistic expectations of officials and settlers.

As early as January 1840, Superintendent La Trobe could write that 'the state of affairs at the present date is far from being calculated to flatter the hopes which have been entertained.' Already he was inclined to blame Chief Protector George Robinson:

Instead of sitting still in Melbourne for seven months, and writing to the Assistant Protectors, he should have visited them in their districts, and by pointing out to them the practical part of their duty, have yielded them that instruction and encouragement which they could expect from none but himself.'

Again, on 3 February 1841, Governor Gipps reported to London: 'I feel it my duty to declare that my hopes of any advantage being derived from the employment of the Protectors are every day diminishing.'

Officers in the field were even more scathing. Crown Commissioner Fyans, writing from Portland, said that before the Protectors arrived, he 'seldom visited a station without witnessing the employment of Aborigines.' Since the establishment of Protectors' Stations, however, 'the character of the Native has changed, with a continued scene of open thefts . . . cruel murders . . . reckless destruction.' Blankets given to Aboriginals could be found 'laying through the country, rotting on the ground.'

Even when Robinson was given the fullest possible facilities, persuaded to leave his desk, and instructed to 'open a friendly communication' with western tribes, Police Magistrate James Blair hotly criticised his activities at Portland—particularly the distribution of 'a large quantity of knives' to the natives.

Early in 1842 La Trobe wrote to Gipps reminding him that the Protectorate had now enjoyed a three-year trial. During that period it had spent £16 000 in public funds, could show few beneficial results, and still displayed 'the same spirit of internal distrust and dissatisfaction'. Gipps sent La Trobe's opinion to London, agreeing with him that the Protectorate was tending 'rather to increase than allay the irritation' between the races. Robinson, thought Gipps, was 'far beyond the prime of life' and 'quite unequal' to his task. The other Protectors' attitude was one of 'feeble action and puling complaint'.

Secretary of State Lord Stanley replied: 'I cannot conceal

from myself that the failure of the system of Protectors has been at least as complete as that of the Missions.' He authorised Gipps to close down the Protectorate Department if he could see no prospect of future benefits.

During the depression of 1842–43 Crown land sales practically ceased and the government was forced to constrict all public expenditure. Gipps took the opportunity of cutting back the Protectorate. On 4 February 1843 he instructed La Trobe to find ways of making continuous savings. Robinson submitted a report showing that annual savings of £2590 could be made on various aspects of the Assistant Protectors' operations. However, he did not propose any reduction of his own salary or expenses.

La Trobe thereupon wrote to Gipps suggesting that the whole of Robinson's office could be abolished without ill effect. Cautiously considering the power of Robinson's supporters in London, Gipps did not accept this proposal. Regarding the Assistant Protectors, La Trobe proposed they should be cut back to their basic salary of £250 a year, with only the smallest allowance for transport of rations to distant stations. Handouts of flour, tea, rice and sugar to Aboriginals would practically cease. Native families would become dependent on local meat supplies, and whatever grain could be grown on the stations. The £3000 spent on rations in 1842 would drop almost to nil. In other words, having persuaded and forced the blacks to congregate on Aboriginal stations, and made them dependent on charity, the government would now remove the enticements which kept them reasonably tranquil.

Since Gipps did not dare to sack Robinson, La Trobe suggested that the Chief Protector, who lived in Melbourne, might as well take charge of the few blacks remaining close by at Narre Warren and Merri Creek. This would clear the way to dismiss William Thomas instead. 'The fact is,' wrote La Trobe, 'I have never been able to consider the employment of Mr Thomas in any other light than as an almost useless expenditure of the public money.' In addition, William Le Souef had proved himself so unsuitable at Goulburn River that he might as well also be transferred or dismissed.

Let us now see what actually happened at each station, and how it affected the Aboriginal population.

Goulburn River Station

The first result of government cuts at Goulburn River Station was that the six white men employed by the Protector quit in a body. Le Souef persuaded some to stay, by offering to pay the difference in wages from his own pocket. Since the services of a smith were essential to continue farming operations, he replaced the former blacksmith John Grady with John Pike.

Le Souef continually attacked Robinson for failure to support the station, claiming that appeals for help were 'treated with the most perfect neglect'. The only letter he received, said Le Souef, was a direction regarding special buttons to be worn by Protectors as a means of identification. The station 'shall not be rusted up if I can prevent it,' Le Souef swore, 'and if I cannot, the public shall know by whom it was done.'

Le Souef's own position became untenable in the latter part of 1843, when he was shown to have misused government stores and equipment. Another replacement blacksmith, Michael Lynis, had informed Robinson that Le Souef had rewarded Mrs Lynis with ten shillings for washing and cooking services, by issuing the equivalent to her in government stores. The blacksmith added that he had shod Le Souef's private horses during government time, besides ploughing and sowing three acres of oats for the Protector's own use. John Pike, whom Le Souef had promoted to overseer, stated that offal from slaughtered sheep, which the Chief Protector had ordered to be given to Aboriginals in lieu of rations, was 'invariably taken down to the quarters of Mr Le Souef and given to his dogs . . . and the fat was made up into candles for his own private use.' William Shackerley, station carpenter, wrote that he had tried in vain to get £32 in wages owed to him by the Protectorate, even though the money had been sent from Melbourne. Now he was 'in great distress', and 'under the necessity of selling part of my clothes to support myself and wife.' Further investigation by Crown Commissioner Airey and Protector Parker showed that Le Souef was indeed guilty of these peculations.

Le Souef was unable to furnish receipts for £110 worth of provisions and clothing he had claimed. Nor was he able to account for £34 worth of food he said he had issued to employees. At harvest time Le Souef had removed men from the fields 'to make a bathing house for his private use'. A quantity of government canvas was used to line the sides. Sub-Treasurer Lonsdale had allowed Le Souef an additional £82 for employees' wages, but they had not received the money. In these circumstances, Le Souef was fortunate only to be dismissed with little publicity, instead of facing criminal charges which would have destroyed the Protectorate's remaining credibility.

After a period of near-destitution, Le Souef was so far forgiven in 1850 as to be appointed secretary of the Victorian Industrial Society at £100 a year.

Le Souef was not replaced after his dismissal from Goulburn River Station. Protector Parker was forced to ride constantly between the Loddon and Goulburn River Stations in an attempt to control both institutions. Parker reported that after Le Souef's removal natives returned to Goulburn Station in larger numbers; average attendance from July to September 1843 was about eighty men, women and children. The potato crop failed, but Parker was able to supply seed potatoes from his Loddon River stocks. The new wheat crop was in 'a healthy and promising state', while the previous year's harvest supplied sufficient flour for the whole of 1843.

Loddon River Station

Under Protector Parker the Aboriginal Station near the Loddon River showed hopeful signs. Hundreds of natives usually lived there, earning rewards such as food and clothing for work in the fields.

La Trobe expressed 'great satisfaction' in March 1843. He informed Gipps that 'not a single case of homicide' had occurred, while 'the property of the settlers for a very considerable circuit appears been altogether exempt from outrages of any description.' Parker himself claimed that continuation of the Station gave 'some compensation to these unhappy people for the loss of their country.' About 350 natives had been 'prevented from roaming about the country', and taught to 'employ themselves in cultivating the ground.'

Produce during 1843 included 650 bushels of wheat, 50 bushels of barley, and 11 tons of potatoes, equivalent to £300 in rations. The adult natives, wrote Parker, were showing 'united and persevering exertions' in manually reaping, threshing and grinding the grain for their own use.

All station blacks attended Sunday services at the Loddon River Station. 'I have prepared a few simple prayers in their own language', wrote Parker: soon he hoped to translate suitable biblical passages.

The Protector added he had been 'deeply affected by the repeated and earnest entreaties of many youths' that he would teach them to read English. He tried to devote an hour each morning and evening to the project, but suffered many interruptions to his schedule. The eager students were sometimes 'reproached by the older Aboriginals for having become so like "white fellows" as not to be able to hunt game like their forefathers.'

Conversion of the young to European ways, said Parker, meant that serious affrays with local squatters had ceased. In fact, the settlers gave Parker 'most encouraging expressions of approbation'.

Fifty wild natives of the Mallegoondeet tribe came south from the Murray River in 1843 to see what was happening. They were delighted by their courteous reception, said Parker, and 'promised to respect the property and lives of white people' on returning to their own country.

It all seemed too good to last. When government cuts removed cherished rewards like tea and sugar from the hard-working Station blacks, Parker reported that 'Some dissatisfaction has in consequence existed.'

Worse was to come. After Le Souef's dismissal from Goulburn River in 1843, Parker was given the task of controlling both Stations. To assist him, Robinson sent up his own son-in-law, 30-year-old Dr James Allen. Allen had worked with Robinson for many years, mainly as a surgeon on Flinders Island, where he had won a reputation as an honest, hard-working officer who displayed great sympathy for the Aboriginals. In the early 1840s Dr Allen was running sheep near Melbourne. He married Robinson's daughter Maria, but in the crash of 1842–43 went bankrupt. The Chief Protector arranged for him to become medical officer at Narre Warren Station in August 1843, transferring him to Loddon River Station in February 1844.

On arrival, Dr Allen found that conditions had seriously deteriorated during Parker's unavoidable absences. The overseer had quit and been replaced by the constable, but that officer knew next to nothing about farming. Most of the seed wheat had been lost: only 150 bushels of dirty wheat remained in store. The station was nearly £900 in debt to neighbouring squatters for meat supplied.

Worse yet, the constable and convict bullock-driver had begun breeding their own pigs behind the bark storeroom. Dr Allen claimed they were giving to the pigs most of the food meant for 'the hundred sick and destitute Aborigines'. The result was that the blacks were drifting back to squatters' runs and 'subsisting on the miserable fruits of vice'. Captain John Hepburn of 'Smeaton Hill', for instance, reported that contrary to his orders, five of his shepherds were harbouring native women in their huts, and had raped a young girl. They were fined £5 each on the first charge, no admissible evidence from white witnesses being available on the second. This was not the only bad example set by whites. Protector Parker reported in 1843 that G. D. Smythe, formerly of the Survey Department, was living on a run in the Pentland Hills with 'several Aboriginal women and girls cohabiting with him, under circumstances outraging public decency.'

In July 1844, when Dr Allen was visiting Goulburn River Station, a Murray River native came to him with a tale that ten women, five men and seven children had been shot by Native Police along the Murray. Protector Parker hastened to investigate, but found the rumour was 'totally without foundation'.

At this period, unfortunately, Dr Allen began showing symptoms of severe mental disturbance. He tried three times to murder his wife, and was dismissed from the public service. His reports, which still seemed rational enough, were largely ignored.*

With the partial failure of agricultural efforts, Parker decided to supplement them with wool production. For some years he had privately run a small flock of wethers, which were 'carefully tended by Aboriginal youths' at Parker's expense. Early in January 1844 he was officially permitted to buy 500 ewes from W. H. Bacchus junior at 5s. each. Friendly local squatters, led by Captain Hepburn and Laurence Rostron, donated eleven valuable rams. The first year's result was 350 new lambs. Parker's books at the end of 1844 showed that 1900 lbs of wool had been shorn and sold for nearly £100. A similar return for March 1845 showed 1988 lbs of wool sold to James Cain in Melbourne for £99. Bales were branded with a broad arrow above the letters A.B.O.R.

Despite its problems, Loddon River Station could still be accounted a modest success.

Mount Rouse Station

At Mount Rouse Station in the Western District, Dr John Watton continued his policy of living as quietly as possible,

---

* Dr Allen and Maria later settled on Clark Island in Bass Strait, where they raised ten children. Allen was drowned in 1856.

while rendering what succour he could to natives who happened to come to the Station.

Intermittent efforts were made to attain self-sufficiency. These were not assisted by the government's economy drive of 1843, when £25 a year was saved by dismissing the best white employee, George Hamilton. In addition, the Station's three convict servants were removed in October.

By 1845 Dr Watton was left with only one white assistant, James Harden, who was paid £20 a year. Since local squatters were paying up to £26 in wages, no other white servant would remain on the Station. The result, wrote Watton, was that 'Our crop of potatoes is now spoiling in the ground.'

At the end of that year, the Station's last employee quit. 'I am quite at a loss how to proceed', wrote Watton. Without skilled labour it was impossible to sow crops: the station was subsisting on a few hundred bushels of wheat reaped the previous January.

Only about twenty blacks were now living at the Station. Others preferred to work without pay for local squatters, where at least they were better fed and given quantities of 'merrijig' (tobacco). Of course their wives had to be made available to the whites for sexual and/or domestic purposes.

Health at Mount Rouse had been reasonably good, said Watton, the main problems being nine cases of syphilis and seven cases of psoriasis (an itchy, scaly skin disease).

Dr Watton added he had heard that in the bush 'mortality has been very great during the past winter.' He attributed this to accidental self-poisoning by the Aboriginals—'their having eaten too freely of sheep which died after severe [arsenical] dressing for the scab.'

Merri Creek Station

After all William Thomas's efforts and sufferings, the expenditure cuts of 1843 affected him more harshly than any other Protector.

In July 1843 Robinson advised Thomas that he would take personal control of Narre Warren Station. As a result, Thomas's ration allowance of 7s. a day was cancelled. This was equivalent to a salary reduction of about one-third. Thomas complained bitterly to La Trobe, asking why he was the only Protector singled out for such treatment. Thomas said he had always done his best to follow Robinson's instructions, working every day with the blacks and writing his reports late at night. In four years he had only taken two days' leave, and that because of illness. Thomas claimed that when he asked Robinson for reasons, 'the Chief replied "that I had brought it all on myself, that I was too conscientious, that by my reports I had been my own assassin".' La Trobe replied through Robinson that each of the Protectorate districts had to bear a burden of reductions. Thomas in particular had failed in his duties: he had never attained sufficient control over the blacks 'to guide their movements'.

The main task left for Thomas was to attempt to manage the blacks camped at Merri Creek—and especially to prevent mendicant lubras and their diseased dogs from 'stalking through the streets of Melbourne.' Often, wrote George McCrae, the women were merely on their way to the lower Yarra, 'to assemble at the slaughter-houses to collect sheeps' heads and plucks which they roasted at their fires by the Merri Creek.'

Thomas made renewed efforts to follow the tribes which moved in and out, as they continually broke up into smaller groups, then coalesced again. But most of the Protector's facilities had disappeared in the economy drive. His convict servants and bullock team had been removed. He was forced to transport food, tent and bedding on horseback, walking alongside in all weathers. Thomas complained that on 12 August he had 'travelled 22 miles on foot and a subsequent day 26 miles.'

Returning despondently to Merri Creek, Thomas began school lessons on 18 August for the few black children left there. He built his hut near the junction with the Yarra River, on a bend upstream from Dight's mill. Thomas's other main duty was to attend gaoled Aboriginals awaiting trial, and attempt to instruct them in legal procedures. In his journal Thomas reflected that 'The poor blacks may be said now to be at the mercy of the settlers . . . We have no commission from the Lord to destroy the people . . . '

Early in December numbers of Barrabool and Buninyong tribes arrived at Merri Creek. They told Thomas they were there 'to settle their differences'. A furious battle between the two groups broke out on 5 December. Dozens of spears and other weapons flew through the air, seriously wounding six natives. Then the women joined in, 'howling and jabbering', beating each other with yam-sticks. Ten women suffered broken knuckles and other wounds. One Buninyong native, Turrenuk, struck by a wonguim (boomerang), died a fortnight later from loss of blood.

In January 1844 hundreds more natives and their children swarmed to Merri Creek. Thomas counted their numbers as 185 from Campaspe and Loddon tribes, 164 Goulburns, 95 Murray tribes, 86 Yarra tribe, 46 Barrabools, 42 Western Port tribes, 38 Werralims (a sub-section of Goulburns), and 20 Native Police—a total of 676 Aboriginals camped along the creek.

Thomas observed that the visitors were 'much more free than formerly from that vile disease [syphilis] introduced among them by base characters, an evident proof of the blessed effects of wholesome Emigration.' He had 'never observed a finer and more wholesome race of children' than his new scholars. For a few months, attendances at school and church services increased markedly, with Thomas doing his best to translate psalms into various dialects. But the tribes were actually there to participate in what Thomas called traditional 'judicial proceedings'* against two tribal leaders, De Villiers

---

* In later years, Thomas gave a garbled version of this event from memory to R. Brough Smyth, who published it in *The Aborigines of Victoria*, vol. 1, pp. 81-2. Thomas's contemporary journal, a preferable source, was by that time well hidden in the official records.

and Billy Lonsdale, for killing a young Werralim black some months earlier on Charles and Frederick Manton's station at Tooradin, on Western Port Bay.

Thomas at first attempted to have the accused blacks arrested and kept in safe custody at Melbourne Gaol. They went into hiding and easily eluded the Chief Constable. Even the Native Police disobeyed orders to assist the white police: these were solely matters for tribal justice.

On 8 February, as soon as Thomas had left on an errand, the Werralim blacks insisted on satisfaction. The brother of one of the culprits and the uncle of the other, painted with white ochre, stood to receive sentence in their stead. They waited about ten yards in front of their accusers, protected only by shields, standing unflinchingly while a shower of spears flew around them. Both men were severely wounded. Pinterginner, an original member of the Native Police in 1839, took a spear through the chest. He later recovered in the government hospital. With this form of justice satisfied, most of the blacks dispersed peacefully enough to their homelands.

The result of the government's economy measures would have satisfied an accountant if nobody else. Instead of the Protectorate costing more than £5000 a year, by the end of 1845 its expenditure totalled only £2089 for the twelve months. Robinson continued to draw £590 in salary and allowances, but spent little else. Thomas drew his £250 salary, and was allowed £16 to repair his family's leaking hut. At Loddon and Goulburn River Stations, Parker was paid £455 as full salary and allowances. At Mount Rouse Station, Dr Watton was allowed £165 as salary, and small amounts for rations.

Scarcely any food or clothing was handed out anywhere to Aboriginals. The Protectorate Stations, with their once-vaunted agricultural produce, now seemed to exist mainly to support the white government employees manning them.

Aboriginals and Homosexuality

The idea of homosexuality aroused special horror in the minds of most 'respectable' European settlers. Not only was it associated with the evils of convict transportation: it was also known to be one of the main causes of incurable venereal disease.

Nobody knows whether Aboriginal males practised sodomy before the arrival of white men. It seems possible but unlikely, for women were usually freely available to tribesmen who had passed their initiation ordeals. However, after a few years of interaction with whites, doctors began to report cases of sodomy and accompanying anal syphilis among black men.

In Port Phillip the first report came from Dr William Baylie, medical officer at Goulburn River Station. On 24 January 1842 he reported to Chief Protector Robinson that 'the awful crime of "Sodomy" prevails in some degree amongst the Aborigines . . . The consequence of this practice is to increase disease of a most virulent character.' The usual symptom seen by Dr Baylie was a secondary stage of syphilis known as condylomata-lata, characterised by moist, round, wart-like papules, which coalesced around the anus.

Protector Parker wrote the same year from Loddon River Station that he had 'long suspected that unnatural offences were not uncommon among these degraded people.' Parker found 'that most of the single men are guilty of this horrible crime, and that the young boys are brutally forced to become its victims.' However, the practice was 'regarded as shameful by the generality of the people, and they are reluctant to speak about it.'

Dr Baylie spent several years in private practice at Geelong. In 1849 he repeated his allegations on the spread of sodomy. He put forward a plan for compulsory enlistment of all young black men into an 'Aboriginal Corps de Garde', where they could be strictly disciplined and prevented from indulging in 'unnatural contact'.

La Trobe circularised the Protectors for their opinions.

From the Goulburn River Station, Dr James Horsburgh said that although syphilitic ulcers were common, he had seen no recent cases of condylomata-lata. However, Protector Parker had now developed a theory that the disease was indigenous: 'though not introduced by Europeans ... it has been greatly aggravated since the races were commingled.' The main reason was 'the prostitution of females to the Europeans', causing 'a most unequal distribution of women'—that is, the whites were taking over most of the black women. In every instance of sodomy detected by Parker 'the crime has been committed by single men, and has invariably been discontinued when the parties have obtained wives.' Sometimes Parker was forced to take into his own house 'the boys who were sought to be made victims' of the dreadful vice. The sodomites were generally ostracised by the tribes, and would not come near the Protectorate Stations. Parker thought that Dr Baylie's idea of a disciplined life for young men was based on a fallacy. He would believe it practical only 'when it can be shown that the drill sergeant's cane is a more effectual instrument of moral reformation than the Word of God.'

Protector Thomas said he had seen little sign of the unnatural crime which had 'caused Sodom and Gomorrah to be razed to the ground'. On the contrary, 'the Australian savages, in all their attacks on others to gratify nature, their invariable object is to secure the females.' Chief Protector Robinson scoffed at Baylie's proposed solution. 'The associating together of young men in the way Dr Baylie proposes, is more likely to increase than suppress the disgusting practice', he wrote.

12

AFFRAYS ALONG THE MURRAY, 1840–43

Natives along the Murray River had been feared by white men since 1830, when Charles Sturt's exploration party narrowly escaped death at the hands of several hundred war-painted warriors. But the irresistible tide of squatting expansion saw settlement spreading up and down the mighty river, with the usual results for the black race of disease and decimation, and vain reprisals against the white invaders.

In June 1840 the brig *Maria* from Adelaide was wrecked near Murray Mouth, Lake Alexandrina. All twenty-six male, female and juvenile passengers were slaughtered by local tribesmen. Inspector Alexander Tolmer of the South Australian Police located two blacks who were said to have led the killing, and hanged them in front of the tribe as a lesson in white vengeance.

Further up the Murray, an overland party droving 5000 sheep to Adelaide was attacked on 16 April 1841. All eleven white men, several suffering spear wounds, were forced to flee. A strongly armed group which set out from Adelaide to recover the sheep was met by a force of about 500 tribesmen, who again routed the whites. South Australian Governor George Grey warned that all overlanders should be prepared for the worst.

Port Phillip Superintendent La Trobe tried a more pacific approach in April 1842, commissioning the Reverends Francis Tuckfield and Benjamin Hurst of Buntingdale Mission to make contact with the Aboriginals along the central Murray. Near today's Echuca the missionaries discovered a tribe living on the flood plains which they called Moama. The blacks were peaceful enough, subsisting mainly on fish caught in brush-wood traps 'displaying remarkable ingenuity'. The whites presented them with a few tomahawks and knives.

About 130 natives from further downstream appeared. Hurst told them that 'the great Governor would do the same for them as he has done for others'—that is, establish stations to protect and assist them. 'As soon as they heard this,' wrote Hurst, 'their countenances began to brighten and there was a spontaneous expression of surprise and joy.'

Hurst felt that the Moama blacks were 'not such a warlike race' as those further south. These were so 'tractable, peaceable and kind' that they gave the missionaries fresh fish every day, and took them to see many places of interest. He was struck by the 'unusually large proportion of children among those tribes which had no previous intercourse with Europeans.' One group of twenty-seven women all carried babies on their backs. They were 'entirely free from loathsome diseases'.

The missionary suggested establishment of a new refuge for the blacks on the lower Campaspe River. It would have to subsist mainly on sheep and cattle grazing, because of the generally poor quality of the soil. Unfortunately local Wes-leyan authorities decided they could not do more than continue to subsidise their existing mission station at Buntingdale. La Trobe similarly found that no government funds were available, but promised to 'leave the field open for future missionary exertions' by discouraging squatters from settling near the junction of the Campaspe and Murray Rivers.

None of these pious hopes prevented squatters from intruding into tribal lands. One such newcomer was Edward Curr, for many years manager of the Van Diemen's Land Company's pastoral interests, who decided in 1841 to transfer his family to Port Phillip. Aged forty-three, Curr made his home at 'St Heliers', Abbotsford, placing his sons in charge of extensive grazing leaseholds. The family found some of the best land at Tongala, south-east of Echuca. Here the eldest son, Edward Micklethwaite Curr, 22, assisted by his younger brother Richard, established 'Moira' station on the beautiful Moira Lakes.

During the winter of 1842 local blacks began stealing sheep and proceeding 'to cook mutton chops on a large scale'. Curr wrote that 'Such feasting and greasing of heads had probably never been known.' Late that year two Border Police troopers seized one of the tribe, leaving him fastened to a slab hut with a bullock-chain until he agreed to lead them to the thieves' hiding-place. When near the Murray, however, the prisoner made a bolt for it, was shot down, and killed. According to Curr, the troopers 'placed the body in a canoe' and set it adrift down the river. No hint of this matter seems to have survived in the official record.

In January 1843 Henry Dana and some of his Native Police arrived to patrol the area. Curr told Dana that large numbers of hostile natives had assembled on the south bank of the Murray. They were still 'daily threatening the lives of his men and attempting to take the sheep.'

Dana proposed a plan in which his four black troopers would stay behind to protect 'Moira' homestead, while he and three white NCOs would attempt to seize the tribe's leaders. Curr went ahead on 1 February with a bullock dray and sheep to act as a decoy. He succeeded in enticing many of the blacks from their reed-bed shelter. Before they could spear any sheep, Curr pointed out a chief named Warry. The white NCOs charged from their hiding place and seized him, despite the fusillade of spears thrown at them. The other blacks retreated to the reeds, where they 'kept their ground in a very determined manner'. When Dana pursued them, he was speared in the thigh, but managed to wheel his horse around and escape.

There is little doubt that much more occurred than was revealed. When Protector Le Souef arrived on the scene a fortnight later, he found that several natives in the reed-beds had been wounded by gun-fire, one so badly that he was not expected to live.

No hint of this appears in Dana's reports to La Trobe for the period. Dana was more concerned with his estimate that there were about 2000 natives on this part of the Murray. 'I had communication with a very great number,' he wrote, ' . . . on the whole they appeared well inclined and not very mischievous, numbers of them working at the different settlers' stations and being well treated in return.'

But when E. M. Curr came to write his memoirs many years later, he recalled that Dana had shown him his report on the episode. The officer, thought Curr, 'omitted some incidents which I thought should have been mentioned.' Dana's hearty reply was that 'persons unconnected with the public service know nothing of reports . . . being apt to blurt out statements more properly held in reserve.'

Meanwhile, back at the river, the prisoner Warry had been secured with a rope around his neck to a trooper's horse, and dragged off to 'Moira' homestead. From there a wool-dray took him to Melbourne. On 24 February Police Magistrate St John committed him for trial. Warry was brought up before Judge Willis in March. The jury decided that 'the prisoner was not at present of sufficient mental capacity' to be tried. Warry, in fact, took little interest in the proceedings, 'the only matter which appeared to arrest his attention being the barristers' wigs, which seemed to puzzle him a good deal.'

After one remand, a now-friendly Curr succeeded in obtaining the native's release. Warry lived with Protector Thomas for a time, then returned to the Murray. 'Ever after he and I were the best of friends', wrote Curr, adding that Warry's tribe became 'quite reclaimed characters'.

Chief Protector Robinson turned up at 'Moira' station on 26 March. One of the Curr brothers told him that the local tribe 'never had venereal until one of his men brought it and gave it to seven women and they gave it to the rest.' E. M. Curr failed to mention this sombre fact in his memoirs.

With relations between most settlers and blacks gradually worsening, the Native Police were sent back to patrol the central Murray region late in 1843. Here they joined forces with Border Police commanded by Henry Smythe, a former surveyor, and brother-in-law of former Police Magistrate William Lonsdale, now head of the Treasury in Melbourne.

Smythe took up his appointment as Crown Commissioner of the Murray District in September. On 15 December he mustered the combined force of white and black police, accompanied by three local settlers, Henry S. Lewes, James Hogg and John Oldbury Atkinson, whose stock had been speared on several occasions. That evening, according to one of the participants (Sergeant Edward Broderick of the Border Police), the heavily-armed band attempted to surround the blacks' fishing camp by the 'Moira' reed-beds. The natives 'immediately deserted their camp and spears, took the river and reeds.' The troopers pursued them, and allegedly shot them 'like wild dogs, without their making the slightest resistance, even the young children was shot out of the canoes on the river.' Broderick claimed there was 'more than a probability that the individuals shot were not those who committed the outrages [spearing of stock].' He said 'there was not the least endeavour made to arrest them, or even to ascertain if any of the offenders . . . were of the party.'

Broderick's evidence may be treated with some reserve, for he did not give it until five months later, after he had been dismissed for drunkenness and immorality, and replaced as sergeant by Johnstone Thornhill.

Smythe's defence to the accusations was that he had required the white settlers to identify the wanted natives before attempting to surround them. 'Almost immediately every man became invisible to his neighbour, being in a bed of reeds of great height and density', wrote Smythe. He admitted that 'some lives were unfortunately lost.' One trooper, seized by a black, 'had in self defence shot him.' This was all of substance that Smythe had to offer. To supplement his thin defence, La Trobe requested that he obtain statements from other participants.

The next piece of evidence came from Protector Parker, who reported that Trooper F. Bush of the Border Police told Dr Neil Campbell at Loddon River Aboriginal Station that 'the blacks had been fired upon indiscriminately and several shot.' One native, 'wounded by ball', came to Campbell for treatment: he told the surgeon that two women and a child had been killed. Parker sent the evidence to his chief, but Robinson apparently did not act on it.

Next came a statement from J. O. Atkinson, one of the settlers who had been present at the battle. Spears had been thrown, said Atkinson, and 'I saw the bodies of two natives who had been shot', but no corpses of women or children.

By June 1844 ex-sergeant Broderick was becoming impatient. He demanded a full inquiry, threatening otherwise to complain to the Aborigines Protection Society and the Secretary of State in London.

Two months later Gipps wrote to La Trobe that he saw 'no reason to suppose that Mr Smythe encouraged or sanctioned the exercise of any unnecessary severity towards the natives.' Broderick, who had complained 'from vindictive motives only', was unworthy of further attention.' Smythe was safe.

13

INCREASING CONTROL OVER THE WESTERN AND WIMMERA DISTRICTS, 1844-45

Clashes in the Western District in 1844 began with attacks on the flocks of William H. Pettett and W. J. T. Clarke, partners in the 'Dowling Forest' run near Lake Learmonth (north-west of today's Ballarat).

On 13 January the natives seriously wounded a shepherd and drove away his sheep. They were tracked by Commissioner Powlett and four Border Police, accompanied by 'Captain' Henry Dana and four Native Police, to a distance of about eighty miles. The blacks, caught in the act of 'regaling themselves on the sheep', hurled spears, wounding Dana and one trooper. The police retaliated, killing one native and wounding two others. The survivors fled, leaving thirty sheep to be recovered. Powlett claimed later that 'some of the natives were from Mr Parker's Aboriginal Station.'

The blacks returned to the attack on Pettett and Clarke's run on 10 May. They approached a shepherd named William Higgins, demanding a 'big belly-full' of mutton. Higgins refused. One 'very tall middle-aged black with large bushy whiskers' took a spear from behind a tree, threw it, and hit the shepherd. Higgins was able to pull out the spear and fire his double-barrelled gun, hitting one native. As this wounded man came crawling towards him, said Higgins, the other blacks were able to drive off 780 sheep.

The shepherd, although dying, made a deposition before the nearest JP, J. Allan Cameron of 'Decameron' station, previously a lieutenant in the 13th Light Dragoons. Powlett's and Dana's police were quickly summoned. They chased the raiders to the northern end of the Pyrenees, and there, on 16 May, killed their leader, a Mallee black called Lillgona.

La Trobe then warned Powlett that he must be careful to proceed lawfully in all such confrontations. He realised that occasional collisions with hostile natives were 'almost inevitable', but instructed that Commissioners in charge of Border Police must first try 'mild measures', such as using Protectors to persuade tribes to give up offenders voluntarily. Harsh actions like those adopted by Major Lettsom in 1840 should not be undertaken 'without some hope of convicting the parties', La Trobe added. Whenever loss of life occurred, inquiries must be instituted immediately, and depositions sent to the Crown Prosecutor for action.

Further to the west, meanwhile, natives were again on the rampage. During March 1844 Koort Kirrup led raids on Henty and other out-stations in the Mount Gambier area. Dana's Native Police pursued the black leader for months, finally arresting him in August (chapter 8).

On 'Fulham', a Glenelg River run owned by Simeon Lord and Sir John Owen, 29-year-old overseer George Fairbairn had been plagued by raiding parties for nearly a year.

In July 1843, when sixty-five sheep were stolen, Fairbairn's shepherds disobeyed orders to report first to the head station. Instead, they immediately attacked the blacks' camp, 'rushing into the middle and discharging all their firearms at the same time.'

The following month the blacks attacked again, driving 1000 sheep forty miles to the Wimmera River. Fairbairn and his men surrounded and rushed the native camp. 'Some of them were shot', he reported laconically, without adding much detail.

Attacks on 'Fulham' run resumed in March 1844, when Fairbairn was absent giving evidence on earlier affrays. 'During the last three or four weeks an immense number of sheep have been driven off in this neighbourhood', he wrote.

On 1 April the blacks pinioned a shepherd, removed his coat and pistol, and drove away 130 lambs. This time the marauders took the sheep to a piece of burned ground, 'and kept wheeling them about so infernally' that trackers could not follow.

Due to these continual losses and mounting debts, the estate of Owen and Lord was put into receivership. The run fell into the hands of a new squatting dynasty, the Armytage family.

Natives along the Glenelg River struck again early in April. This time they crept up to 'Dunrobin', a 150 000 acre property four miles north of today's Casterton, leased by James Addison and William Murray. It adjoined a smaller run called 'Nangeela', privately leased by Henry Dana (Commandant of the Native Police) and Robert Savage.

One day in mid-April the overseer, William McPherson, was shocked to see a wounded sheep, with a spear driven through it, bleating and stumbling its way back to the homestead. He rushed to the out-station, to find 700 sheep missing and no sign of the shepherd or his double-barrelled gun.

After a three-day search in wet conditions, most of the missing sheep were located in thick scrub on the banks of the Glenelg. Nearby, in a shallow grave, lay the shepherd, Thomas Casey, the back of his skull broken, three wounds on his forehead, his nose broken off, two spear wounds through his heart, and another through his neck. 'I believe', wrote McPherson, 'the above case is the first on record in which the natives have covered their diabolical murders by burying.'

Police Magistrate James Blair conducted an inquest, but found the body in an advanced state of decomposition, 'accelerated no doubt by its being badly affected with venereal disease.' The murder', said Blair, had 'created such a panic' that squatters now had to send out two armed shepherds with every flock.

William Ryan, a shepherd on Benjamin Boyd's 'Ledcourt' run in the Grampians, reported that on 16 April a party of nine blacks approached and demanded that he hand over the flock. The raiders were led by old Billy Billy, who had been badly treated on his arrest by Border Police the previous year, but released after appearing before Judge Jeffcott (chapter 10). In this latest confrontation, Billy Billy threw his spear at a sheep and killed it. The others threw spears at Ryan, who fired his gun twice, killing one man and wounding another.

La Trobe sent Ryan's statement to Crown Prosecutor Croke, who felt a thorough investigation was required. La Trobe sent the papers on to Protector Parker, asking him to make inquiries. But Parker's time was more urgently required at the Goulburn and Loddon River stations.

The Protector did not reply for nearly two years. With the event so far in the past, Parker could only report vague rumours among the tribes that a black had been shot on Boyd's property. There was even a rumour that the shepherd had cut himself with a knife and pretended it was a spear wound.

La Trobe washed his hands of the affair, concluding that Ryan's whole story was 'factitious' and undeserving of further notice.

A settler in the Portland district, James Shepherd, shot an Aboriginal on 13 July, and informed Police Magistrate Blair of the circumstances. No trace of his deposition, or any further information, can now be found in the official files.

Early in 1844 a squatter named Charles Kiernan formed a run

which he named 'Berrat'. It was located on the lower Gellibrand River, north-west of Cape Otway, near Moonlight Head.

In mid-July Kiernan went off to Melbourne, leaving his shepherd in charge. A squatter named Scott, visiting from Lake Colac, later found the hut burned down, with 'small pieces of burnt bone apparently human' lying in the ashes. There were, however, no remnants of the station's tomahawks, knives or the shepherd's double-barrelled gun. The sugar cask was found empty in the creek, surrounded by fresh barefoot tracks.

The only tribe in the area consisted of four women, three boys and two infants, led by a fierce warrior named Meenee Meenee.

In 1846, two years later, George D. Smythe, with a party of seamen and convicts, was attempting to survey the Cape Otway area. On 25 July a seaman, James Conroy, left the camp and walked along the beach. When he failed to return, his mate, another seaman named John Smedmore ('Kangaroo Jack'), tracked him and found his naked corpse lying on a sand hummock. Conroy's body had a deep four-inch cut on the forehead, another gash which divided his left jaw from nose to ear, and blows on the chest.

Surveyor Smythe was sworn in as a special constable with a warrant to arrest Meenee Meenee. Late in August he took a party of whites and Barrabool black-trackers towards the spot, being joined on the way by a heavily armed posse consisting of squatter William Roadknight and his men. The trackers went well ahead of the whites. Smythe deposed that he 'heard some shots, and hurried to get up as soon as I could, and only in time to save a female, a young girl.' The eager trackers had obliterated the remainder of the tribe. Meenee Meenee lay dead, wearing James Conroy's pea jacket, blue cap, and one boot. Around him lay eight other bodies—women, boys and infants.

La Trobe returned from a trip to Sydney to find this horrifying deposition lying on his desk. What could he do? Nothing, without involving his administration in a scandal as bad as anything which had occurred in the whole disastrous history of white–black relations. The documents were simply stuffed away in a file: nothing was ever done. There is not even a trace of the massacre being reported to the Sydney authorities.

William Saunders, a squatter near today's Torquay, south of Geelong, sent out his 14-year-old brother James on 28 September 1844 to look after a flock of sheep.

That evening, Saunders found the sheep 'scattered about'. His wife told him she had seen natives on the station. Saunders searched the grazing area and found his brother lying face downwards, naked, his head 'so fractured that I could not look at it.' In response the squatter's calls for help, a sawyer, William Elton, came out of the bush. Elton described the body as having 'two large cuts I suppose from a tomahawk, on the back of the head', and a blow on the chest as though from a waddy.

Commissioner Fyans concluded that the boy had been murdered by blacks, merely to obtain his clothing and a small gun he carried.

Aboriginals on the Wimmera River near present-day Horsham enjoyed an interesting talk with the Native Police one day in the spring of 1844. Their leaders, Jim Crow, Old Tom, Mister Lock, Charley, and Old Man Belgium, told the black constables there were 'immense numbers of natives down the river which the settlers have never seen.' As soon as river levels fell, leaders proposed to muster all the tribes, 'murder all the settlers in this quarter', spear all their horses, and 'carry off all the stock'.

They made a good start in September by throwing several spears at a shepherd on William Taylor's vast 'Longerenong' run and driving off his sheep.

The raiders continued on 21 September by attacking C. J. Sheppard's hutkeeper north of the Grampians, and driving off his flock. Sheppard immediately armed his men and set off on horseback to 'make an example of the blacks'. 'I should most decidedly have shot one or two of them', he told the local magistrate. Returning without success, Sheppard enlisted the aid of Native Police in the area. Their sergeant-major, Peter Bennett, had been looking for Jim Crow ever since the native stole a bag of sugar from his dray some months before.

On 12 October Bennett's force found Jim Crow with his tribe. When the troopers burst on the scene, the blacks fled into the river, giving Bennett the opportunity of breaking up and burning their spears and other possessions.

The Native Police immediately proceeded to Dugald McPherson's 'Ashens' station (east of Horsham), where spears had been thrown at a shepherd. There they met a party of Border Police under Sergeant James Daplin, and told them of the previous week's encounter. On 19 October Daplin's men tracked down Jim Crow's band, hiding in dense scrub by the river. They shot and wounded Charley, who was still clinging to the upper branches of a tree when last seen by McPherson's overseer, Daniel Cameron. Then they surrounded Jim Crow himself, who stood proudly with spear poised, shouting that he would 'kill all the white fellows'.

Sergeant Daplin ordered his men to charge, but they refused. After about an hour's parley, he ordered them to fire on the defiant savage. This time they obeyed, felling him.

The civilian eyewitness, Daniel Cameron, walked over: 'I found him with his weapons in his hands apparently dying', Cameron deposed. 'We then left him.'

Although Sergeant Daplin held a warrant to arrest Jim Crow, he was now in considerable trouble. His initial statement, sworn before J. A. Cameron, JP, was that as soon as Jim Crow's band saw the police, they 'began immediately to throw their spears', which were 'very near proving fatal.' After Jim Crow himself was cornered, said Daplin, 'I used every effort for him to lay down his spear.' His only reply had been 'Borack gibbert white bugger.'

Crown Prosecutor Croke considered that Daplin should be prosecuted for manslaughter. The officer had departed from 'discretion, sound judgment and humanity'. On his own showing he had not made out a case 'amounting to that degree of personal danger and inevitable necessity which would warrant him to order the men under his command to fire.'

Sergeant Daplin and two of his troopers, William Sparrow and Frederick Bush, were indicted at the Criminal Sessions of August 1845 for killing Jim Crow. Funds for their defence were quickly raised by sympathetic private individuals. After evidence had been given on both sides (by Redmond Barry on behalf of the Aboriginals), Judge Therry made a strong summing-up in favour of the accused. They had been handed a warrant, he said, and their duty was to execute it. If any party resisted legal arrest, the arrestor was authorised in opposing force to force. Without even retiring, the jury returned a verdict of not guilty.

By the end of 1844 Commissioner Fyans was able to report that the whole of the Portland District had become 'extremely quiet'. The natives, thought the Commissioner, were enjoying 'a state of improvement'. Many had found constant employment, being fed and clothed by squatters in return for their labour. 'The greatest punishment felt by the native', wrote Fyans, 'is for a settler to forbid him staying on his place.'

The newly settled Wimmera area would also settle down, particularly now that pairs of mounted troopers were lodging on stations exposed to attack. There too, wrote Fyans, 'I feel that ere long the natives will become quiet and orderly.'

'Peace' in the Western District lasted until April 1845, when cattle were killed on William Learmonth's run at Darlot's Creek.

Fyans blamed the outbreak on the activities of a Sydney black named Bradberry, whom he claimed had left the Learmonth's employment and taken a gun with him. 'The character of Bradberry has been changing for some time, attaching himself to the natives, thereby leading them on to mischief', Fyans wrote.

After talking to Fyans, Bradberry decided to return to Learmonth's service. A short time later he was speared to death by vengeful blacks while trying to protect his master's cattle.

As a result of these episodes, two Border Police were stationed at Learmonth's run. A year later Fyans complained that the natives were still 'very numerous' but the police 'seem to have effect'. He recommended that they could be safely withdrawn.

A group of blacks on 'Squattlesea Mere' run on the Eumerella River attacked Thomas Pye, overseer to Thomas Browne, on 12 May. Several natives threw spears at Pye and attempted to surround him, while others drove off his master's cattle. Pye fired shots before fleeing for his life.

Browne and Pye rode for help to the neighbouring station, 'Eumerella East', managed by Robert Crawford for Benjamin Boyd. They also enlisted the aid of settlers on 'Eumerella West'. These included Samuel Gorrie, described by Browne as 'a stalwart, iron-nerved, elderly Scot, the envied possessor of a rifle of great length of barrel and the deadliest performance.' With Gorrie came his nephew, Samuel McGregor.

The posse set out in pursuit of the blacks on 15 May. They followed the tracks of cattle leading into the Mount Eeles rocks. Next day they came across the native camp. 'On our approach,' said Robert Crawford, 'they shipped their spears and threw them at us, which obliged us to fire upon them in self-defence.'

Thomas Browne later wrote a more colourful version of events:

Two aboriginals bolted out of their cover immediately in front of Mr Gorrie. Running their best, and leaping from side to side as they went, the nearer one made frantic signs to the effect that the other man was the real culprit. 'Bide a wee,' quoth the calm veteran, as the barrel of the old rifle settled to its aim. 'Bide a wee, laddie, and I'll sort ye baith.' Which the legend goes on to say he actually did, disposing of the appellant at sight, and knocking over the other before he got out of range of 'la longue carabine'.

Forwarding the evidence to Dr Watton at Mount Rouse Station, William Campbell, JP, of 'Dunmore' station, complained that since the Native Police had been removed, 'the settlers are obliged to protect their property from the attacks of the natives, however unpleasant the duty.'

At the same time, a petition went to La Trobe from settlers on the Wimmera River, further to the north, asking for Native Police to be sent back urgently to that area. The settlers claimed that although the tribes 'have in no way been molested', severe stock losses were occurring. The natives drove the sheep into 'almost impenetrable scrub', goading on the animals with spears 'much quicker than it is possible to track them'. The result was that Robert Hamilton and Lady Mary Baillie (represented by her son Thomas Baillie) had lost 800 sheep, Messrs G. S. Brodie and A. R. Cruikshank 700, Major William Firebrace 150, and William Patterson 40.

By this time the government had authorised expansion of Native Police numbers. La Trobe had informed Gipps in July 1844 that his favourable opinion of the force 'has been greatly strengthened by the experience of the last 18 months.' He wanted to double its personnel, appoint additional sergeants, and extend the pay of 3d. a day currently allowed to the two native corporals.

In March Gipps authorised 'adding nine men to the twenty-one already composing the party of Native Police', but said nothing about extra pay.

Joseph Maes emigrated from the south of France to seek his fortune in the new land. He obtained a job as a hutkeeper for James Horsfall, owner of 'Rich Avon' station (south of today's town of Donald).

Unfortunately, Maes had a deep olive complexion, and displayed violence in his dealings with the natives. The notion spread that he was 'a foreign black' who should be killed anyhow.

Late in May two Wimmera blacks, named Dick and Peter, came to the station, building their campfire near the hut. They remained there quietly until 3 June, when all station hands except Maes went out on their duties. One man, Richard Munt, recalled later that 'Peter had a waddy or thick stick in his hand.' When the shepherds returned that evening, they found Maes lying dead, with the back of his head beaten in. Nearby was a bloodstained waddy and spade. Food, bedding and a gun were missing.

Protector Parker and the Border Police attempted to find the murderers, but were unsuccessful.

Soon after the affrays in the Mount Eeles area, Samuel Gorrie reported worriedly to Police Magistrate Blair that the blacks were now using spears bearing sharpened steel tips, obviously manufactured by white men. 'I would rather meet the blacks armed with muskets', Gorrie wrote.

Blair investigated, and discovered that an unnamed Portland blacksmith in fact had manufactured the spears, believing they would be used for eel-fishing. He promised to make no more.

However, those steel spears already in existence were helping the blacks to terrorise settlers near Mount Eeles. During June and July 1845 stock was killed, and shepherds threatened, on J. H. Butcher's and George Fairbairn's stations. The same aggressors drove thousands of sheep off Mount Gambier runs. On E. P. S. Sturt's 'Compton' station, they killed two white men and one woman.

Steel-tipped spears were also used in renewed attacks on 'Dunmore' station during July. In the first affray, several natives armed with these spears chased William M. Campbell's partner, James Irvine, back towards the homestead. A few days later, on 21 July, a spear grazed the shoulder of a gentleman named Arthur Cunningham, who was staying at the station.

He deposed that he had given 'no provocation of any kind.' Early next morning the six white men on the station armed themselves and rode towards the blacks' camp. The natives saw them coming, 'raised a shout, and laid hold of their spears, putting themselves in an attitude of attack.' The whites fired in unison at a distance of about 100 yards, but apparently hit nobody. The blacks 'retreated precipitately into a dense scrub'. The settlers set fire to their mia-mias, burning all the spears, tomahawks and stolen beef they had left behind.

A major problem in policing the outback was that the forces of law and order could never quite catch up with the expansion of squatting settlement.

A 35-year-old squatter named William Brown had been forced out of his partnership at Deep Creek, north-west of Melbourne, by the prolific lambing of the firm's flocks. Brown decided in 1845 to drove 1000 sheep to the Western District. He found all good grazing country filled up, until he got past Edward Henty's 'Muntham' (north-east of today's Casterton). There he settled in what was called 'the new country', in partnership with John Oliver.

Both men claimed they exerted themselves to stay on friendly terms with the local tribes, but always carried guns and stayed within each other's sight. On 1 July they broke this sensible rule. Brown went alone towards some scrub to bring the flock closer to the homestead. When he failed to return, Oliver investigated and found his partner's naked body lying near a waterhole.

'I immediately alarmed my neighbours', Oliver wrote. Next day a search party found a black woman of the tribe, who told them that the chief had waddied Brown without warning, killing him instantly, and had taken his coat and gun. The search party pursued the black warriors, discovering them still carrying the dead man's possessions. 'I have reason to believe these paid dearly for their temerity', Oliver added cautiously.

What happened was described in detail many years later by James C. Hamilton, whose family worked on 'Bringalbert', some distance to the north:

A call to arms was made—the footmen going one way and the horsemen another. They were all armed with flintlock muskets and pistols of the same sort—heavy, clumsy weapons they were, but effective enough. (I have put a ball into a tree at a hundred yards with one of these pistols, and used the musket successfully as a fowling piece.)

It was a bad day for the ill-fated darkies. The horsemen came up with them in the ranges, behind Narracoorte, and saw one fellow carrying poor Brown's gun, and a lubra wearing his coat. They opened fire, and many of the blacks went under. They made no show of resistance, but scattered and ran for their lives . . .

One black, who was mortally wounded, made his way into a cave and died there. He was found years after sitting in an upright position, petrified, and was one of the sights of those wonderful caves, until he was stolen and taken to England, where he was exhibited.

Further attacks occurred in July 1845 on Baillie and Hamilton's station 'Polkemmet', a 96 000 acre run on the Wimmera River (north-west of today's Horsham).

Just before sundown on 10 July several natives emerged from the Mallee scrub and drove about 300 sheep into the trees. Thomas Baillie immediately sent for help from Dana and his Native Police, now quartered at Major Firebrace's station close by.

On 12 July Dana and his men tracked Baillie's sheep about thirty miles into the scrub. They came across a strongly constructed brush yard holding most of the sheep. A little farther on they found the marauders, who 'uttered a yell and commenced threatening us with their spears, and threw a number of waddies and other missiles at us.' Dana ordered his men to fire. Three blacks were killed on the spot, and several others wounded. Their leader, Yanem Goona, was 'cut down after a long resistance'. Suffering severe sabre wounds, he was taken prisoner. The surviving blacks fled.

When Protector Parker came to investigate these events,

he protested to La Trobe that while the Native Police were en route to the Wimmera, they 'openly boasted that they were not going to take prisoners, but to shoot as many of the blacks as they could.' Dana's answer was that it was his duty to arrest offenders where possible and 'make an example of them'.

After recovering from his wounds, Yanem Goona was tried in Melbourne on 17 October for sheep-stealing. A man named Burchett* was found who could speak his language and act as interpreter.

William Thomas, who attended Yanem Goona throughout the trial, believed there was 'not a tittle of evidence' that he had stolen sheep. He criticised Judge Therry's summing-up, which said that 'if the prisoner was a member of the community where the sheep were found . . . he was equally guilty.'

The jury had no hesitation in reaching a verdict of guilty. Before passing sentence, Judge Therry remarked that the prisoner was 'without education, intelligence, or knowledge of the rights of society, and devoid of everything connected with civilisation.' He then sentenced him to ten years' transportation to Van Diemen's Land, where he experienced a type of civilisation in which men could be flogged almost to death.

On 19 October 1845 a hutkeeper named Margaret Bazzle, employed by C. J. Dennys on his Moorabool River run, saw three blacks come over the hill towards her hut. They demanded that she give them damper, tea, sugar, powder and shot. She told them she had none, and they went away. 'Being frightened, I went for my master', said Bazzle. Dennys came and searched the area, but could find no one. He tied up his dog to guard the hut and left.

Next morning five blacks besieged the hut, smashing open the locked door with their tomahawks. They stole a joint of meat hanging from the ceiling, then seized one of Bazzle's children by the feet and swung it around as though to smash out its brains. The mother took a shovelful of hot ashes from

---

* Probably one of the Burchett brothers of Penshurst.

the stove and threw it over the blacks. One of them, whom she identified as Kunnin Koombra Kowan, pointed his gun at her, but an older man seized it so that the shot went harmlessly into the air. The brave mother then rushed to the door and 'beckoned as if I saw a man near,' causing the blacks to flee.

Dennys brought the police, who succeeded in arresting Kowan. However, the black managed to escape from custody, summoned his tribe, and burnt down the woman's hut by throwing a firestick into the thatch.

Early in November Dennys happened to sight Kowan again, and took him at gunpoint to the lockup. The Aboriginal was tried in Melbourne on 21 January 1846, found guilty of stealing the meat, and sentenced to ten years' transportation to Van Diemen's Land.

14

FAILURE

OF

THE MERRI CREEK

MISSION

The much-maligned Aboriginal Protector William Thomas, now fifty-two, his pay cut by one-third and his government horse removed from under him, continued during 1845 to visit the blacks camped around Melbourne, earnestly persuading them not to drink the white man's liquor, not to waddy their own lubras, and at all costs to stay out of trouble.

In July 1845 the Ryrie brothers complained that 300 blacks camped on their Upper Yarra run were becoming 'very troublesome'. Thomas could only reply that he 'had no means of following the natives, my daily journeys were on foot, that I followed the blacks generally as far as Brighton to the south, Heidelberg to the east, and Campbellfield to the north, but no farther.'

A few weeks later a large number of Aboriginals returned to the Protector's camp near Merri Creek. Here they conducted themselves in 'a very disorderly manner', Thomas reported. 'When inebriated they are like maniacs . . . one so severely treated his lubra that she has been removed to the hospital for treatment by the government surgeon.'

During the second half of 1845, several blacks died at Merri Creek of disease or old age, but only one healthy child was born.

With these recurrent crises, it was not surprising that religious and school attendances at Merri Creek dropped away. The previous year, the Protector had sometimes counted up to seventy blacks at Sunday services. By early April 1845 this figure had declined to twenty-five, and by late April to nil. Lessons for children were also abandoned: 'no inducement could entice them to school', wrote Thomas.

Into this vacuum stepped members of the Melbourne Baptist Chapel. Their minister, the Reverend John Ham, raised enough money in 1845 to engage Edward Peacock of Richmond, who had previously taught native children at Narre Warren Station.

On 30 November Thomas encountered Peacock near Merri Creek. The teacher was leading a procession of a dozen children, 'all clean as tho' they were going to chapel.' Asked for an explanation, Peacock replied that he was 'going to Mr La Trobe's to know why the blacks were forced away from their school.' When the children failed to return, the lubras commenced 'a general crying and howling'. Thomas accompanied them to Richmond, where Peacock was persuaded to give up his young charges.

The Baptists then won from La Trobe permission to take over educational efforts at Merri Creek. Peacock at first used Thomas's hut as a schoolroom, but was soon given Dr Peter McArthur's abandoned 30 ft x 12 ft homestead, 'Arthurton', near the junction of Merri Creek and the Yarra River. With a full-time teacher on the job, attendances grew to more than forty. Lessons were conducted in two daily periods of ninety minutes each. By 12 May 1846 Peacock was able to present the best of his scholars, well scrubbed and dressed, to a public display in Collins Street Chapel. They read from the Bible, performed spelling tests, and sang hymns. The audience of 600 was 'quite stirred with emotion' at this evidence that primitive people could probably be civilised, if caught young enough.

La Trobe took new heart from the apparent success. A few days after the meeting he authorised Thomas to draw rations for those of Peacock's scholars 'steadily in attendance'.

Under this scheme, enrolments remained fairly steady at between eighteen and thirty pupils. Every month Thomas drew 500 lbs of flour, 300 lbs of meat, 50 lbs of sugar, 10 lbs of tea, 6 lbs of salt, and 5 lbs of soap, at a cost of about £6 6s. 0d. a month, doling it out equally among the students.

Signs of fresh problems came in September 1846, when native constables enticed several of the older boys from school, with the promise that they too could become 'soldiers' supplied with 'horses, guns, swords, pistols, fine red-striped clothes &c.' Thomas immediately pursued the absconders to Narre Warren, and persuaded them to return home.

A few weeks later six Native Police, led by Beruke, went to Merri Creek and enticed two boys and a little girl to follow them. Peacock tried to interfere, whereupon Beruke 'spat in the teacher's face, forcing the children before him.' The parents followed the procession, crying and pleading to at least 'let the little girl remain.' Beruke sent her back that evening, but retained the two boys. The parents persisted, bringing back the lads on 9 October.

Seven weeks later, when Henry Dana returned from distant service, he replied to La Trobe's demand for an explanation. Beruke, said Dana, 'most emphatically denies' the charge. And that was that.

Meanwhile, 'some dissolute character' insinuated to tribal elders at Merri Creek that the school's true object was 'to arrest the boys and send them on board a vessel to another country'— an obvious reference to the practice of transporting felons to Van Diemen's Land. Thomas met with the elders on 1 November, and told them the rumours were nonsense. The boys who had begun to drift away from school again returned to their lessons.

Now episodes of drunkenness in the camp and insubordination in the classroom began to disrupt signs of progress.

Even more seriously, Western Port and Devil's River blacks began visiting Merri Creek to demand that some of the girls (pupils of eleven to twelve years of age), who had been promised to them in marriage, must fulfil the tribal contracts. The Baptist committee uncomfortably took the easy way out, reporting in November that 'it was deemed advisable to exclude three of the elder females.' That left seven girls up to ten years old to learn reading and needlework, and fifteen boys aged from seven to fifteen to learn reading and writing.

White men who supplied liquor to tribal elders sometimes asked for payment in the form of sexual services. It is difficult to know how far black girls were 'corrupted' by whites, how far they obeyed their elders, and how far they willingly co-operated for the sake of gifts or money. Protector Thomas reported that a 14-year-old girl named Koorburburdin was so 'inconstant' that she often left her tribal husband to disport in 'the bad houses [brothels] in Melbourne'.

At the end of 1846 the school was costing a total of £300 a year. The government contributed £80, the balance being raised by subscriptions, donations and collections. In view of the apparent fair results, Gipps agreed to increase the official grant to £150 a year.

During 1847, however, attendances began to fluctuate markedly. In January four of the older boys quit, Thomas surmising that they simply 'got tired of the school'. By April average daily attendance had dropped to seventeen. Many of the remaining boys were able to write 'tolerably well', while the girls made all their own clothes.

The authorities decided to supplement formal lessons with agricultural training. Thomas suggested fencing off a 25 acre tract between the two rivers which would include the Baptist school. (Today this forms part of Yarra Bend public park.) La Trobe agreed to the application in May. Within six months the pupils, with the help of one white overseer, had sown four acres of wheat and two acres of potatoes, and established four vegetable gardens. Much of the produce was sold at the Melbourne market on Saturdays. 'Since handling their own money,' wrote Thomas, 'they have been stimulated and taken another piece and planted it with potatoes.'

Early in June five girls left the mission, apparently wishing 'to have a night in the bush by themselves'. Thomas discovered them next morning on the opposite bank of the Yarra, 'almost perished with cold and hunger'. He had little difficulty in persuading them to return.

The Protector reported that the boys' school work and religious observance improved greatly during the year. The girls, however, remained 'listless': 'as soon as they get nine or ten years of age they will be off so the men will have them.' They had also stolen five pounds of tobacco from the store for their male friends. Nevertheless, the girls proved 'very handy in household work.' Two washed the clothes and cleaned the house, while one could even 'iron like a white woman'. Their output included four large patchwork quilts.

Although enrolments were now down to ten boys and four girls, La Trobe judged the results 'satisfactory'.

Without warning, on 23 November, the blacks broke up their encampment near the school, burned the European clothes donated to them, and marched off towards the north-eastern ranges, taking many of the pupils with them. Only seven young boys remained. Five of these quit two weeks later, leaving behind two 'foreign' boys from Port Fairy. When Thomas tried to discover the reason for the exodus, one aged black left behind told him, 'Black boys work like government men [convicts] long time ago and girls too much work.' Perhaps the real reason was a serious epidemic of influenza which had swept through the camp a short time before, affecting mainly the women. Native doctors forecast that 'all white and black people would die at Melbourne.'

Thomas pursued the missing children up the Yarra River, finding nothing until after he passed John Gardiner's station, 'Mooroolbark' (near today's Lilydale). The Protector carefully approached the blacks' campfires, but was unable to persuade the elders to allow the children to return until the next full moon. Thomas continued upstream to Ryrie's 'Yering' station, where he found more children, who also refused to return for a month.

Even then only three boys went back to Merri Creek. Late in December these boys lit a fire which destroyed half of the mission's ripening wheat crop, then absconded again.

Thomas gave up. 'Their deception in leaving', he wrote, 'removes the last shadow of hope left respecting them; they or their parents seem bent on destroying the mission.'

Despondently, Thomas took 'a turn around the bush' on 31 December. He found a party of seven Yarra blacks at Worrowen (today's suburb of Brighton), who took him to their carefully tended cemetery. The blacks told Thomas that 'when seven more of their tribe are laid in their graves, all would be gone.' The Protector reflected sombrely that 'these people are awfully minishing from the face of the earth without any apparent cause.'

On hearing of the events at Merri Creek, the Baptist Chapel tried to cut its losses. On 27 January 1848 a deputation asked La Trobe to take over the whole mission, in the hope that one day the Aboriginals could still 'take their place amongst the civilized and Christian portions of mankind.' Ironically, La Trobe had just received a few days before, by slow ship mail from London, a copy of a report by B. Kay Shuttleworth, secretary of a Privy Council committee on education, recommending methods of operating day schools and model farms for 'coloured races of the British Colonies'. These were precisely the tactics which had been tried for years in Port Phillip and shown to be useless.

The Baptists agreed to carry on temporarily. On 25 April their committee visited Merri Creek, reporting that 'the whole place wears an aspect of neglect'. Teacher Peacock, like Protector Thomas, had given up. By noon on the day of the committee's visit, the five boys in residence had not been summoned either to breakfast or lessons. Peacock himself appeared to be removing some of the mission property, including a stable. Three days later Peacock was given a month's notice of dismissal. He was replaced by F. S. Edgar, an

English-born schoolmaster from Hobart, who worked hard to overcome the situation left by his predecessor.

Drunkenness was the major problem faced by whites attempting to ameliorate black suffering. Liquor seemed fatally attractive to Aboriginals, no matter how hard they fought against addiction.

On 15 March 1848 Protector Thomas was deeply affected when Benbow, formerly a tribal leader and a native constable, went up to him and said, 'Me been very bad, two gentlemen yesterday make me drunk, and me break a good white man's window ... me pay and he no sulky, me sorry.' Benbow returned 'with good grace having paid for the window.' But the elder was last heard of on the Yarra bank, dying of alcoholism. Thomas then persuaded him to move with his tribe to St Kilda.

In March when tribes made their usual descent on Melbourne for the autumn racing season, Thomas addressed them, pointing out that intoxicated blacks had been killed on similar occasions. But on 3 April he reported, 'Windberry, a Yarra black and notorious drunkard, was with his lubra, both drunk on the racecourse. They quarrelled and he began to beat her.' White men interfered and knocked Windberry senseless. Before the bruises had healed, wrote Thomas, he was again drunk, lost his opossum cloak, and had to be ordered out of Melbourne.

In July most of the Yarra blacks departed from Melbourne on their annual hunt for bullen-bullen (lyre-birds). Melbourne exporters had again supplied them liberally with powder and shot for their ancient muskets. Thomas found the blacks forty miles away, on Commissioner Tyers's new line of road to Gippsland, where lyre-birds were still plentiful.

The Protector heatedly criticised the government's failure to renew distribution of blankets: 'Most of the poor females and some of the males were awfully destitute of covering', he wrote. The influenza-ridden blacks, he thought, would 'soon be beyond the pale of commiseration or supplicancy.'

The government's response to Thomas's plea was to provide six blankets, Thomas gave one each to very aged and ill females who had no other covering. 'The general dissatisfaction of the others can be imagined', wrote Thomas. To comfort them, he gave money from his own meagre salary.

During August Thomas found a group of twenty-nine Gippsland blacks in the Dandenong ranges, some in 'a wretched state.' One 11-year-old girl was badly affected with 'mundil (venereal)'. Thomas left mercurial ointment to be applied to the girl by the other females. He reminded the Chief Protector that such medicines had to be provided at his own expense. 'I am destitute of even [forage] allowance for my horse', he wrote.

The battle against alcohol and prostitution continued. About thirty members of the Yarra tribe were now camped at St Kilda, 'principally employed by the residents there'. On 20 September these natives begged Thomas to 'get two lubras from an inn on the beach.' The Protector succeeded in persuading the straying women to return to camp.

Tommy, one of two Port Fairy boys who had continued their education at Merri Creek, disappeared from the camp after an altercation with the teacher on 24 October. Thomas searched for the 13-year-old boy at camps far up the Yarra. Eventually he was told by two former pupils that Tommy had been murdered not far from Merri Creek by Goulburn River and Devil's River blacks. The Protector located an aged tribesman named Tobin who had been near the scene of the killing. Another aged black, Old Billy, had told him: 'My blackfellows kill em bopup [boy] sit down school . . . Old Billy show em me how cut him and take em marmbulla [kidney and fat] tie em legs and arms put em stone in belly and throw em in water Yarra.' Three other blacks said they had been told a similar story. La Trobe could find no other motive for the crime than 'heartless subserviency to detestable Aboriginal usage.'

Later in November Thomas reported that 'the most objectionable characters' had quit Merri Creek, leaving five boys at school. Visiting the mission on the 18th, he was 'much pleased': 'From the rise beheld the five boys with their teacher hay making, their appearance would gladden the heart of any philanthropist . . . thinking their wildness was at an end.' By the end of 1848 these few boys had built a gum-tree bridge across Merri Creek, giving easier access from the north. The vegetable gardens were repaired and cropped, and fruit trees and vines planted. When the neighbouring Yarra Bend Lunatic Asylum opened, the farm supplied it with eggs and butter.

Lessons were now limited to the afternoons, with prayers and elementary instruction in reading, writing and arithmetic. 'I consider them as apt to learn as Europeans', wrote Francis Edgar optimistically. 'They keep the schoolroom clean, cook in weekly rotation, and wash and mend their clothes.'

But neither Francis Edgar nor William Thomas could persuade some black girls to leave the streets of Melbourne. Edgar's daughter Lucy wrote in her memoirs some years later that in fine weather the girls spent most of their time window-shopping, but 'in wet weather the poor wretched creatures might be seen in their dripping rugs, cowering under trees and in corners for shelter, like beasts . . .'

Nothing could conceal the fact that only four pupils remained at Merri Creek. Chief Protector Robinson suggested in January 1849 that the government should take over the school entirely and move it to the south bank of the Yarra. La Trobe refused.

During 1849 four more pupils enrolled. One male was old enough to marry, and after much pondering Thomas 'united the eldest of the youths in marriage to the young widow of the late Bungeeleen', an elderly chief taken as hostage in Gippsland (chapter 18).

Various tribes again flowed back into Melbourne in March 1849 for the racing season. Thomas was given the thankless task of breaking up their camps. By May he had succeeded in persuading all but twenty-eight blacks to return to country areas.

That winter was particularly wet and harsh on the

wandering tribes. During the worst weather sixty Gippsland blacks drifted into Melbourne. Thomas praised their behaviour: 'They would ask alms without further importunancy, show their card, blanket, tomahawk &c., state how good we had been to them, and pass on.' But influenza 'raged severely'. Thomas recorded nine deaths among the Gippslanders in Melbourne, including two of the three children born that winter. La Trobe was able to allow a more liberal supply of blankets; unfortunately, wrote Thomas, 'it was impossible to render them further assistance in the way they were living, moving almost daily thro' swamps &c., dragging their sick with them.'

The Baptist mission closed down in 1850, Edgar taking his family back to England. One pupil was apprenticed to a tailor in Melbourne, and seemed to give satisfaction; later he was sent to Narre Warren to make uniforms for the Native Police. Two children who had been abandoned by their mother were transferred to the Pentridge (i.e. Coburg) Episcopalian School. That was the end of Merri Creek as a missionary enterprise, and the end of any hope that Aboriginals could be easily integrated into suburban Melbourne.

15

TERROR
COMES
TO
GIPPSLAND

After pioneering explorations like those of George Mackillop in 1835, and of Angus McMillan in 1839–40, white men gradually began to settle the rugged district of Gippsland.

The same kind of confrontations with native tribes began to occur as elsewhere in Port Phillip. Any initial curiosity and goodwill disappeared as squatters drove their flocks into traditional hunting and ceremonial areas: Aboriginal resistance was again interpreted as barbarous opposition to the enlightened forces of white civilisation.

No real evidence survives about early clashes. All that can be learned from official records is C. J. Tyers's vague information given later to a NSW Legislative Council committee. Tyers said that Angus McMillan's early exploration parties were attacked several times, in particular on 22 December 1840, 'when one Aborigine is said to have been shot.' In December 1841 an unnamed shepherd of Lachlan MacAlister was killed, and strips of his flesh carried away. In 1842 a hutkeeper of John Foster's was killed while shifting the sheep hurdles. Finally, said Tyers, two men on Loughnan and Taylor's station were killed in 1844 while moving their goods from one hut to another.

A notable representative of white civilisation in Gippsland was 28-year-old Scottish-born John Campbell, who in 1843 took up 16 000 acres, which he named 'Glencoe', along the La Trobe River (opposite today's Sale). On first arrival by boat, Campbell and his companions were said to have scared off native observers by firing at them a nine-pounder gun loaded with nails and broken glass. Settling in at 'Glencoe', Campbell trained a savage deerhound to chase Aboriginals. According to George Dunderdale, later Clerk of Courts in the area, 'This dog acquired great skill in seizing a blackfellow by the heel, throwing him, and worrying him until Campbell came up on his horse.'

Known black resistance began with a major tragedy in July 1843, when young Donald MacAlister, the nephew of Captain Lachlan MacAlister of 'Boisdale' station (north-west of today's Stratford), was sent south to make arrangements for shipping stock. According to Dunderdale:

> The day before their arrival Donald saw some blacks at a distance in the scrub, and without any provocation fired at them with an old Tower musket, charged with shot. The next day the drovers and shepherds arrived with the stock, and drove them over Glengarry's bridge to a place between the Tarra and Albert rivers, called the Coal Hole, afterwards occupied by Parson Bean.* There was no yard there, and the animals would require watching at night; so Donald decided to send them back to Glengarry's yards ...
>
> The drovers started back with the cattle, Donald helped the shepherds to gather the sheep, and put them on the way, and then he rode after the cattle. The track led him past a grove of dense ti-tree, on the land now known as the Brewery Paddock, and about a hundred yards ahead a single blackfellow came out of the grove,

---

* Reverend Willoughby Bean, Anglican minister at Port Albert from 1848.

and began capering about and waving a waddy. Donald pulled up his horse and looked at the black. He had a pair of pistols in the holsters of his saddle, but he did not draw them: there was no danger from a blackfellow a hundred yards off. But there was another behind him and much nearer, who came silently out of the ti-tree and thrust a spear through Donald's neck.

Lachlan MacAlister, previously an officer of the 48th Regiment in Sydney, vowed revenge. With Angus McMillan's help he formed a private army known as the Highland Brigade, and set out after the tribe. 'The blacks were found encamped near a waterhole at Gammon Creek, and those who were shot were thrown into it, to the number, it was said, of about sixty men, women, and children; but this was probably an exaggeration', wrote Dunderdale. According to another writer who claimed to have spoken to two survivors, up to 150 blacks were shot: 'as fast as they put their heads up for breath, they were shot until the water was red with blood.'

During the time of these events, Crown Commissioners based at Western Port reported no serious affrays in the Gippsland area—as far as they were aware. G. S. Airey could not see any need for Aboriginal protection by means of stations or reserves. F. A. Powlett's report for the crucial year 1843 said that the natives 'upon the whole conducted themselves peaceably'. However, Powlett added cautiously, an Aboriginal Station in Gippsland might be useful as 'a place of refuge', and a centre where 'the ringleaders of any [black] outrage can be detected'.

As rumours of the MacAlister/McMillan massacre began to trickle back to Melbourne, La Trobe became concerned. In June 1843 the Sydney authorities agreed with his proposal to appoint the noted surveyor C. J. Tyers as Crown Commissioner for the whole Gippsland district. Tyers wound up his survey duties on 31 August, and La Trobe allowed him four mounted Border Police—all ex-convicts—a free constable, a bullock-driver, and three convict servants.

While Tyers was setting up his first establishment at Port

Albert, La Trobe prevailed upon Chief Protector Robinson to
leave his comfortable Melbourne base and investigate race
relations in Gippsland.

Robinson eventually got away on 22 April 1844, taking
with him four black troopers of the Native Police and the
author G. H. Haydon. After a difficult passage through the
bush they reached Port Albert, Haydon reflecting scornfully
on Robinson's self-centred behaviour. Robinson continued
with two troopers along the coast as far as Twofold Bay,
returning through part of the Snowy Mountains and down the
Murray River. He tried to report enthusiastically about the
results of his trip, in mastering local dialects and 'obtaining
correct information', but in fact his official reports were almost
valueless.

The sole responsibility for pacifying Gippsland fell to
Commissioner Tyers. But Tyers was not inclined to be
communicative. La Trobe wrote to him on 16 November 1844
demanding a report. Tyers did not reply until 1 July 1845,
blaming the long delay on 'ignorance of the dialect of the
Gippsland tribe, and the wildness of their habits'. Tyers
reported that a few Corner Inlet blacks had been employed on
stations early in 1843, but 'since the unprovoked murder' of
Mr MacAlister, they had 'not been seen in the neighbourhood'.
He did not add that they had been slaughtered by the Highland
Brigade. In other parts of the district, continued Tyers, the
blacks had 'occasionally come into collision with the settlers—
the consequence was the murder of four shepherds, and as far as
I can learn, without any provocation.' The Commissioner gave
no names, offered no details, took no depositions.

Four black troopers under Sergeant Samuel Windridge
were added to Tyers's force in December 1844. Tyers found
them at least the equal of the Border Police. Although the
black recruits were 'naturally averse to restraint', Henry Dana's
'kind yet firm system of discipline' worked wonders for their
efficiency. Yet, said Tyers, 'little or no moral improvement
seems to have attended their association with Europeans'. The
only solution, he thought, was to separate black children en-

tirely from their parents, and educate them European-style.

The first serious affray in which Tyers admitted personal involvement occurred in November 1845 near 'Clyde Bank', the run of Robert Thomson and Robert C. Cunninghame, on the Avon River near today's Stratford. Tyers reported that Gippsland blacks were now carrying out 'continued aggressions' on settlers' stock, causing serious losses on runs. 'No sooner have the police succeeded in driving the blacks from one, than their services are immediately required on another station', he wrote.

On 3 November Tyers and several Native Police tracked Thomson and Cunninghame's depredators to Lake Wellington. They pursued a group of about sixty Aboriginals into a thick belt of tea-tree scrub around the lake. One of the blacks threw a spear ('a formidable weapon, with a jagged glass head'), narrowly missing a trooper. The constable fired his gun and killed the man. A second warrior poised his spear to hurl it at Tyers, when another trooper fired and killed that man as well.

Two months later, in his capacity as JP, Lachlan Mac-Alister took depositions from two native troopers named Dan and Cobawn Johnny. These more or less confirmed Tyers's reports, but like those earlier reports, failed to specify who had fired the fatal shots. Upon transmission of these reports to Sydney, the Governor pointed out that no inquest on the dead blacks had been held according to standing orders.

La Trobe sent the file to Crown Prosecutor Croke. That official was scathing on Commissioner Tyers's failure to follow regulations. 'The evidence of Mr Tyers (if it may be so called) is extremely vague and indifferent', wrote Croke; '... I cannot collect from it, who the persons are who ought to be subpoenaed as witnesses ... I cannot see any chance of a conviction with such evidence.'

Unusually, La Trobe did not forward Croke's damning opinion to Sydney. Instead, he simply reported that 'the circumstances ... were such as to render a further prosecution of the case useless.'

The Governor accepted La Trobe's advice, replying that 'the matter must rest where it is.' British law, and all the well-meant instructions from officialdom, once again proved useless in protecting the native population against squatters.

One of the most brutal squatters in the Port Phillip district was Frederick Taylor, who arrived in March 1836 and took up a run at Cowie's Creek, near Geelong.

Six months after his arrival, Taylor captured a native named Curacoine, who was believed to have assaulted Captain James Flitt with a tomahawk. Taylor tied the native to a tree, and told one of his shepherds, John Whitehead, to 'do as he pleased'. The squatter walked away, then was surprised—so he told the magistrate—to hear a shot ring out. Whitehead had killed Curacoine, then dumped his body in the nearest creek. The employee was arrested, but Taylor decamped to Van Diemen's Land before the trial, and so escaped giving incriminating evidence.

Taylor returned cautiously to the Western District in 1839, taking up a different run north of today's Terang.

About August 1839 Taylor, with an unnamed squatter and several of their servants, all well armed, advanced quietly on a native tribe camped on Taylor's run. According to one black survivor, the whites 'immediately fired upon the natives who were asleep . . . killing all they could see, amounting to thirty-five.' Men, women and children were slaughtered without mercy.

Three survivors, Karn, Worgeemoni and Wangigamon, hid in long grass nearby. The last-named watched helplessly as his lubra and child were murdered. All three saw the whites throw the bodies into a waterhole: 'the water was much stained with blood', they said.

Two days later, still hiding, Wangigamon saw Taylor, Anderson and Watson return to the scene. The other two men asked Taylor, 'Why did you kill so many lubras and children?' His reply was not recorded.

The squatters' servants, named Charles Courtney, James

Ramslie and James Hamilton, dragged the decaying bodies out with bullock teams, made a bonfire, and burned them to ashes. After another two days, the squatters returned with a sack, removing all bones not consumed in the fire.

A few months later, in December, the Scottish settler T. F. Hamilton was searching for a suitable run for his friend Niel Black. One evening Hamilton arrived opposite Taylor's hut on Emu Creek, and shouted for someone to guide him across. There was no answer. Crossing, Hamilton found the hut hastily abandoned, with dinner still cooking. Taylor and his men, apparently concluding that the Border Police were about to arrest them, had fled.*

The next report of Taylor came from squatter Henry Monro, who told G. A. Robinson in January 1840 that Taylor had 'absconded in an American whaler at Portland Bay'. From there he went to India, and lay low for some years.

He need not have bothered, for in March 1840 Crown Prosecutor James Croke concluded that although the circumstances of the massacre were 'of a very suspicious nature', the evidence of the Aboriginal survivors was useless in court. White evidence provided by Charles Courtney, Stephen Moore and William Blake, said the law officer, was 'more of an exculpatory than inculpatory character'.

While hiding out in India, Taylor recruited a number of coolies as labourers for the new district of Gippsland. In 1843 he formed a squatting partnership with London-born John and Henry Loughnan, to take up 'Emu Vale' run at Lindenow (between today's Stratford and Bairnsdale).

Taylor returned to official notice in April 1844, when two employees were killed by Aboriginals on the property. To avoid fuller investigation, Taylor made out that the deaths were due to natural causes, but failed to account to Commissioner Tyers for £12 missing from the bodies.

The squatter next began ill-treating his coolies, to the

---

* The property later became part of Niel Black's famous 'Glenormiston' station.

extent that they fled northwards over the Snowy Mountains to escape to Sydney. G. A. Robinson met the coolies by accident on the Monaro high plains in May 1844, and reported their miserable condition.

Tyers then discovered that Taylor was occupying twenty square miles on the Mitchell River in excess of the partnership's legal entitlement. Tyers ordered Taylor's shepherd to remove his sheep. The squatter countermanded the order, whereupon the Commissioner told the partners that Taylor 'would not be permitted in future to superintend any station in this district.' When Tyers reminded La Trobe that Taylor was the alleged murderer of Aboriginals in the Western District, both La Trobe and Governor Gipps supported the Commissioner's ruling. Taylor wrote from Geelong in August 1844 protesting his innocence of all charges. But the Reverend Tuckfield was able to produce another living witness to the massacre, a lad named Larkakok, then living at Buntingdale mission, who said he had 'stood up and begged Mr Taylor to spare his life.'

J. M. Loughnan, one of Taylor's partners in Gippsland, wrote to Governor Gipps on 1 February 1845 to appeal against the alleged ill-treatment of Taylor. Gipps replied that although the allegations against Taylor were based solely on Aboriginal evidence, 'he is not in the position of a person who has never been accused'. Although charges could not be laid, the ban on him as a squatter must remain. Loughnan answered with what Gipps described as 'rather a saucy' letter, threatening legal action for the wrongs allegedly done to him.

A year later Taylor made a new attempt to obtain a squatting licence. Commissioner Tyers held an inquiry and examined witnesses at Alberton. On 17 March 1846 he wrote a curious letter to Superintendent La Trobe, explaining that he had found Taylor 'not guilty of the charges made against him'. Tyers requested 'permission to withdraw my letters relative to those charges'.

At the same time Taylor boldly applied for a refund of nine guineas duty on a hogshead of British Plantation Rum, which he claimed had been lost on the road between Port Albert Custom House and Tarraville. La Trobe refused.

Governor Gipps disowned Tyers's remarkable change of heart towards Taylor. Gipps expressed 'very great surprise' at Tyers's 'assumed authority' to try the squatter and to pronounce him not guilty, disclaiming 'in the most explicit manner any participation in such proceedings'. Privately, Gipps wrote to La Trobe exclaiming that 'Men on becoming Crown Commissioners seem to take leave of their Senses.'

All of that was very fine, but it did not bring thirty-five dead Aboriginals back to life, nor avenge their deaths.

In 1847 a new governor lacking Gipps's colonial knowledge, Sir Charles Fitzroy, was in power in Sydney. That year Taylor was licensed to hold 'Deighton No. 2' station on Tom's Creek, Lake Victoria, in Gippsland. For some ten years he lived a full and happy life there, in a fresh partnership with the Loughnan brothers. He even led a petition to La Trobe in 1849 requesting immigrant labour to be dispatched to Gippsland, and received a courteous letter in reply. In the end, most white murderers of blacks were forgiven their sins.

16

CONTINUED DECLINE

OF THE

PROTECTORATE,

1845–48

We have already seen in chapters 11 and 14 how the Protectorate was saddled with most of the blame for the failure of Aboriginal–European relations. Protectors were a convenient scapegoat: the more public money they spent in trying to overcome a deteriorating situation, the easier it was to claim that all such humanitarian efforts were useless.

In August 1845 39-year-old barrister and landowner Richard Windeyer, a prominent member of the Aborigines Protection Society, persuaded the NSW Legislative Council to appoint a Select Committee 'to consider the condition of the Aborigines, and the best means of promoting their welfare.' Windeyer's motives in chairing the committee seemed sound enough, but the evidence backfired to finish up doing further harm to the Aboriginal cause.

The only Port Phillip squatter who bothered to attend was James Malcolm, a settler of 1836 on the Sydney Road, twenty miles north of Melbourne. Malcolm claimed the 'universal impression' throughout Port Phillip was that Aboriginals 'do not like to work', and that the Protectorate was responsible for 'a great deal of harm instead of good'.

Next came Crown Commissioners Addis, Smythe, Powlett and Fyans. Fyans, the most experienced among them, recalled that on first white settlement, many natives had been gainfully employed on stations. However, 'Immediately on the appearance of the Protectors and Missionary gentlemen, the natives left these employments', he said. They went 'wandering and pilfering throughout the country.' Fyans did not consider 'that the slightest good has been effected by the appointment of the Protectors.'

Realising that a political crisis was upon them, Chief Protector Robinson submitted evidence from himself and each of the Assistant Protectors. Robinson estimated the existing Aboriginal population in Port Phillip at about 5000, a decrease of about twenty per cent over the six years since his arrival. He did his best to defend the Protectors' work, in particular reciting the alleged benefits of his own travels throughout the district.

Edward Parker admitted that most natives avoided Protectorate Stations except in emergencies. On the credit side, he felt that 'a numerous Aboriginal population, once turbulent and dangerous, have been conciliated, and induced to live in amity with the European inhabitants.'

William Thomas attributed the great decrease in the Aboriginal population almost entirely to syphilis: 'I have known hapless infants brought into the world literally rotten with this disease', he said. This Protector could find little improvement in native affairs: 'They can talk more English, but in filth, dress, and habits, they are precisely the same.'

John Watton of Mount Rouse thought that Aboriginals should be forced to remain at Protectorate Stations for compulsory training in behaviour: 'I fear that nothing short of a system of absolute coercion for a time can effect any change worthy the name of civilization', he said.

No Aboriginal leaders were invited to give evidence to Windeyer's committee. Just as they were barred from giving evidence in court, so their views on the white invasion of their land were considered irrelevant.

Due to Windeyer's premature death, his committee failed to reach firm conclusions. When the Secretary of State called for further suggestions, Crown Commissioners favoured coercion as an essential preliminary. Major St John wrote:

> In the history of all savage nations, you find the first steps towards civilization have been made by conquest, and bringing the natives into due subjection; and that done, you may hope to give them some instruction moral and religious.

F. A. Powlett thought the attempt to govern by religious instruction was 'a pleasing speculation, but . . . chimerical':

> Coercive measures, gradually training the mind of the Aboriginal to the restraint necessary for the welfare of all civilized communities [was the only way] in fact, much the same as boys at school are treated by rewarding good conduct and punishing bad.

H. W. H. Smythe's opinion was that the Aboriginals were 'gradually becoming more quiet and inoffensive and altogether less troublesome to the stockholder . . . They war upon one another and not on the Europeans.' With the high native death rate, low birth rate, and 'unconquerable aversion' to regular employment, Smythe believed 'any scheme for their amelioration to be hopeless': within a short time 'few would remain to claim European sympathies.'

As the year 1846 wore on, G. A. Robinson amused himself with a journey from Melbourne to Adelaide lasting nearly five months. Acting Superintendent William Lonsdale attacked Robinson's report of the trip, saying it had 'little or no aim', that 'no advantage has accrued to the peculiar service for which he is employed', and that it more resembled 'the excursion of a man of leisure, remarking any thing that chances to come in his way.'

When Superintendent La Trobe returned from duties in Van Diemen's Land, the new Governor of New South Wales, Sir Charles FitzRoy, asked on 26 February 1847 for his opinion of the Chief Protector's activities, and whether the whole Protectorate system should be abandoned. La Trobe replied in April that Robinson's expeditions had proved 'almost utterly useless', that he performed 'no duties whatever that could not be discharged by a much less costly agency', and that the Protectorate had 'failed in all its higher and more important objects.' However, before closing down the operation, La Trobe felt he should make one further personal inspection of Protectorate stations. In his busy life, this could not occur for some time.

Robinson used the reprieve to submit a glowing report on the state of each station. At Goulburn River Station, he said, a new slab hut had been built and 'a quantity of excellent wheat was on hand'. Although only twenty natives were in residence, he believed that another 200 were on the way. At Loddon River Station, although only seven natives were present, a new paddock had been enclosed with a post-and-rail fence; the area was peaceful. At Mount Rouse a large paddock was also being fenced. Thirty-seven natives were present, although Robinson admitted that 'The greater part left before my departure.'

But when the details of events in and around each station are studied, a somewhat less impressive picture emerges.

Goulburn River Station, 1845-48

Edward Parker of the Loddon River Protectorate continued to supervise Goulburn River Station as well during most of 1844 and 1845. His report for September 1845 showed an average daily attendance at Goulburn of about fifty natives.

To relieve the pressure on Parker's time, Dr W. B. Atkins then took over at Goulburn River. His more detailed returns showed similar total attendances, but only six women and one boy as willing to work in the fields. Rations were allotted strictly in accordance with work performed: those issued to blacks totalled some 5 lbs of meat and 7 lbs of flour per day— the five Europeans in residence were eating nearly double this amount.

Occasional outbreaks of violence still occurred in the area. Major Alexander Davidson's run on the Acheron River, a tributary of the Goulburn, was attacked by four Devil's River warriors on 13 November 1845. An East Indian coolie, Raddy, tried to prevent the raiders from stealing three blade razors, flour, tobacco and soap from his hut. They cut open his stomach with one of the razors and left him with intestines protruding. Another coolie, Sutchman, found Raddy before he died, and heard his evidence.

La Trobe despatched Commissioner Smythe and his Border Police to the scene, followed by Henry Dana and his native troopers. By the time they arrived, all hope of tracking the murderers was lost. The remaining Hindus, convinced the warriors would return, told Smythe their contracts had expired and that they wished to return home immediately. La Trobe concurred, instructing G. A. Robinson to make arrangements.

Dana meanwhile received information that the killers had joined up with a group of Goulburn warriors and proceeded to their old haunt near the Ryries' station on the Upper Yarra. Dana found their camp, but could not get them to talk, and 'did not consider it prudent to arrest any of them.'

On Dana's return to Melbourne, La Trobe appealed to Robinson to try to find evidence such as the missing razors. Robinson passed this dangerous task to William Thomas, who reported vague rumours on the subject but could discover nothing definite.

Major Davidson reported in December that when one East Indian accompanied by a white man were driving his dray near Kilmore, they were threatened with death by Goulburn blacks. Davidson identified the Goulburns as Jackie Jackie, Lanky, and Long Bill, all notorious for earlier raids and killings. La Trobe sent a white trooper to help protect Davidson's station, and a strong party of Native Police under Dana to escort all the coolies back to Melbourne for repatriation to India.

At Goulburn River Protectorate, meanwhile, Dr Atkins disappeared from the government payroll and was replaced by Dr James Horsburgh. Early in May 1846 Horsburgh reported a daily attendance of about eighty blacks, but by late May this had dropped to only sixteen.

With few willing workers available, sowing of wheat did not take place until July, resulting in a meagre crop. The storeroom and other huts built only a few years earlier were in a sad state of disrepair, said Horsburgh.

From May to November Dr Horsburgh treated eight men and seven women for spear wounds. He also treated 140 women, 133 men, and 118 children for syphilis and syphilitic ulcers.

Several lubras at the Splatt brothers' property nearby who cohabited with whites were speared by their black husbands in December. Dr Horsburgh took the women by dray to the Protectorate station, but they vanished into the bush as soon as they were able to walk again.

Two Aboriginals died on the station late in December. The remainder fled, and settled on Wilson Holker's run, 'Warranga' (near today's Beechworth). Dr Horsburgh was left totally bereft of labour to harvest his ripening wheat crop. Fortunately he was able to hire four itinerant white workers to do the job.

An influenza epidemic swept the wandering tribes in January 1848, with 'many fatalities' along the river reported to Horsburgh.

By May about sixty natives had returned to the station, in time to help eat the flour from the eighteen acres of wheat which Horsburgh's men had harvested. The remaining wheat was black with smut: despite attempts at washing, it had to be thrown out.

In June Horsburgh admitted he was £800 in debt, mainly for wages paid, and that he needed extra rations urgently from

Melbourne. Meanwhile other natives he had visited up and down the Goulburn were now dying from an infection which what they called 'yagabua'—an enlargement of the liver.

Late in June the ex-convicts who comprised Horsburgh's main work force complained about the tedious task of hand-grinding the wheat into flour. 'Most "old hands" do not like this job . . .', Horsburgh reported. 'There appeared to me to be a regular conspiracy amongst them, each one striving how little he could possibly do, and how much insolence they could give me.' Horsburgh dismissed the worst offender, whereupon all packed up and left the station. The doctor asked for two replacements, besides employing a former commercial travel-ler from Manchester at his own expense as tutor for his children.

Matters improved slightly after that. When Robinson visited the station in October he reported that sixteen acres of smut-free wheat were growing. More than forty natives had returned and their medical condition had improved.

Lubras then took over the task of grinding wheat, although relieved of this labour when a steam grinding-mill opened at Kilmore. The male natives stripped 500 sheets of bark, sufficient to make new roofs and walls for the station's decaying huts. In return, they were given complete suits of clothes, blankets, and ample rations.

Loddon River Station, 1846-48

The modest success of Edward Parker's efforts in the Loddon River area were marred by isolated killings in 1846 and 1847.

The pioneer squatter Charles Wedge reported to Parker that a native named Wypurnin was shot on one of his out-stations on the Avoca River (west of today's Maryborough) on 28 June 1846. The killer was one of his shepherds, an expiree convict named John Fox, described as of 'dark complexion, low stature, and either blind in one eye or a serious defect in it.' His only previous offence as a freed man seems to have been drunkenness and riotous behaviour at Portland in 1841. Wedge said the murder was 'of a most wanton and unjustifiable character'. All squatters were anxious to bring Fox to justice, to prevent reprisals.

Parker told La Trobe he would immediately travel the 120 miles to arrest the shepherd, were it not that the Chief Protector had taken away the horses assigned to Loddon River Station. La Trobe despatched native troopers with a spare horse to assist Parker but by the time they arrived Fox had absconded towards South Australia. It appears that he made a clean getaway.

On their way back to Melbourne, the Native Police rested a while at Loddon River Station. Two of the lubras, Tootur-rook and Muthamurrum, attracted by their dashing ways and smart uniforms, absconded with them to Melbourne. Parker sent one of the husbands after them with a letter to William Thomas. After investigation, Thomas replied that since the lubras had gone willingly, nothing could be done to make them return.

Early in 1847 the wife and brothers of a tribal leader named Booringumin were killed in a brawl outside Anderson's Inn at Burn Bank, a tiny settlement near Talbot (south of today's Maryborough). They were, said Parker, 'victims of the drunkenness and debauchery there prevalent'.

After that event, Booringumin lapsed into 'a state of savage frenzy'. He recruited five warriors from his tribe in the Pyrenees and went on a rampage. In November 1847 the group attacked Alexander McCallum's 'Mount Hope' station east of the Loddon River, spearing to death an elderly chief named Abraham, wounding another native, and severely wounding a white employee. Parker feared the result would be a fresh outbreak of warfare between the Loddon and Pyrenees tribes.

Both Parker and Robinson complained about the effects of licensed public houses in the district, which had increased from two to ten in eighteen months. This had caused 'scenes of debauchery of the most frightful character'. Outside one inn, wrote Robinson, 'there were congregated at one time upwards of 300 natives and about fifty designated Europeans; the infatuated Aborigines were encouraged by the latter in every kind of vice.'

Apart from these events, the Loddon district remained reasonably quiet during the late 1840s.

Half-caste children, who had previously been killed out of hand by their black mothers, were now often allowed to survive. Edward Parker left a list of three boys and three girls of mixed parentage who were growing up under his family's care.

The next development was intermarriage between blacks and whites. In 1847 the Reverend William Hamilton of Kilnoorat asked Superintendent La Trobe whether it would be legal for him to marry a 40-year-old stockman named Michael Sullivan to a 16-year-old black girl in domestic service. Sullivan seemed 'steadfast and earnest', said the minister, and spent all his money on the girl. La Trobe replied that because the girl was 'in a state of heathenism', she must be baptised before the marriage could go ahead.

Meanwhile, the Protectorate's lambing and wool production was making progress. Surplus sheep were sent from the Loddon to the Goulburn River Station. For the year 1845–46 wool grown on the two Stations sold for £140. During 1846–47, this figure rose to nearly £160. In addition, 150 wethers were killed each year to supply the stations with meat.

Despite these encouraging signs, the Loddon natives still decided at the end of 1847 to go walkabout. When G. A. Robinson visited the Station late in March 1848 he found there were no blacks at all left there. The wheat was smutty, the potato crop had failed, and neighbouring squatters were beginning to encroach on the Protectorate area.

In his half-yearly report, Parker gave two reasons for the natives' unprecedented absence. First was the severe sickness and mortality on the Station. More important was the 'frantic hostility' displayed by Pyrenees tribes, forcing the Loddon blacks to flee northward and eastward. Not until the middle of 1848 did some of them dare to return.

During their absence, Parker's eldest son died at the age of eighteen. 'The recital of his dying expressions and his triumphant departure from this world', wrote Parker, 'has produced a deep impression' on the minds of those blacks who had returned. Having 'seen the big tears rolling down the cheeks of those who are too indiscriminately deemed uncouth, unfeeling and unimproveable savages', Parker concluded that 'it is not an utterly hopeless work in which I am engaged.' The young blacks in particular displayed 'the most cheering alacrity' in returning to their Station duties, fencing a 200-acre paddock with little help from whites.

Robinson's reaction to Parker's touching report was to censure him for forgetting to send in a duplicate copy. The Chief Protector promised La Trobe that such a flagrant breach of the regulations would not occur again.

By the second half of 1848 things seemed to be going so well on the Loddon River Station that Parker regained his habitual optimism. Average daily attendance of natives stabilised at fifty-five. They showed 'less disposition to wander' than ever before, especially while Parker was able to remain on the Station.

White employees were still reluctant to teach blacks the details of agricultural work, mainly because they feared the effect on their own wages. Parker overcame this problem by using his surviving sons (now 17, 16, 14, 13 and 11 years of age) as instructors. This cost the government nothing.

Nor did it cost the government a penny for Parker to use his second wife, Hannah, as instructor for the native girls. Under her tuition they made all their own clothes, and some learnt to read. Even the young men were taught to make their own canvas trousers. After the day's farm work was done, Parker's elder sons taught the native boys to read.

Parker said he had begged suits of old clothes from neighbouring squatters. The men were happy to don these and attend Sunday afternoon services, conducted in their own language in a new chapel built by an anonymous private donor. But there was a problem with the women: 'I have found increasing difficulty in inducing the females to join regularly in the services', wrote Parker. He felt it necessary to condemn 'the wickedness and danger of certain immoral practices' among them. 'Some of the women have consequently displayed resentful feelings, others have manifested levity, and most, I regret to say, have shown great indifference.'

On the station, conditions were prosperous. The flocks had multiplied to about 3000 sheep. Half were kept near the homestead; half around a newly-built out-station manned by a married white couple and a boy. The season's wool clip amounted to 6627 lbs.

The natives themselves had built a substantial earth-and-timber dam, creating a sheep-washing pool where the flocks were spout-washed by native labour before being handed over to itinerant white shearers.

Seven tons of hay had been harvested by the natives for sale, and wheat was growing well in the 34 acre paddock. Whites and blacks together had built a substantial mill-dam, sufficient to operate two steel mills for grinding the wheat into flour.

All that was needed, said Parker, was proper educational facilities so that young blacks could be trained to continue the good work.

La Trobe was stunned by this excellent report. In forwarding the report to Governor FitzRoy, he remarked how it contrasted with the scene of 'neglect, disorder, and discouragement' found by himself and the Chief Protector on earlier visits. Anyhow, thought La Trobe, the apparent improvement at Loddon River made no difference to the fact that the Protectorate arrangement 'should give place to one more simple and manageable'.

Mount Rouse Station, 1846–48

While dear old Dr Watton slumbered at Mount Rouse Station, sporadic violence continued to flare throughout the Western District.

On 25 January 1846, while Thomas Barrett, a stockman employed on Walter Birmingham and Owen O'Reilly's 'Mullagh' run (north of today's Harrow), was taking a flour bag full of the men's rations past a honeysuckle forest, an Aboriginal named Jim grasped his horse's bridle and the ration bag, saying he should have it: 'he no frightened, plenty black fellows all about.' When Barrett refused, Jim raised his leanguil over the man's head. Barrett aimed his gun and fired both barrels, killing the native.

Depositions were sent to Melbourne, but no trace of further action can be found.

The following month blacks again attacked William Learmonth's cattle run, 'Ettrick', on Darlot's Creek (near today's Heywood). Learmonth reported that during the last weeks of February he and his neighbours had been subjected to continual raids. Their men were forever 'bringing cattle in, dressing their wounds, and withdrawing spears from them.' One man who was riding along the road to Learmonth's house was challenged by a large group of natives brandishing spears, and was forced to flee.

After hearing this, Learmonth armed two of his men and started off in search of the war party, 'determined to dislodge them if possible'. The posse found about fifty blacks on 'an almost inaccessible island surrounded with boggy swamps'. The whites retired, found a long route around to the same spot, 'and got within 20 yards of them unperceived.' Learmonth shouted to the blacks, asking why they had speared the cattle. He was 'answered by threats and the brandishing of spears'. The squatter told his men to fire, but when two of his small party were wounded, was forced to retreat.

The massacre of settlers' cattle continued through March

and April 1846. The natives often broke up into smaller war parties, able to conceal themselves successfully in the rocky country between Heywood and Mount Eeles.

As a temporary measure, Commissioner Fyans stationed two of his Border Police at Learmonth's station, the squatter paying half the cost. This had the immediate effect of reducing native depredations.

In May Superintendent La Trobe ordered Dana and his Native Police to take over this duty. The move simply diverted the native attackers westward to properties on the lower Glenelg River. Two squatters there, Allan R. McDonald of 'Glenaulin' Station (near today's Dartmoor), and William Lang of 'Mornbeong', complained in July 1846 that their stock was 'completely at the mercy of a daring band of Aborigines . . . led by two or three half-domesticated blacks—possibly the same blacks who had deserted Mount Rouse Protectorate the previous month, telling Dr Watton they were no longer willing to hand-grind the wheat in order to obtain food.

Patrolling by the Native Police finally quietened the district. Twelve leading squatters signed a letter of thanks to La Trobe, stating that their properties were 'effectually protected' by their presence, and congratulating the black troopers for their 'orderly conduct' while quartered on their stations.

By the end of 1846 about thirty natives had returned to Mount Rouse. Dr Watton reported that he possessed only about fifty bushels of wheat, and that was so smutty as to be 'scarcely worth the trouble of thrashing'. Unless money was made available for fencing paddocks and employing white labour, he could see no hope of conducting the station 'with credit to myself, satisfaction to the Government, or essential benefits to the Aborigines.'

With the desultory attendance of natives at the Station, neighbouring squatters began to utilise its pastures. Dr Watton reported that Alexander Donaldson of 'Purdeet' run on nearby Black Creek was grazing his stock and cutting what little timber remained on the Protectorate area. In addition,

Donaldson's cattle were infected with 'black-leg', putting the station cows in danger. There is no indication that the Chief Protector took much notice of Watton's complaints. His report to La Trobe on the state of Mount Rouse Station during 1846 was a masterpiece of evasion of the real issues.

La Trobe himself visited Mount Rouse in 1847. He concluded that the Station had largely failed in influencing 'the habits of the tribes', and that 'no amount of bribe in the shape of food or clothing would . . . lead the Aborigines to forsake their natural habits.' Nevertheless, thought La Trobe, the Station was costing so little that Dr Watton might as well remain there, for the sake of the 'slight influence' for good he could exercise.

Several atrocities took place in the Western District during 1847. On 20 May an unnamed shepherd was murdered by blacks on H. A. Elms's run on the Glenelg River. John Cox, JP, authorised a punitive expedition, during which two natives were killed. Cox then sailed to Van Diemen's Land, delaying further investigation.

When Cox returned five months later, he was interviewed by Dr Watton. All that the Protector could discover was that the two natives had been shot after throwing spears at their pursuers, and that the murdered shepherd's clothes were found on one of them. No other action seems to have followed.

Further north, in the Wimmera, overseer John Stokel, who was employed on George Armytage's 'Murrandara' station (south-east of today's Apsley), was infuriated to learn that one of his Aboriginal shepherds had been murdered by a wild black named Mister Mark.

Stokel found Mister Mark on 12 October 1847 at Robert Officer junior's 'Mount Talbot' run (near today's town of Harrow). Officer had lent a double-barrelled gun to Stokel, and when Mister Mark fled from him, Stokel fired, hitting him in the left ear and jaw. Stokel then ordered his men to drag the wounded black to a dray, secure him with a bullock chain, and attach a padlock. Mister Mark was left there bleeding profusely. Despite attempts by Officer to dress the wound, Mister Mark died that night. 'A more brutal disgraceful act was never perpetrated', wrote local squatter-magistrate, Major William Firebrace.

La Trobe ordered Dr Watton 'instantly to take steps to arrest the murderer and bring him to justice.' Before Watton could get there, another local settler, Dr Edward Barker, exhumed the body and described the injuries. By this time it was impossible to give positive identification that it was Mister Mark. Nevertheless, Stokel was committed at Horsham Police Court on 27 November for trial on a number of charges, including murder.

James Croke prosecuted Stokel in the Supreme Court in February 1848 on six counts: the jury found the overseer guilty on one count only, that of causing grievous bodily harm. Judge à Beckett wrote on the trial documents:

> The jury would have acquitted prisoner altogether, if I had not told them that his moral conviction that [Mister] Mark had killed his boy was not sufficient in point of law to justify his firing. The prisoner received a very high character, and as he had evidently acted without malice, and there was no proof of the death of Mark or that he had received any fatal wound, I did not think it a case calling for a severe sentence.

The judge therefore imposed a sentence of two months' imprisonment in Melbourne Gaol.

Early in 1850 Protector William Thomas compiled a list of Europeans tried for offences against Aboriginals since the beginning of white settlement in Port Phillip. There were nine white men on the list. John Stokel's two months' gaol was the only penalty of any kind imposed.

With the Stokel affair especially in mind, Chief Protector Robinson wrote in his annual report for 1847: 'Those parties are now mostly in possession of large runs, i.e., immense tracts of country, and laugh at what they have done as a good joke.'

Robinson added in his 1848 report: 'The ruffians' boast is that shooting blackfellows is good sport, that they must be got rid of, think no more of shooting them than crows.'

In December 1847 Protector Thomas learned that Charles Johnstone (also known as George Johanstein), a bullock-driver from H. J. Miller's run on the Glenelg River, had brought an eleven-year-old Aboriginal girl with him to Melbourne.

Thomas took a constable to Clare Castle public-house in Exhibition Street and arrested the man. The landlord testified the pair had slept in the same bed. The girl was found 'huddled up in a corner', and put in the care of the watch-house keeper's wife.

In Melbourne Police Court on 22 December, to Thomas's 'utter astonishment', the bullock-driver was freed, the Protectorate system castigated, and the little girl given back to her abductor. By the time Thomas stirred the Crown Prosecutor into appealing the decision, 'the fellow made off with the child', and was never seen again.

Dr Watton's summary for the year 1847 was just as gloomy as his earlier reports. Native attendance at Mount Rouse was low, he said, because those working for squatters received far more food and clothing than they could get from the Protectorate. Although two small paddocks had been fenced, there was 'no produce of any kind on hand.' The few residents were existing on salt beef, which the natives hated. Without funds to make repairs, 'the buildings on the station are rapidly hastening to decay.' Watton had to pay from his own pocket for essential repairs to the main homestead in which he lived.

Watton supplemented this litany with a letter complaining that his annual salary had remained at £120 since 1843, despite a government promise that it would be raised to the normal Protector's rate of £250. The Chief Protector's retort was that Goulburn River Station, also managed by a medical officer on exactly the same terms, produced far better results.

In April 1848 Watton pleaded for extra white men to carry on the Station work. 'The potatoes are now to be dug, every building on the station requires new thatching, the cultivation paddock to be ploughed and sown', he wrote. In addition, the home paddock fences needed repair, and a thrashing floor was essential for the wheat. A medical hut was also required, 'instead of bringing the blacks with their disgusting diseases into my own residence.'

By the end of 1848 Watton had to confess almost total failure of the new wheat and potato crops. Only about twenty natives were now occasionally attending the Station, mostly for medical treatment. There was no food for them: 'No supply of any kind on hand', Watton reported.

Fortunately few tragedies were heard of in 1848 throughout a more sedate Western District.

The worst case occurred on 23 September, when a 'wild' native woman who had come out of the bush to seek refuge was killed by blacks living on William Lonsdale's station, 'Upper Grange' (just to the north of today's Hamilton). Edwin Partridge, bullock driver, deposed that he saw a station black named Jimmy throw a spear at her from a few yards away. John Stot, a labourer, said he saw Jimmy then strike the lubra violently with a large waddy, knocking her to the ground. Another black man, Jack, ran up, and tried to prevent Jimmy from making further assaults. While they were grappling, a third black, Jackey, 'took a spear and thrust it into her', then hit her three more times with a waddy. A fourth black named Old Man Johnny struck her several times on the shoulder and ribs. By this time her groans had ceased and she was probably dead.

The white men, who said they were too frightened to interfere, later emerged from their hut, buried the body, and sent for help. Hamilton's Chief Constable Peter Tighe located and arrested Jimmy soon afterwards. He was tried at the Supreme Court on 18 October, but acquitted. If a black man's death meant little, a black woman's death meant even less.

Complaints about the Protectorate's lack of success which reached London led Secretary of State Earl Grey to instruct Governor FitzRoy to re-examine Robinson's activities. 'If the result of such examination should prove unfavourable to the continuance of the Office, you will act at once to abolish it', wrote Earl Grey.

The Governor omitted this crucial passage in a partial copy of the despatch sent on to La Trobe. All that was seen in Port Phillip was Earl Grey's description of the reserves as 'the most successful of the experiments which have hitherto been tried.' In this alternative approach, Grey commended FitzRoy to pay 'immediate attention to the suggestion of the Chief Protector' for expansion of the system, and to open more schools for Aboriginal children 'on the principle of combining the arts of industry with the elements of ordinary and religious education.'

La Trobe must have sighed when this cheerful extract was transmitted to him in September 1848. Nevertheless, he circulated it to his Crown Commissioners, again asking for their opinions.

Commissioner Edward Grimes replied that 'the suggestion of the Honorable the Secretary of State appears to be based entirely upon the present Protectorate system, which I am fully convinced so far from attaining the desired end, has aggravated the very evils it was intended to remedy.' Distribution of rations had merely encouraged the natives' 'indolent habits' and 'mutual jealousy'.

Grimes attributed any improvement in racial relations to 'the cessation of any intercourse between the natives and the Protectors, the Protectorate stations being notoriously the last place at which you are likely to meet any number of the Aborigines.'

La Trobe finalised his reply to FitzRoy on 18 November 1848. He traversed the whole history of governmental attempts to assist the native population of Port Phillip—going to this trouble because Robinson had presented the 'most voluminous' reports over the years 'without conveying any distinct idea of the actual position of the Aboriginal natives . . .'

La Trobe pointed out that the government had spent a total of £61 000 on native welfare in thirteen years of white settlement in Port Phillip. Of this, the Protectorate had cost £42 000; the Native Police more than £11 000; the Wesleyan Mission at Buntingdale nearly £7000; and the Merri Creek school nearly £1000. 'The result of all this outlay may be stated in few words', wrote La Trobe. 'Every one of these plans (with the possible exception of the Native Police) . . . has either completely failed, or shows at this date most undoubted signs of failure.' As regards the Protectorate, 'if no such establishment had existed, the state of the Aboriginal native within the District would not have differed very greatly from what it now is.'

On the subject of Christianisation of the natives, the Protectors had 'talked and written, and the Wesleyan missionaries have faithfully labored in vain', noted La Trobe. They could not show even one example of success. Similarly every attempt to train natives to support themselves by agriculture had failed. Shown how to build comfortable huts, they persisted in living under 'a few sheets of bark'. When exhorted to remain at a station, La Trobe observed, the only result was 'production of a more than ordinary accumulation of filth, and a greater air of squalidity.'

All in all, thought La Trobe, the Aboriginals 'are, I fear, pretty much as they were . . . They have their feuds, their superstitions, observances, preposterous and cruel murders, and abominable vices . . .'

All these things necessarily led to 'a gradual extinction of race'. The coming of the European 'converted what may have been a gradual decline into a rapid fall.' La Trobe, of course, did not know that the Aboriginal race had already survived successfully for at least 40 000 years.

The Protectorate, continued La Trobe, had taken on an impracticable task, using the wrong people. Robinson was 'totally unsuited' to management, a function 'quite beyond his powers'; his efficiency, 'such as it was', had been destroyed.

The Assistant Protectors were of 'incongruous and ill-assorted character, and they never at any time 'understood each other, or had mutual confidence'.

La Trobe had come to agree with his Crown Commissioners that coercive measures were necessary, even if these were 'not consistent with the spirit of the age'. The older natives were 'past reclamation', but all young males, when they reached an appropriate age, should be enrolled in a body like the Native Police, and subjected to 'strict military discipline', including forced inculcation of 'Christian and moral principle'. With the children, 'nothing short of an actual and total separation from their parents', and education away from all tribal influences, held any hope of their ultimate civilisation.

For the tribal remnants themselves, additional reserves should be created throughout Port Phillip, under the control of medical officers, where rations could still be available in emergencies in return for exertion 'at some passing occupation'.

Robinson himself had now come to feel that Aboriginals should be given legally enforceable land rights. Surveying the squatting scene at the end of 1848, he wrote that 'every spot where water and grass is found is occupied and overrun with stock . . . Such is the cupidity of some persons that they would not leave the Aborigines any available country.'

Robinson believed, at a time when few others did, that 'The Aboriginal natives have a right to a reasonable share in the soil of their Fatherland, and ought not to be driven from their haunts and homes at the caprice of any person.' He thought that 'Free access should be allowed the Aborigines to lakes, rivers, swamps, lagoons, and to their favourite hunting grounds at their season for hunting.' Too late, too late.

17

FAILURE OF THE WESLEYAN MISSION AT BUNTINGDALE

Pacification of the near Western District between Geelong and Colac was assisted by Wesleyan ministers working away quietly at the Buntingdale Mission (near today's town of Birregurra). This mission was the idea of Reverend Joseph Orton, a noted British anti-slavery evangelist, who visited Port Phillip in 1836 when Van Diemen's Land squatters were first landing large flocks of sheep in the Western District. Wesleyan authorities selected two ministers, the Reverend Francis Tuckfield, 31, and the Reverend Benjamin Hurst, 28, to open the mission in 1839. The government allotted a tract of land, and a £1 for £1 subsidy up to £600, instructing Crown Commissioners that squatters must keep their men and flocks at least five miles distant from the mission buildings.

The main Aboriginal tribe in the area was known as the Dantgurts. According to Hurst, 'Two years ago this tribe was a numerous one, but nearly the whole of the fighting men have been butchered in cold blood by Europeans.'

The same fate would have overcome the Coligan tribe at

Colac, wrote Tuckfield, 'were it not for some humane settlers in the vicinity of the Lakes to have thrown around them the shield of Protection.'

Reverend Hurst was able to report to La Trobe by May 1840 that several huts had been erected at Buntingdale, sixty natives were usually in attendance, cultivation of paddocks was under way, and twenty-five black children were being taught to read and sew. With further instruction, high hopes were held that the blacks would become 'useful members of civil and religious society'.

By the end of the first year, after expenditure of £1200, the natives improved further in 'habits of cleanliness and industry', were imitating Europeans at sabbath services, and were often used by local squatters to assist at sheep-shearing time. Unfortunately the mission homestead burnt to the ground that year, destroying a dictionary of tribal dialects compiled by the missionaries.

These good-hearted ministers soon found that Aboriginal traditions were not easily set aside. Early in 1841 a visiting tribesman died of disease at Buntingdale. An inflamed war party of 200 natives descended on the mission huts on 13 July 1841 'in order to be revenged.' Most of the station blacks fled into the bush. One who remained was speared to death in his mia-mia. This would have led to further retaliatory murders, had not one of the Aboriginals settled matters by agreeing to give up his wife.

For some time after that the mission remained deserted, except for six young boys attending school. 'We shall have much of our work to do over again', wrote a chastened Hurst.

The missionary asked for La Trobe's understanding of the 'alarming extent to which the females are prostituted'—a practice 'not confined to the lower order of Europeans.' In other words, some squatters as well as former convicts also played a part. This had led, said Hurst, to the 'almost universal prevalence' of syphilis among the blacks. The consequent enfeeblement made them 'almost incapable of performing any manual labour.' Only two healthy black babies had survived within a forty-mile radius of the mission, while practically every half-caste baby was killed at birth in a desperate attempt to preserve tribal breeding customs.

La Trobe felt the missionaries should not 'shrink from the duty of openly exposing the vicious connexion which too often exists between the Europeans and the native women,' despite 'great difficulties in the way of obtaining positive proof.'

Yet, said Hurst in his annual report for 1841, 'the Spirit of God . . . is striving with them.' Many natives listened seriously to Sunday sermons, while on weekdays the men had learned to yoke bullocks, plough, and cultivate a ten-acre paddock. La Trobe visited the mission twice that year, and authorised continuation of the government subsidy.

The missionaries laboured on faithfully against many odds during 1842, with attendances fluctuating greatly. On 28 November they called a meeting of 120 survivors of local tribes, warning them that the station might have to be abandoned unless they became more regular in attendance and work habits. The natives promised to improve, but pleaded that 'the great Governor ought to send the Police to protect them from the violent and revengeful attacks' of wilder tribes, which made them seek refuge in the bush.

Attendance figures improved considerably after this, to an average of ninety-five a day. Following prayers at seven o'clock each morning, the blacks went off to school or to work in the fields in 'peace and harmony'.

Then, on the evening of 4 January 1843, Derederesbarn, a young warrior of the Tolerbollock tribe stole into camp and 'drove a large spear through the body' of a young Dantgurt woman. She died after moaning in agony for several hours. All her tribe again fled from Buntingdale, creeping back only when the danger had passed.

Reverend Tuckfield advised Superintendent La Trobe that he had decided to limit the mission's operations to the Dantgurt and Coligan tribes, which were interrelated by marriage. He asked for better police protection against armed attacks. La Trobe agreed, instructing Commissioner Fyans to send Border Police to Buntingdale whenever a crisis threatened.

By the spring of 1843, Tuckfield felt able to report 'auspicious and encouraging' results. The fifty-two natives now in residence had fenced and sown fifty acres with wheat, potatoes and vegetables. Some had built their own slab huts. Others supervised a small flock of ewes donated by friendly squatters. The children became particularly adept at catechism and geography lessons. Under Mrs Tuckfield's tuition, they made '32 pairs trousers, 18 shirts and 26 dresses'. 'Thank God and take courage', wrote Tuckfield.

New problems occurred. With reduction of government income during the economic depression, the annual subsidy of £600 to Buntingdale was cancelled. Its own funds depleted, the Wesleyan Missionary Society in London was forced to order the closure of Buntingdale.

The day was saved only when Tuckfield was able to submit a further glowing report. The mission's flock of sheep had grown to 550, besides keeping the station in mutton for several months. The blacks had also made themselves self-sufficient in grain and vegetables.

One native youth, Koymonanen, had shown distinct signs of religious conversion. He told Tuckfield: 'I have two spirits within me, the good spirit and the bad spirit, and they are talking to me every day, they never stop. One of them tells me to be bad and the other tells me to be good.'

Encouraging progress continued during 1845. The government now had sufficient funds to allow an annual subsidy of £150. Private donations added nearly £100, plus more sheep and clothing. The mission's flock increased to 900, and a small herd of cattle was added: 'work with which the natives are at all times delighted.' By the following year, the mission's own sheep increased to 2000, with another 3000 being grazed on agistment. The cattle increased to 120 head.

However, at the end of June 1846 Tuckfield underwent 'the painful duty' of telling La Trobe that many of his station blacks had gone off to join the wilder tribes, or were existing by begging offal from nearby squatters. If anything, this was an understatement. La Trobe revisited the mission in August, and 'with great regret' was forced to inform Governor FitzRoy that despite all the missionaries' efforts, they had 'most signally failed in operating the desired change in the habits and character' of the natives. 'I cannot consider the experiment otherwise than as a total failure', La Trobe wrote.

Crown Commissioner E. B. Addis sent in a separate report, confirming that the position of Buntingdale blacks had 'become nearly hopeless, from their wandering and indolent habits.' Their numbers continued to diminish. Addis attributed this mainly to their fondness for spirits, and 'the promiscuous intercourse of the women . . . with the servants of the settlers.'

In his report for the year ended 30 June 1847 Tuckfield admitted that most of the blacks had fallen back into habits of 'unrestrained vagrancy'. Only half a dozen natives remained on the station, and these displayed 'the greatest apathy and indifference'. This reacted 'very injuriously' on the young, who had grown tired of school and 'relapsed into careless indifference'.

This state of affairs could not last. In June 1848 Tuckfield informed La Trobe that he had been 'instructed to wind up the affairs of the mission and resign the reserve into the hands of the Government.'

The circle with a five-mile radius around Buntingdale, into which squatters were not supposed to penetrate, had long been marked with ploughed furrows. This did not stop settlers' employees from driving stock through the mission land to reach water in the Barwon River or Pennyroyal Creek.

In 1845 Tuckfield complained that flocks belonging to James Austin, the Dennis brothers and J. M. C. Airey were gradually encroaching on his land. For this reason he made an agreement with W. H. Bowden on 12 November to depasture his flocks at Buntingdale, in return for an increasing number of lambs each year.

Once the imminent closure of Buntingdale became known in 1848, squatters around the five-mile circle applied for a share. A joint application for possession went to La Trobe from the Austin brothers, William Roadknight, G. T. Lloyd for Thomas Ricketts, the Dennis brothers, and George Armytage.

La Trobe had other ideas. He recommended to Governor FitzRoy that the whole of the mission 'should be looked upon as a Reserve ... with a view to the future if not present advantage of the Aboriginal natives.' Surveyor Robert Hoddle said he did 'not see why any portion should be reserved for Aboriginal purposes'. La Trobe insisted. Hoddle therefore reserved some four square miles for Aboriginal use, and marked out the rest of the land for sale.

The old mission station was completely destroyed in the bushfires of 'Black Thursday' in February 1851. The town of Birregurra later arose on the north-western edge of its original land holding, and whites took over all the grazing areas. In the mid-1850s there were believed to be only ten men, five women and one child of Aboriginal birth left in the entire district. The dreams of missionaries and government officers alike had failed.

18

WHITE WOMAN CAPTURED BY GIPPSLAND BLACKS

In the frontier society that was Port Phillip, respectable women were rare and precious. So a particular thrill of horror ran through the community whenever it was feared that white women had fallen into the hands of black tribes.

Ignorance of the fate of people shipwrecked on remote coastlines added a new dimension of terror. During 1839 and 1840 several vessels sank after leaving Melbourne, and few traces of their passengers were ever found.

The first intimation that a female survivor might be held captive in Gippsland came in a letter from squatter Angus McMillan in December 1840. McMillan and his men found in one hastily abandoned native camp 'several pieces of women's wearing apparel'. As the blacks retreated into the bush, McMillan saw one woman 'continually looking behind her, at us.' Examining the shelters, he concluded that 'the unfortunate female is a European.'

Speculation ran riot on the woman's possible identity. Some thought she was a woman named Anna MacPherson, lost when the *Britannia* sank off Gippsland in 1839. Others thought she was Mrs Thomas Capel, wife of a Sydney brewer, also on the *Britannia*. Possibly there were *two* white women being held captive. Other theories abounded.

The next piece of evidence emerged in 1841, when a party of settlers routed a native camp near Port Albert. In one of the canoes, they noted that an article of women's attire had been used to block up an opening.

Two years later another party of whites, sailing on Lake King, were attracted to a group of blacks on shore. As they drew closer, they 'distinctly saw the upper part of the body of a white woman as if violently pressing forward to reach the beach, and as violently dragged back under cover of the sand hill.'

Even more significant evidence came early in 1846 from an 8-year-old native boy, Jackawadden, who had joined the whites when squatter J. R. Wilkinson drove tribal blacks off his run at Lake Wellington about six months earlier. Jackawadden went to live at 'Boisdale' station with John Paine, storekeeper to Captain Lachlan MacAlister, who taught him to speak English. The boy told Paine that a white woman with two half-caste children was living with his tribe. He used to play with one of them, who was then five or six years old. Jackawadden's own mother used to tell him that the white woman 'came from a big canoe' called Bunga-Bunga, with several white men who had been 'sent away' towards Sydney while the tribe 'kept the white gin'.

A party of ten Native Police under W. H. Walsh (Henry Dana's brother-in-law) happened to be in Gippsland. In April 1846 Crown Commissioner Tyers placed the force under Sergeant Windridge, now of the Border Police, ordering him to take Jackawadden, John Paine, and troopers in search of the white woman. La Trobe warned that 'great difficulty and danger ... must attend any attempt to rescue her and her children by force', and advised 'the greatest caution and prudence'.

When Windridge and the black troopers arrived at

'Boisdale', they found that the storekeeper and Jackawadden were frightened of being speared in the bush. Eventually the boy was persuaded to go.

After some false leads, in May the party found part of Jackawadden's tribe encamped between Lake Wellington and Lake Victoria. The tribesmen told Windridge that the white woman had crossed the backwater the previous day in search of food. Windridge offered them 'blankets, and anything else they might want, if they would give up the white woman.' They agreed to fetch her, but failed to return.

On 25 May Windridge spoke to an old man of the tribe, who told him the woman 'had gone into the mountains with a wild black named Bungeleena.' The boy Jackawadden said this was 'a man of some consideration with his tribe, but not chief.'

Searching a native camp at Lake Reeve, Windridge found portions of a lubra's body 'being cooked at the several fires, and some pieces from the thighs and other parts of the body put away in some bark.' Jackawadden told him it was 'not uncommon for the men to kill their gins and eat them.'

For some weeks Windridge's men continued their search by boat around the Gippsland lakes. On 24 June they captured one native who told them (through the boy) that 'he had left the white woman and the blacks the night before.' But when the tribe saw the boats approaching, they 'left the camps precipitately.' The troopers followed the blacks overland towards the Snowy River, locating them again near today's Lake Tyers.

Again the blacks retreated, leaving behind seven women, who agreed to accompany the party back to the Border Police station. Asked if they wanted to return to their tribe, Walsh reported, 'they say no—that they would get nothing to eat, and have to go naked—The last time I asked them they began to cry.'

On receiving these reports, La Trobe instructed Tyers to spare neither effort nor expense to find the white woman. Even greater caution than before was essential, for 'The blow of a waddie is soon given . . .'

By this time, the whole of Melbourne was convinced that a white woman was being held against her will. The phlegmatic Sub-Treasurer, William Lonsdale, wrote: 'I have not the slightest doubt of such a person being there.'

From conversations Lonsdale himself had with Walsh and Jackawadden, he learned that

> the female appears to be about 24 or 25 years of age, that her hair is light brown, and now cut short; that when wrecked she seems to have been well dressed, her shoes being described as of thin material; that she had on a boa; and that part of a silk dress which was found some time after, belonged to her.

Bungeleena was apparently kind to her, and mostly she lived contentedly. 'She sometimes cries, yet joins in the amusements and pursuits of the people she is with; and that she has good health.'

La Trobe agreed that the woman's existence was 'now confirmed beyond a doubt'. He instructed Tyers to purchase 'a sufficient number of blankets, tomahawks or such other articles as may be most attractive', take them to a camp as near as possible to the tribe, and remain there 'until the female was brought to you'.

This idea nearly succeeded. In November Tyers despatched the women living at police headquarters with a message to their tribe that plenty of goods would be handed over in return for the white woman. The tribe agreed to negotiate with Bungeleena, 'making a condition that during their absence no party of white men should be sent out.'

Meanwhile, a party of Native Police placed temporarily under Sergeant Windridge was investigating the spearing of cattle on Lachlan MacAlister's station. On 20 October 1846 the troopers encountered a tribe of 100 blacks carrying freshly killed beef. They attempted to handcuff some of the blacks, but were attacked with waddies and tomahawks. Windridge ordered his men to fire. Two blacks were killed and another wounded.

Was this all that happened? According to a story told by Clerk of Courts George Dunderdale, Tyers took some friends sailing around one of the lakes. When they neared land

the air was filled with a stench so horrible that Mr. Tyers at once put the boat about, and went away in another direction. Next day he visited the spot with his police, and he found that the dead wood covered a large pile of the corpses of the natives shot by his own black troopers, and he directed them to make it a holocaust [i.e. burn the bodies].

If true, Tyers did not report the matter to headquarters.

A group of well-meaning amateurs from Melbourne had already entered the scene. A public meeting on 2 September presided over by the mayor, Dr J. F. Palmer, had begun to raise funds for a private expedition to locate the woman. The *Argus* added fuel to the fire on 29 September by reminding readers of 'The horrors of such a captivity—an educated white female forcibly detained by a savage, cannibal black—the helpless misery of her wretchedness . . .', and so on.

The result was that a party of five whites and nine blacks was recruited under C. L. J. De Villiers, a South African bushman who had failed in an attempt to form the first Native Police corps in 1837. Now a squatter near Dandenong, De Villiers was apparently anxious to salvage his reputation.

Before leaving Melbourne, De Villiers purchased a large number of linen handkerchiefs printed with the following message in both English and Gaelic, to be nailed to trees throughout Gippsland:

WHITE WOMAN!—There are fourteen armed men, partly White and partly Black, in search of you. Be cautious; and rush to them when you see them near you. Be particularly on the look out every dawn of morning, for it is then that the party are in hopes of rescuing you. The white settlement is towards the setting sun.

Arriving in Gippsland in November 1846, De Villiers was prohibited by Tyers from proceeding until conciliatory attempts had concluded. This time came on 9 December, when, wrote Tyers, 'two natives of the friendly tribe ... returned from their mission with broken heads—Bungeleena being determined ... not to give her up without fighting.'

Tyers sat down to write his annual report on Aboriginals of the district. Those living in friendship with whites, he said, had become useful as sheep-washers, stock-keepers and bullock-drivers. They were paid about a shilling a day, spending it on tea, sugar and other stores. Unfortunately, wrote Tyers, 'They have no idea of a Supreme Being—nor does their moral condition appear to have been bettered by their intercourse with white people.' The second class of natives, Tyers added, called wild blacks or warrigals, lived by fishing, hunting kangaroos, possums and native bears, and stealing about 150 head of the settlers' stock each year.

Tyers did not say what had been discovered by the young settler Henry Meyrick, who arrived early in 1846 to take up 'Glenfalloch B' run (north-west of today's town of Stratford). Meyrick wrote that:

Men, women and children are shot whenever they can be met with ... what they can urge in their excuse who shoot the women and children I cannot conceive ... these things are kept very secret as the penalty would certainly be hanging ... For myself, if I caught a black actually killing my sheep, I would shoot him with as little remorse as I would a wild dog, but no consideration on earth would induce me to ride into a camp and fire on them indiscriminately, as is the custom whenever the smoke is seen ... I am convinced that not less than 450 have been murdered altogether ... I am become so familiarized with scenes of horror from having murder made a topic of everyday conversation.

Meyrick's observations were probably near the true state of affairs when young William Dana arrived to take charge of the Native Police. They were first off the mark in renewed search for the white woman, arriving at the Snowy River mouth on 18 December, and camping about ten miles upstream.

Taking native canoes, they paddled on 20 December to a small island where the white woman was said to be. The blacks rushed them with spears, wounding Trooper Owen Cowen in the hand. He drew his pistol and shot one assailant dead. Another black man and woman were captured and handcuffed together around the ankles, but managed to escape.

De Villiers and his private expeditioners took up the quest. On 22 December they rowed up an eastern tributary of the Snowy, where William Dana had warned De Villiers not to go. Seeing the grass trampled down, they went ashore and found the native who had been shot dead. Next day they found the handcuffed man and woman and struck off the cuffs. That was all De Villiers had to say, apart from reporting his return to Tambo Bluff on 27 December.

A red-hot version of the affray was given to Melbourne newspapers by James Warman, second-in-command of De Villiers's force, who had returned home. Relying entirely on hearsay, Warman claimed that fourteen blacks had been killed. The Native Police, he claimed, were 'the most cruel bloodthirsty wretches alive'.

Commissioner Tyers discovered that these extravagant claims had been spread by a man called Yorky, in the service of John Foster, licensee of the Heart Inn at Port Albert, 'as he terms it, "for a lark".' Unfortunately they have been taken seriously by several subsequent historians, although formally denied by La Trobe.

Sergeant Windridge and his Border Police, now thoroughly refreshed, decided it was their turn. On 4 January 1847 they proceeded to the islands in Lake Reeve with a great quantity of blankets, shirts and tomahawks to be given in exchange for the white woman. They found about 100 blacks camped there, who promised to send a party to the mountains where Bungeleena had the woman hidden. When nothing further was heard, Windridge decided on 15 January to take his police to the mountains.

The party proceeded northward up the Tambo River. At dusk on 19 January they encountered a tribe of 200 natives, who promised to send for the white woman. Bungeleena sent back a message from his hiding place next day, 'stating that he would not give up the white woman.'

The main result of the meeting was that the boy Jackawadden was able to see his father again. Tears of joy ran down the old man's face as the boy told him how he had visited Melbourne, and liked the white folk.

Jackawadden asked his father why the tribe would not give up the woman who belonged to the whites. The man replied that 'the whites were always savage' towards the Aboriginals. Besides that, 'the blacks were very fond of the white woman and a little boy she had, and therefore would not give them up.'

By January 1847, therefore, all three parties—Native Police, Border Police and De Villiers's force—had failed even to sight Bungeleena and his woman. All they had done was to make the blacks suspicious of further parleys.

The Melbourne committee, having spent the £170 it had raised, appealed to the government for further aid to De Villiers. Surely, they wrote, the government was not prepared 'to adopt the distressing alternative of leaving the wretched woman to her fate'? Acting Superintendent William Lonsdale agreed to supply further food and clothing, provided the committee felt that 'positive good will result from another immediate attempt.' To the Governor, Lonsdale wrote that De Villiers's attitude of 'prudence and energy' seemed preferable to the alleged damaging efforts of the Native Police.

De Villiers and his party set out again in mid-January 1847, accompanied by Sergeant Windridge, but no other black or white police. Guided by friendly blacks from Lake Victoria, they spent a further eighteen days searching the mountains. Bungeleena again sent messages which 'positively refused to give up the white woman'. When De Villiers persevered, the tribes 'appeared determined to oppose themselves as a barrier between the party and Bungeleena.' Under these circumstances, Commissioner Tyers feared her rescue was 'far from probable'.

Both De Villiers and Windridge suggested to Tyers that they should capture some of the tribe's leaders and hold them as hostages. Tyers warned that such proceedings 'would most likely be attended with great loss of life', and possibly death of the woman herself.

With provisions again exhausted, De Villiers and party returned to Melbourne.

Several men of the Border Police and Native Police remained in the Lakes district. On 18 February a group of about 100 blacks of Bungeleena's tribe approached their quarters. One grey-haired old man, about six feet tall, claimed he was Bungeleena. He offered the troops a lubra, calling her by the white woman's tribal name of Loondigon, in return for gifts.

The boy Jackawadden was brought forward to identify Bungeleena. He trembled violently and refused to talk until the blacks had gone away empty-handed. Then he confirmed that the blacks were trying to 'gammon' the whites by offering a black instead of a white woman.

Tyers recommended abandonment of the whole search. However, feeling in Melbourne was still high. La Trobe promised a deputation of citizens on 26 February that the search would vigorously resumed, 'without regard to expense'.

To Tyers, La Trobe wrote that no further assistance should be given to private expeditions over which the government had no control. Nor should the Native Police be used again. Tyers himself should employ any other possible method to get the woman back, using 'great discretion, and prudence, and patience'.

Since white settlers in Gippsland were no longer willing to spend time in lengthy searches, La Trobe sent Sergeant

Windridge back to the lakes with a newly recruited force of five experienced white bushmen of good character, to be paid £30 each per year plus rations.*

While Windridge's party was on the way, Tyers heard from blacks named Toby, One-eye, George and Jack that the white woman was being held by Bungeleena's brother, Koogaljine, in the mountains. Bungeleena himself was said to be on an island in the lakes.

On 6 April Tyers despatched Windridge's party in two whale boats to the outlet of the lakes, following himself in another boat three days later. Arriving on the evening of the 9th, Tyers found that Bungeleena had been persuaded to camp with the whites. The native confirmed to Tyers that the white woman had been taken from a party of survivors of a ship wrecked on the Ninety Mile Beach, and was now held in the mountains.

Tyers offered him 'articles of greater value' than before. Bungeleena agreed to give her up, and sent messengers to his tribe. When nothing happened by 24 April, Tyers accused Bungeleena of bad faith, and took him and his black family into 'compulsory detention'.

After weeks of negotiation, the two men made a formal agreement which the native signed with a cross:

> I, Bungeleena, promise to deliver to Charles J. Tyers, the white female residing with the Gippsland blacks, provided a party of whites and Western Port blacks proceed with me to the mountains at as early a day as may be convenient for the purpose of obtaining her from my brothers.

Bungeleena also agreed 'to leave my two wives and two children with the 'said Charles J. Tyers, as hostages . . .' In turn, Tyers agreed to give Bungeleena a boat with oars, a tent, four blankets, a guernsey frock, some fish hooks and lines, and

---

* La Trobe named these men as Thomas Hill, McLeod, Peters, Dingle and Hartnett.

a tomahawk; with other gifts for any tribesman who helped to find the woman.

A party headed by Sergeant Windridge, and including Bungeleena and the boy Jackawadden, left Tyers's camp at Eagle Point on 19 May. After a fatiguing journey between Mount Wellington and Mount Buller, along the headwaters of the Macalister River, on 29 June they found a grass rope which one of Bungeleena's sons said had been used to tie the white woman by the legs to a log.

Next day the boy told Windridge that Bungeleena was deceiving them: that he had arranged for his brothers to take the woman in the opposite direction, towards today's Buchan. On hearing this, and being out of provisions, the party returned empty-handed on 4 June.

With winter closing in, further expeditions were impossible. Tyers disbanded the party, and asked Henry Dana to take charge of the hostages at Narre Warren Native Police camp.

La Trobe realised that Bungeleena and family 'cannot be detained by legal forms', but told Dana to feed and guard them for the time being.

Four months went by. In October Tyers interviewed a wild black named Pateo, a son of Bungeleena. Pateo claimed that the white woman had been *his* wife, and had borne him a half-caste child. But, he said, the woman had been drowned in Lake King about the previous June or July, 'by the upsetting of a canoe, during a gale of wind, while crossing from Tambo Bluff to the opposite shore.' Pateo said he recovered her body and placed it in a tree, in the traditional manner.

Tyers sailed off with several volunteers but could not find the spot. He sent four native troopers, who returned with bones they said were a white woman's, being different in shape from a black woman's, especially the skull. 'The deceased appears to have been about 5 feet 4 inches in height, of middle age, with black and grey hair', Tyers concluded.

La Trobe felt the case for the white woman's existence and fate was fairly well established. He suggested to Tyers that more conclusive proof would be to find her half-caste son, but nothing further was recorded on this line of investigation.

As far as the official records show, all other accounts of the woman's end are imaginary. Yet one is left with the feeling that Tyers was rather too anxious to close the file.

The tale was not quite finished. Even after the assumed death of the white woman, Bungeleena and his family were kept at Narre Warren, amid scenes of idle drunkenness. Protector William Thomas visited them on 21 March 1848, and found them 'woefully destitute' of covering. 'I cannot see the justice or utility of detaining this unfortunate man', he wrote.

Five months later, one of Bungeleena's native wives died at Narre Warren. Bungeleena himself died soon afterwards, on 21 November. Henry Dana wrote that 'The poor old man was one of the least troublesome, and showed more intelligence, than any of the old natives who have ever been on this station.'

One of Bungeleena's sons, Thomas, was taken to be educated at Merri Creek, but died from alcoholism in 1865. The old man's remaining wife and three sons were raised with the Native Police at Narre Warren: their fate seems to be unknown.

The boy Jackawadden, who had done so much to establish the white woman's existence, was taken to live with Europeans in Melbourne. He attended school there until late in 1850, when he was reported as having absconded and 'again taken to the wandering habits of his race'. Commissioner Tyers thought this 'a bad augury of our success to civilize even the children of the Aborigines of Gippsland.'

During the late 1840s the 'warrigals' continued to spear stock in Gippsland. Responding to settlers' appeals, La Trobe agreed in April 1848 to return sixteen Native Police to Port Albert.

This force remained in Gippsland from May to November, being split into small parties to guard stations on the lakes and in the mountains. Immediately they went back to Narre Warren for inspection and re-equipment, attacks began again, especially on the flocks of Loughnan, Taylor and McLeod, notorious for ill-treatment of the blacks.

A few Native Police returned briefly to Gippsland in February 1849 to escort Dr Charles Perry, Bishop of Melbourne, on his tour of the district. William Dana was sent with a further detachment in April to assist the Crown Commissioner and local magistrates in maintenance of public order.

Some Gippsland natives visited Brighton in 1849, became intoxicated, and staged a battle in which two warriors died. The following year they visited the Melbourne tribe, had to fight to protect their women, and killed several Melbourne blacks before police could intervene.

A small detachment of eight native troopers and one officer, William Dana, returned to Gippsland in 1850 to occupy their old station at Green Hills. By that time the vitality of Gippsland tribes had been practically exhausted in their long struggle for survival. The native troopers were soon disbanded, and a few white constables were able to police the district to the satisfaction of the now firmly entrenched squatters.

19

THE LAST STAND: BATTLES ALONG THE MURRAY

With closer settlement of older established areas, the final phase of Aboriginal resistance to white incursions shifted to remote regions of Port Phillip.

The last stand of the black warriors was made through the central and lower Murray River districts, especially in the area where the Loddon River joins the Murray near today's Swan Hill. By a curious twist of history, it is also here (mainly in the Lake Boga region) that conservationists of the 1990s conduct their yearly confrontations with white shooters at the beginning of each duck-hunting season.

The state of Murray tribes in the mid-1840s was summed up by Crown Commissioner H. W. H. Smythe in one annual report. Although 'generally intelligent', and in a few instances becoming 'useful members'of white society, they were said to be 'universally indolent', and hence 'becoming more dependent on the Europeans for food and clothing every day'.

During summer they were able to catch abundant fish, but when the river rose during the rainy season the fish disappeared. The Aboriginals' hunger during these winter months caused repeated raids on the settlers' stock.

Smythe estimated native numbers in the area at about 1000 men, women and children. However, they were fast disappearing, due mainly to 'their murderous custom of supposing that they are appeasing the names of the dead by sacrificing the first innocent and unguarded victim of a neighbouring tribe they can meet with—and also to the circumstance of there being few or no births among them.'

The Commissioner felt there was only one method of preserving a remnant of the tribes: 'The children should be removed to where they can learn habits of industry, and forget, or rather be prevented thereby, from ever acquiring the habits of the present adults.'

Smythe's observations were supplemented by a petition from the Huon family and other humane squatters along the Murray, asking for 'a little medical attendance' for the tribes. The blacks were, said these settlers, in a 'fearful state of disease ... suffering under the various stages of Venereal ... and propagating the disease amongst the labouring men of the district to a very great extent.' So it was the fault of infected black women, not of the white working men who cohabited with them!

Here was a fertile field for the ministrations of Protectors, especially those knowing how to prescribe mercury pills and ointments. G. A. Robinson in fact suggested formation of a Protectorate in this troubled area of the Murray. The new Governor, Sir Charles FitzRoy, was pleased to approve the idea. Obviously primed by his advisers, he authorised Robinson to go ahead, 'if that gentleman will undertake the duty of residing there.' Robinson did not take up the vice-regal suggestion.

Instead, the old dreadful saga of inter-racial aggression and revenge unfolded along the Murray.

In 1845 James Cowper, a squatter at 'Boramboot' station near the Campaspe River, formed a distant station near the junction of the Loddon and Murray Rivers. However, reported Crown Commissioner Powlett, Cowper failed to appoint an experienced overseer. The result was that his shepherds used their rations to entice Aboriginals near the hut, 'for the purpose of obtaining their women'. Once that was achieved, the whites stopped supplying food to the black men, who 'then began to help themselves to the sheep.' When the blacks crept near the folds at night, shots were fired and spears thrown. The shepherds began to carry arms at all times, waiting for an excuse to rid themselves of the constant fear of being speared.

One day in May a number of Cowper's shepherds concealed their guns and called out in friendly fashion to a group of blacks on the far side of Murrabit Creek to come across for food. While the blacks were crossing in a canoe, the shepherds uncovered their guns and let fly. At least one black named Bimbite was known to have been killed.

Five months later, in October, William Britton, one of Cowper's shepherds, came into conflict with a native who had broken a sheep's back. The native ran away but his dog stopped behind: Britton promptly shot it. Another native stepped from behind a bush and aimed a blow at Britton with a nulla-nulla. Britton's dog caught the attacker by the leg, while Britton smashed his gun butt over the man's head.

A few days after that, on 8 October, Britton and another shepherd, Thomas Henning, failed to return with their flocks in the evening. Next day Britton's body was found: 'naked with spear wounds, opened, and his entrails taken out, and beaten about his face and head apparently with a tomahawk, and his ears cut off.' Henning's remains were found in a similar state two weeks later.

William Dana and a detachment of fourteen Native Police were sent to 'pacify' the area. On the afternoon of 1 February 1846 they were riding through a swampy bed of reeds between Cowper's and Campbell's stations when they encountered a group of perhaps 200 warriors.

Dana said he tried to avoid them, but was pursued on to

dry ground. Two of his horses and one man were speared. Dana ordered his men to wheel around and charge. During the mêlée the troopers fired 'one hundred rounds of ball cartridge' before the attackers retreated. 'I saw several dead bodies; there must have been a great many wounded', Dana reported.

La Trobe ordered Henry Dana to take reinforcements up to his brother. He also ordered Chief Protector Robinson to investigate. Robinson took Protector Parker with him from Loddon River Aboriginal Station. At Lake Bael Bael they met up with the younger Dana, who refused to give them any information. Parker left Robinson at Lake Boga and proceeded to visit every station up the Murray, but could learn nothing from either whites or blacks.

Superintendent La Trobe confessed himself 'quite unable to reconcile this' with William Dana's reports. To one squatter who complained about Aboriginal raids on his stock, La Trobe replied curtly that stations should not have been established in the area in the first place.

A breakthrough in Cowper's case came in August, when Sergeant William Johnson took a party of Border Police to the district. He had a good description of a black leader named Warrigal Jimmy, who was alleged to have been involved in murderous attempts on shepherds' lives. Johnson located his quarry at George C. Curlewis's head station, 'Bael Bael', also known as 'Reedy Lake'. Warrigal Jimmy tried to stab the sergeant with a pair of sheep shears but was subdued after a struggle. A carbine and pistols were found in the native's net bag.

Warrigal Jimmy was committed for attempted murder of John Forrester, another of Cowper's shepherds. On 17 October he was found guilty in the Supreme Court, and sentenced to transportation to Van Diemen's Land for life.

Robinson and Parker wrote to Judge à Beckett praying for mitigation of sentence. The judge replied that the sentence was 'indeed intended to be exemplary'. Aboriginal attacks, he wrote, had placed settlers 'in a constant state of insecurity'. It was therefore a matter no less of policy than of justice, that when the Law has been so far successfully appealed to, as to lead to the trial and conviction of an Aboriginal Black, that it should be followed, if the offence be a serious one, by punishment of the most exemplary kind.

Thus spoke the Supreme Court.

After a group of Gippsland blacks were brought to Melbourne in February 1847 in connection with the case of the 'missing white woman' (chapter 18), Protector Thomas took them to visit Melbourne Gaol, 'to give them an idea of the effect of our laws on transgressors.'

When they saw Warrigal Jimmy languishing in irons, 'the youngest Gippsland black seemed much affected and agitated.' The others looked around with 'composed coolness', noting 'black and white identical in crime mingled together.' Prayed Thomas: 'May it have some effect upon them.'

Edward Mitchell, pioneer of 'Therguina' station (near today's Albury), employed a black girl, Jesse, in the kitchen and an Indian coolie, Neddy, to assist her.

On 6 March 1846 Mitchell heard Jesse screaming, and ran to see what had happened. She told him that 'the black-fellows were after her coolie Neddy.' Saddling his horse, Mitchell galloped to the river, but could find nothing except abandoned native weapons. Next morning the squatter found Neddy's body some distance down the river, opposite Ebden's station, with two severe wounds in the head.

John Pierce, stockman on Mitchell's station, deposed that two Murray blacks, named Darby Murray and Sodyer, had asked him early on 6 March where they could find Neddy. But he had not seen the actual murder: nothing further seems to have been done in the case.

Henry Dana and his Native Police toured much of the Murray area in April and May 1846. He reported that the region was now 'perfectly quiet'. Reports of depredations on stock were,

he claimed, 'much exaggerated, and in many instances un-
founded'.

Alas for such comforting words. Every white person in
Port Phillip was horrified by the next murderous event on the
northern frontier.

Andrew Beveridge senior had arrived from Dunfermline,
Scotland, in 1839 with his wife and five children. At first he
leased land on the Sydney Road near Wallan, then opened an
inn at Mercer's Vale (today named Beveridge). In April 1845
Crown Commissioner St John discovered that Beveridge was
grazing his sheep on part of 'Glenvale' run, leased by J. B. Kirk
and John Harlin. He ordered Beveridge to remove his flocks
immediately.

Beveridge conferred with other neighbours, the Kirbys,
who had arrived from Northamptonshire in 1840. The two
families then joined forces, bought bullock drays and herds of
cattle, and all (except Andrew Beveridge senior and his wife,
who stayed behind at Mercer's Vale to run the inn) set off for
the Murray River. Andrew Beveridge junior notified Commissioner Smythe in February 1846 that he wished to occupy
vacant land on the south bank of the Murray River between
Redfern's and Boyd's out-stations, between today's Echuca and
Swan Hill. The request was refused, partly because police
protection could not be provided.

The Beveridge and Kirby families trekked their cattle
further downstream until they were about twenty miles past
today's Swan Hill. Here Beveridge squatted on a tract of
30 000 acres, part of which was later called 'Tyntynder'
station. According to one story he cohabited with an Aboriginal girl, but refused to return her to her tribe after an agreed
period.

Protector Parker visited the area in April 1846. In an
excess of zeal, he paid for a bullock and asked young James
Kirby to shoot it dead with one shot—partly to show the
Aboriginals the power of white men's guns, partly to provide
them with food.

It was a terrible mistake. 'Up to this time we were getting

on very nicely indeed', Kirby wrote many years later. After Parker's visit he refused to give the blacks any more beef, and a few days later for the first time found one of his beasts speared and butchered. 'They used to kill cattle sometimes in sight of our own hut', said Kirby. Some of Beveridge's sheep were also taken.

Through a 'tame' Aboriginal, Black Beveridge, young Andrew Beveridge warned the tribes that 'if they took the sheep again he would shoot them dead.' They replied that they would kill him on the following Sunday morning—and they did.

On Sunday, 23 August, Beveridge was asleep in his men's camp at the furthest out-station (today the town of Piangil). Soon after dawn a coo-ee was heard. Beveridge went out to investigate, and was immediately struck with several spears, one penetrating his stomach, and another his back. Black Beveridge carried his master back to the camp, but he died almost immediately. He was twenty-four years old— just the heroic type of young settler idolised in towns and seaports.

The shepherds fled to 'Tyntynder' homestead. Peter Beveridge rescued his brother's body, and abandoned Piangil to the blacks.

Commissioner Powlett recommended to Superintendent La Trobe that since the murderers were known, a strong force of police should be sent to the area 'as soon as the floods have subsided'. La Trobe replied: 'Let every exertion be made.' On 16 September Powlett despatched his only available men: two Border Police troopers, Patrick Farrell and Thomas Dollard, under a sergeant named William Johnson.

Before the police could arrive, however, an overseer named F. J. Byerley, acting on behalf of the Coghill brothers of Monaro, drove stock to the Piangil area. Finding that the Beveridges had abandoned the run, Byerley took possession. A few miles further downstream, past Piangil, Byerley's men built a strong slab hut which became the nucleus of 'Burra Burra' run. Around the hut they erected a substantial palisade of saplings, with only one entrance.

The Border Police arrived at 'Burra Burra' on 30 October. Sergeant Johnson, a life convict, was a man of great resource and cunning. He instructed his men to change into stockmen's clothes, and roll their uniforms and carbines into swags. They pretended to be new settlers, offering food to any Aboriginal who would strip bark for the building of huts.

On 2 November the cook began to prepare a great feast of 'bubble-bubble'—a mixture of flour, sugar and water—within Byerley's palisade. Each white man had a rope noose concealed in his clothing, while two shepherds armed with the troopers' swords hid in the bedroom.

When about twenty-five blacks had been enticed by the smell of cooking into the enclosure, Byerley quietly pointed out three men, Bobby, Ptolemy, and Bullet-eye, who had thrown spears at Beveridge. The whites circulated behind them, and at a command dropped the nooses over their heads, pulling them tight. Simultaneously the shepherds burst out of the hut swinging their swords. After a desperate struggle the remaining blacks fled, leaving their three fellows half-strangled on the ground. They were then chained to posts within the hut.

Native smoke signals rose through the bush to summon the tribes. Edmund Kirby jumped on his horse and galloped to 'Tyntynder', thence to Lake Boga, to get reinforcements. Veterinary surgeon George James French, George Beveridge and young James Kirby picked up their guns and rode through the night to get back to 'Burra Burra' in time.

At dawn on 3 November hundreds of wild blacks surrounded the hut. With loud yells they launched a volley of spears. Sergeant Johnson fired through an opening in the slabs and wounded one native. Another who was levelling a spear was shot dead by Edmund Kirby. A third native tearing away bark from the chimney was shot in the side by George Beveridge.

'At the fall of the man from the chimney,' deposed Sergeant Johnson, 'the natives gave a tremendous yell and dispersed.' The only white man injured was George French, who accidentally shot himself in the hand while reloading a gun.

Further reinforcements of nine mounted men arrived from George Curlewis's station next day. On 5 November Sergeant Johnson was able to remove his prisoners under strong guard to Melbourne. When Ptolemy pretended to be ill and tried to kill Trooper Farrell, the blacks were tied tightly to the horses' backs for the remainder of the journey.

The three captives were tried before Judge à Beckett on 25 February 1847, with Protector Parker acting as interpreter. Native boys from Merri Creek school attended the trial, their teacher explaining to them as it proceeded 'how it might tend to their benefit in the sequel of their life.'

Unanimous evidence from white men identified Bobby and Ptolemy as among those who had murdered Andrew Beveridge. After only three minutes' deliberation, the jury pronounced them guilty. No such eyewitness evidence existed against Bullet-eye, who was acquitted.

Judge à Beckett condemned the two guilty blacks to death. William Thomas had the task of telling them they would be hanged: 'They wept bitterly on my communicating the sad tidings to them', he wrote. Thomas visited them regularly in gaol, mainly to assure them that they would be despatched to a better world. Bobby was deeply affected, wrote Thomas: 'The colour of his skin the last fortnight got fairer and fairer and his countenance settled down to what artists would call perfect resignation.'

Executions in Melbourne no longer took place quite in public, but behind the new gaol wall in Russell Street. The fall had been made deeper, so that when bodies dropped they disappeared completely from view.

At 8 a.m. on 30 April the two blacks were led out. At the foot of the scaffold they looked upwards and began to weep. Ptolemy mounted the ladder without help, and was quickly hanged without a murmur. Bobby had to be helped to the platform. As he fell he tried to wrench free, and was strangled in 'lengthened and violent convulsions'. William Thomas remarked that in his coffin Bobby was 'as fair nearly as a white.' Was he perhaps a half-caste?

Sergeant Johnson, meanwhile, had become a public hero. He was granted a free pardon from his sentence as a transported convict, tried inn-keeping in the bush, and later was employed by the Crown Law Department. G. J. French was awarded £50 for the wounded hand suffered in the affray on the Murray.

At least one further gruesome result followed the executions. Bullet-eye had been freed, but forced to watch the hangings as a lesson before returning home to the Murray. A little later, a Mr McTier and his two sons, neighbours at Piangil, were captured by the tribe. Nooses were placed around their necks, and they were hanged from adjoining trees. No black was ever taken for these three murders.

The remaining Beveridge brothers retained 'Tyntynder' in their father's name until 1866, when it was subdivided. Mrs Andrew Beveridge senior visited them, and was said to be the first white woman who dared to venture into the Swan Hill district.

A month after Andrew Beveridge's murder, in September 1846, two shepherds on James Malcolm's 'Murray Downs' station near Lake Bingham decided they would enjoy taking a lubra prisoner for the night. Their excuse, a rather feeble one, was that the blacks had been stealing sheep.

The shepherds, John Keefe and Richard Pickett, achieved their object. Next morning the woman's husband, a native named Toby, came to the hut to try and find her. Pickett fired a shot at him but missed. Keefe then fired his gun, wounding him mortally. The whites left the lubra trying to staunch Toby's wounds, and fled to the head station with a nonsensical tale of how they had detained the woman in order to entice the sheep thieves to the hut. Even the superintendent, Andrew Crockett, found the story hard to believe. Warrants were issued for the men's arrest, but by then no trace of them could be found.

Summing up the condition of Aboriginals at the end of 1846, Commissioner Smythe described them as 'gradually becoming more quiet and inoffensive'. He believed that in the whole extent of the Murray district, there was 'less danger to be apprehended from an Aborigine than a white man.'

Smythe's sentiments were echoed by Edward Grimes, Commissioner for the Western Port district, whose area included part of the Murray River. Grimes recommended a semi-permanent police force to patrol the Murray.

The best that La Trobe could do at this stage was to send a detachment of eight native troopers to the Upper Murray. He warned strongly that they were to avoid collisions with the local natives, 'unless under circumstances fully and legally to justify such collision.'

The troopers' constant patrolling kept things fairly quiet until mid-1847. On 7 June overseer Jeremiah Bowes was riding through 'Yarroweya', the Yarrawonga property of Mrs Elizabeth Hume, widow of John Kennedy Hume, who had been killed by Aboriginals seven years earlier. Bowes heard dogs barking, and saw a black named Gentleman Jimmy striking a heifer on the head with a tomahawk. As Bowes approached, the black shipped his spear in preparation for battle.

Bowes retreated to get assistance. With stockman James Short, he took up pursuit, and found another black named Blucher 'in the act of opening a beast with his tomahawk.' The two whites managed to pinion Blucher, and take him to Broken River police station. Blucher's defence was simple: he was station cook to Octavius Phillpotts, lessee of the huge 'Cobram' run, and was taking meat from one of his master's beasts for use on the station. Commissioner Smythe was forced to release him.

Gentleman Jimmy, meanwhile, had been taken by police. He too had a novel defence: 'I was in the act of striking the dogs belonging to the blacks, which were attacking the beast.' This ingenious plea did not succeed. Gentleman Jimmy was committed to stand trial in Melbourne for felony; William

Thomas acted as interpreter. On 28 July 1847 Judge à Beckett sentenced the native to one month's gaol.

James Maxwell Clow, son of the Reverend James Clow, took up a large run known as 'Pine Plains' (north of today's Jeparit), on the edge of the Big Desert and Mallee regions.

In August 1848 one of Clow's employees, John Jenkins, was alleged to have shot an Aboriginal on the station. No police investigation seems to have been made: the Horsham bench simply committed Jenkins on the basis of hearsay evidence.

When the case came before the Supreme Court on 17 February 1849, there was still no legal evidence: 'the jury immediately returned a verdict of not guilty.'

Nearly two years after Andrew Beveridge's murder, ugly rumours began to spread that up to twenty natives had been poisoned on the Beveridge family's run between today's Swan Hill and Piangil. The original information came from a shearer on the Murray, who, according to Protector Parker, 'stated in a neighbouring wool shed that a Mr Beveridge had "settled" the blacks by leaving a quantity of poisoned flour in their way, and that numbers had been killed by it.'

Parker despatched some of his Station blacks to the junction of the Loddon and Murray Rivers 'to make enquiries'. They returned with almost identical information from blacks on Edward Curr's and Archibald Campbell's runs: 'they were informed that seven or eight natives had been destroyed.'

The story fitted fairly precisely with rumours heard by Dr James Horsburgh at Goulburn River Aboriginal Station. Horsburgh's opinion was that the natives had either died of an influenza epidemic sweeping the Murray Valley, or that the story was 'an imagination of the brain of our *worthy* Seymour correspondent of the *Argus.*'

Protector Parker was commissioned to obtain further evidence if he could. In February 1849 he was told by natives from Lake Bael Bael that 'a number of the blacks of

Tarrkgoondeet tribe [the 'reed-spear tribe' of the lower Murray] have been poisoned some months since by white men at a place called Bapparrinok'. Similar stories came from other sources which Parker did not disclose.

When La Trobe pressed the Chief Protector for action, Robinson replied that the rumours seemed 'too vague to enable the Government to take any proceedings in the case.' Robinson felt that Parker should have investigated long ago. Now he was more anxious that the Assistant Protector 'should proceed to the Goulburn Aboriginal Station to balance his accounts.' There spoke the ideal bureaucrat.

Superintendent La Trobe, through the Colonial Secretary, next applied for information to the Bench of Magistrates at Moulamein, north-east of Swan Hill, on the Sydney side of the river. Patrick Brougham, JP, replied on behalf of the Moulamein Bench that he 'certainly some months ago heard a report of the same [alleged poisoning], but took no notice of it, as groundless rumours have frequently been spread of natives having been killed.'

In this unsatisfactory manner, and with further excuses from Robinson for his department's inaction, the whole affair petered out.

Probably more natives died in tribal battles along the Murray in the 1840s than were killed by white men.

Archibald Macarthur Campbell, a raw-boned kindly Scot who arrived in Port Phillip from the Isle of Mull in 1841, moved his stock from the Pyrenees to 'Gannawarra' Station, south-east of Swan Hill, in 1845.

Helping him was Jack, a 20-year-old native of Twofold Bay: 'a merry, agreeable fellow, a first-rate bullock-driver, and an expert horseman'. But when Campbell left Jack alone for a few weeks, he was 'enticed away by other Aborigines, who murdered him the day after.'

Settling in near today's town of Koondrook, Campbell wrote that he continued to cultivate 'a friendly feeling with the natives,' finding them generally 'inoffensive and obedient'.

Campbell showed other settlers just how useful the Aboriginals could be. He quickly trained them to prepare his 8000 sheep for shearing. The flocks were 'put through the water twice, yarded and done clean without the assistance of a single white man', Chief Protector Robinson reported proudly. One of Campbell's station blacks who was trained by him as a stockman was even entrusted in 1849 with the task of driving a mob of cattle 180 miles to the saleyards in Melbourne.

One day, however, seven strange blacks came to the station. One followed Campbell to the river: as the squatter bent down to draw water, he glanced behind to see the native with 'axe uplifted and clasped in both hands.' Campbell fixed his eye upon the black man, 'walked deliberately up to him, and gently took hold of the axe, which he quietly relinquished.' The native was the notorious Warrigal Jimmy, later transported for life.

On another occasion Campbell was surrounded in a reedy swamp by thirty natives brandishing spears. His station blacks persuaded them that Campbell was friendly towards the tribes.

Rumours spread in February 1849 that Campbell had been accidentally speared when, at great personal risk, he broke up a battle between opposing tribes. The wound must have been minor, for Campbell himself did not mention it.

A few months later, more serious affrays took place when Gunbower blacks went to Bell and Wilson's station across the river from today's Swan Hill, murdered 'an old man and two lubras', and carried off strips of their flesh. About the same time, natives of the lower Loddon River shot an unknown number of the Lake Boga and Moorabut tribes.

Campbell reported that his station blacks were 'so much in dread' of going out with the flocks that they were now of no use to him.

Native Police under W. H. Walsh rode to the area, and in May a pitched battle occurred on James Crawford's 'Gayfield' run on the Murray, where a large number of sheep had disappeared. According to Walsh's report, two of his men suffered slight spear wounds but no lives were lost. The troopers succeeded in disarming all natives on Crawford's run.

Protector Parker also visited the area in October after flood waters had subsided. He was able to confirm most of Campbell's allegations, but only through native sources. An Aboriginal Native Evidence Bill had recently been rejected by the NSW Legislative Council, so their word was still as useless in the courts as it always had been.

All that Parker could do was to 'dissuade and interdict the natives' from making revenge raids on other tribes. This they promised to do.

Commissioner Powlett thought it was time that a permanent Police Magistrate's court with a gaol, and six or eight mounted constables on constant patrol, was established on the lower Murray. For the time being, however, La Trobe was forced to rely on sporadic visits to each locality by his existing over-stretched police forces.

In January 1850 settlers on the lower Murray petitioned for return of the Native Police. Henry Dana said his troopers could be ready to move at short notice, and the Jamieson brothers near the confluence of the Murray and Darling Rivers agreed to provision them for 1s. 6d. each per day. Even at the height of summer, Dana was glad to be able to get his men away from Narre Warren, with its constant temptation of intoxication and consequent punishment of imprisonment on bread and water.

By late February fourteen black troopers, under W. H. Walsh and Corporal Owen Cowen, were back at the Jamiesons' station, with orders to patrol constantly along the Murray. Within a few days, a detachment led by Corporal Cowen was in action. Riding through D. J. McLeod's 'Narrung' station near the junction of the Murrumbidgee, they 'saw the blacks busy at work killing a bullock.' The troopers rode down on the men, chasing them into the river and firing carbines as they threw spears. 'We could make no prisoners', reported Cowen.

A native named Bonaparte led an attack on John R. Rae's

flocks near the junction of the Murray and Murrumbidgee on 4 May. Attempting to protect his sheep, Rae was speared in the right breast. He was forced to go to Melbourne for medical treatment, leaving his wife and family unprotected on the station. La Trobe agreed to send in the Native Police, but they were unable to locate the raiders.

Three black troopers continued upstream to meet their commandant Henry Dana at Swan Hill. One of them drowned in the river en route, but his name was not included in Dana's report.

The other two troopers arrived at Swan Hill on 12 May. Trooper Edward went down to the river to fish, about 150 yards from the inn. Some time later a carpenter came running to innkeeper Gideon Rutherford, shouting that Edward had been attacked by blacks.

'He appeared in great pain and seemed quite delirious', said Rutherford. He examined the man's wounds: 'The principal one was in the groin. It appeared to me that his kidney fat had been taken out.'

Trooper Edward regained consciousness, lingering for two days. He described how two blacks, named Captain Denham and Peter, had waddied him, then cut him open to extract the fat.

A search for the two murderers was mounted when Henry Dana arrived with reinforcements on 26 May. If an official report was ever made, it does not seem to have survived. All that is known comes from Peter Beveridge's memoirs, published many years later. The black troopers crossed the Murray, and spotted one of the alleged killers some distance away. Then, wrote Beveridge,

This man saw them coming, tried to creep away, and was pursued ... The foremost trooper at full gallop put a bullet through his head ... The rest rode up, dismounted as one, and smote the carcass with sabres till it was reduced to pieces not larger than a hand's breadth.'

On their way up-river in June the Native Police were summoned to W. H. Mitchell's 'Terrick Terrick' run (southeast of today's Kerang), where bushrangers had driven off several horses.

A party of eight troopers under W. H. Walsh searched for the thieves, when 'suddenly several blacks rushed out of the mallee, seized his horse, pulled him from it, tore his clothes off him, threw him on the ground, and injured him in such a manner that he was insensible.' The black troopers came back to look for Walsh, and 'just arrived in time to save him.'

Henry Dana recommended that 'the natives on that part of the country most certainly require putting down.' If they would attack an armed police officer, 'they would not think much of murdering unarmed shepherds, hutkeepers and travellers.'

One of the most troublesome tribal leaders on the river was given the satirical soubriquet of 'Sir Robert Peel', after the British Home Secretary who had organised the London police so that they became known as 'Bobbies' and 'Peelers'.

Our black Robert Peel went to William Splatt's run, 'Bael Bael', near Swan Hill on 9 May 1850, demanded food, and threatened to spear hutkeeper Joseph Chambers when refused.

Henry Dana issued a warrant for Robert Peel's arrest, and Corporal Cowen went out with five troopers to execute the warrant. They crossed the Murray River, rode to Bell and Wilson's station, and were told that the black was camped further upstream with 120 warriors. He was 'threatening vengeance on all the unprotected whites in the country', Cowen reported.

The troopers rode all night, then smelled smoke from camp fires. They hid behind a thick area of scrub until dawn. Cowen concluded that the only way to capture Robert Peel was by surprise. At first light on 26 June he ordered his five men to charge the encampment, 'which they effected in gallant style, and succeeded in making prisoners of about seventy men without firing.'

But Robert Peel had left the previous day with about forty warriors. Cowen left two sentries over the prisoners, and 'scoured the country round' with his other men, to no avail. On his return to the camp, said Cowen, 'I took a black and made him fast to my saddle, as a guide.' Ten miles away they found Robert Peel's camp. Cowen immediately gave the order to charge. This time the blacks were ready, and met them with a volley of spears.

As Cowen himself approached Peel, the black leader swung his nulla-nulla, but missed. Cowen drew his sword and parried, but Peel dodged and swung at another trooper. This man levelled his carbine and shot Peel through the head.

On seeing their leader fall, the other blacks immediately laid down their spears. Some later told Cowen they were pleased, as Peel 'was in the habit of treating them in the most tyrannical manner.' Before leaving, Cowen warned the survivors that 'punishment would ensue, if they continued in their evil course.'

One week after Robert Peel's death in the Australian bush, the more famous Sir Robert Peel died in London after being thrown from a horse.

Rumours were current along the Murray that the black Robert Peel had murdered several white men before his own death. Corporal Cowen set out to search for any remains. Early in July 1850, near Wilson's station, he 'found one body that had been buried with his clothes—his skull was broken.'

Next day, accompanied by Gideon Rutherford and a native of Peel's tribe, Cowen went to an island near Swan Hill. There they found 'the remains of two men that had been buried; their bodies was in a state of decomposition.'

The unnamed member of Peel's tribe told Cowen that Robert Peel had killed the men, 'and that he himself assisted to bury them.' Cowen added that the native also showed him 'where three other men had been murdered and thrown into the river; their bodies I could not discover.'

Formal depositions were sent to Crown Prosecutor

Croke, who in turn sent them to the Attorney-General in Sydney for advice. The Attorney-General advised Governor FitzRoy that the killing of Robert Peel was 'perfectly justifiable', and that 'there is no occasion to call for any investigation of the case.'

By the end of the 1840s the Native Police corps was in a state of decline. Many of the original recruits had died of drunkenness and disease while still in their twenties. Moonee Moonee, described by Protector Thomas as 'a fine young man', died in the Wimmera in August 1845, aged twenty-one. Billibellary, chief of the Yarra tribe, and generally a good friend to the whites, died a year later. Bungellun died in September 1848, as did Corporal Buckup after amputation of his leg. Many other deaths were recorded in Thomas's regular reports.

Henry Dana continually tried to raise recruits to the level of a highly disciplined European-style force. In 1847 he promulgated a list of Rules and Regulations. NCOs were enjoined to enforce obedience, but with 'forbearance and humanity'. Troopers who complained of ill-treatment were given immediate access to a commissioned officer.

On patrol the men were to 'behave with respect to all settlers and their servants'. They must not discharge firearms without distinct orders, and must take more than ordinary care in patrolling districts 'infested by robbers, blacks and bushrangers'. In the streets of Melbourne, troopers were to be sober, clean, and properly dressed at all times.

La Trobe tried to assist such improvements by calling on Sydney to regularise the corps and permit cash payments to troopers. The NSW Legislative Council agreed in December 1847 that the corps had proved useful against aggressive blacks, but was doubtful of the desirability of employing it against the white population. The question, they thought, was better left until Separation.

A year later, La Trobe seemed less convinced of the value of Dana's black police. Although they had proved of 'greater practical utility than all the other schemes together', yet 'many allowances have had to be made, and many irregularities to be winked at.'

Early in 1849 simmering disputes between William Dana and his elder brother Henry boiled over. William accused the commandant of 'frequent and marked discourtesy' in not answering his reports and applications. Henry replied that his brother was being 'impertinent', and should wait his turn on official matters.

The same month, William Dana took it on himself, during the commandant's absence, to dismiss Corporal Malone for disrespect, insubordination, and keeping a troop horse all night in Melbourne without permission.

The black police attracted great interest at the Separation celebrations of November 1850. All that year, Henry Dana continued his efforts to expand the corps, asking Superintendent La Trobe for six more white troopers to be trained as corporals, in charge of a chain of out-stations stretching from the Broken River to the Glenelg. La Trobe would approve only three corporals at £25 a year, plus uniforms and rations.

In the second half of 1850, reported Dana, 'three of the best troopers' died from disease, and another four men deserted to return to their tribes.

The public was not impressed by a confrontation which occurred in January 1851, when W. H. Walsh accused William Dana of making improper advances to his wife. The two men became reconciled and shook hands, but a few days later Walsh fell into another fit of jealous rage.

On 17 January Mr and Mrs Walsh went riding at Narre Warren. On their return, William Dana stepped forward to assist Mrs Walsh down from her horse. Walsh drew his pistol and shot Dana in the side, severely wounding him.

Walsh was tried for attempted murder in March 1851, and sentenced to seven years' transportation with hard labour. William Dana was forced to take eighteen months' leave of absence on half pay to recover from the wound, and Trevor Winter was employed as a subaltern in his place.

During the first half of 1851, when self-government for Victoria was being implemented, a gradual process of Europeanisation of the Native Police began. Black troopers who died or drifted away were not replaced. New white NCOs were appointed, and the total strength reduced from sixty-nine to fifty. The force was now generally kept away from Melbourne, being dispersed to stations throughout more remote districts.

Fourteen black troopers remained in Melbourne to help guard the Pentridge stockade. On the night of 21 July 1851 they walked away: most were not seen again. Henry Dana shamefacedly explained to La Trobe that he had long felt the blacks were 'unable to stand the wet and cold nights'. He thought they should have been set to guard road gangs during the day instead. La Trobe retorted tartly that since extra white guards would be needed at Pentridge, the expense should be met by reducing the Native Police strength by a further seven men.

The last important task of the Native Police was undertaken in September 1851, when they were sent to the new gold diggings near today's Ballarat to collect licence fees. Their overbearing methods so antagonised the diggers that a flame of rebellion was lit, culminating in the Eureka Stockade three years later.

For Henry Dana, the end was not far off. In November 1852 he fell victim to pneumonia while searching for a gang of bushrangers on the Mornington Peninsula. He died in a bedroom at the Melbourne Club on 24 November, aged thirty-five.

Within a few weeks the Native Police corps disintegrated. Most of its Aboriginal members returned to their tribal grounds—or what was left of them.

Many criticisms now surfaced. Melbourne Police Superintendent E. P. S. Sturt wrote cautiously that the corps's native members were 'not improved by their absence from savage life'. Journalist Edmund Finn, who saw them at first hand, described the corps as a 'simply intolerable' piece of 'useless extravagance'—an 'abominable, costly toy'.

La Trobe felt impelled to defend his long encouragement of Henry Dana's experiment. The corps, he wrote, 'fully answered the main purposes for which it was organized.' Dana himself 'may have had his failings', but he 'spent himself freely in the service with singleness of purpose', and the existence of the corps 'left no excuse for the vindictive reprisals which have been a blot upon the early years of the settlement.'

20

THE STATE
OF AFFAIRS
JUST BEFORE
THE GOLD RUSH

By the end of the 1840s the Aboriginal tribes of what was about to become Victoria had been battered and bribed into submission. Not much fight was left in them. Squattocracy reigned supreme. In the general air of white prosperity which covered the countryside, there seemed little need for further well-intentioned government interference.

District of Bourke

In the areas around Melbourne, Aboriginals gave practically no trouble to whites at the end of the 1840s, simply because the few remaining detribalised blacks went in terror of what they had learned about the implacable nature of white domination.

Crown Commissioner Edward Grimes reported in January 1849 that Aboriginals in the District of Bourke were still 'rapidly upon the decrease in almost every instance'. He felt that a 'good understanding' now existed between blacks and whites, due mainly to 'the cessation of any intercourse between the Aborigines and the Protectors.'

James Simpson, who took over from Grimes as Crown Commissioner for Bourke, reported early in 1850 that Aboriginals around Melbourne were proving even less troublesome, although they had 'not become in the slightest degree more useful to the white inhabitants.' Their numbers now included many aged and infirm who were objects of compassion—'but I am at a loss,' wrote Simpson, 'to suggest a means of relieving their individual cases without bringing down other claims which could not well be considered as within the scope of charitable interposition.'

A year later, as Victoria triumphantly entered its period of colonial independence, and riches flowed from every corner of its lush lands, Simpson reported that the few blacks left near Melbourne were of 'generally obedient demeanour when ordered from the vicinity of the settlement.'

The young men were still keen on joining the Mounted Police Corps, but 'The young females I fear are not yet destined to make much advance in civilization; occasional employment in cutting wood and fetching water is the extent of their occupation . . . '

Western Port

To the south-east of Melbourne, Commissioner Powlett reported early in 1850 that the Aboriginals were 'still decreasing both from natural causes and the murders which are perpetrated among themselves . . .'

A year later Powlett wrote that young blacks had deserted the areas set aside for their benefit and taken to drink at the numerous public houses now licensed through the countryside. Many were suffering from syphilis, liver complaints and skin diseases.

Powlett thought that 'it will be difficult in two or three generations to perceive any traces of the Aboriginal population of this Province.'

Gippsland

Commissioner Tyers reported early in 1851 that the Aboriginals of Gippsland were still divided into two distinct groups.

The 'warrigals' or wild blacks stayed well away from squatters' stations, except when launching sudden raids to spear cattle. Their numbers seemed to be diminishing: they were in 'a very unhealthy state', which Tyers put down to inter-tribal battles and unspecified diseases.

'Tame' blacks of the Buffalo, Maneroo and Omeo tribes still wandered through the district, 'encamping at the several stock stations where they can obtain food.' They led 'an idle life, seldom working for their bread,' wrote Tyers, 'and only take to hunting when driven by necessity.'

The total number of these blacks was now only forty-one: eighteen men, ten women and thirteen children. Two males were employed full-time on stations at £10 a year, plus rations.

Western District

In the previously violent western regions, only one serious outrage marred the scene during 1849–50.

On 26 June 1849 an illiterate white labourer, James Lloyd, was resting in his hut on John Ralston's 'Dergholm' run on the Glenelg River, about twenty miles north-west of today's Casterton. Two native men and a woman entered the hut and asked for tea, sugar and flour. Lloyd told them he had none to spare. They retorted he was 'a big one liar', and, claimed Lloyd, lunged at him with a tomahawk.

'I just had time to pick up my gun,' said Lloyd, 'when in the scuffle and in my fright, my finger being on the trigger, the gun went off; and the native woman rushing between us at the time, she was shot in the belly.' Lloyd ran out of the hut towards the head station, one of the black men chasing him about eight miles.

Dr Watton was ordered from Mount Rouse to seek further evidence. By the time the rivers had gone down and he arrived at Ralston's run, James Lloyd had absconded. A warrant was issued for Lloyd's arrest, but no further proceedings seem to have occurred.

Mount Rouse Aboriginal Station, still practically deserted, continued in its dispiriting way for a few months longer. Dr Watton managed to save some of the 1849 wheat crop, but after heavy winter rains it began to sprout in the stacks. A labourer was employed constantly to thrash the grain and save what he could.

Watton purchased a ton of seed potatoes in July 1849. In view of the projected closure of the Protectorate, he asked the Chief Protector whether they should be sown. Robinson agreed; but when the plants appeared above ground, Watton wrote dolefully, they were 'much injured by frost'.

By September Dr Watton had made up his mind to become a squatter on his own account. He wrote to La Trobe asking for permission to occupy part of the Aboriginal Station with his own stock. No reply can be traced.

Mount Rouse Station, in fact, had reached the end of its inglorious career. In May 1850 Surveyor Robert Hoddle instructed Draftsman Charles C. Horrell to take six assistants to the Aboriginal Station, survey it, and divide it into four portions. In the middle of each portion he should mark out half-acre township allotments, surrounded by small cultivation lots. Elsewhere, the best land should be divided into cultivation farms of 80–640 acres for disposal by public auction.

As soon as the survey teams arrived, surrounding squatters tried to establish 'pre-emptive rights' to the land. On 14 September J. H. Webster, Henry Gottreaux, William Hutton and Matthew Gibb protested to Superintendent La Trobe, claiming that the Survey Department's marking of an area ten miles square (i.e. 100 square miles) impinged greatly on what they had regarded as their lawful leaseholds. Robert Hoddle retorted that although these squatters had been allowed to depasture stock on the reserve, it was 'by sufferance and not by right.'

La Trobe arranged a compromise. In October 1850 he

decided to decrease the government reserve from 100 to 80 square miles. The southernmost portions of the old Aboriginal Station were to be divided into two squatting runs. The northernmost portions would form agricultural parishes with future town centres. Main roads and streets were to be three chains wide, and minor roads one chain wide. Town allotments would be sold in half-acre lots.

In this way today's town of Penshurst arose on the main road to Hamilton, and the Aboriginal reserve disappeared. By the 1880s Penshurst had grown into a town of 600 people serving surrounding grazing areas. It contained four hotels, three churches, two banks, a steam flour-mill, a Mechanics' Institute, an Old Bushman's Home, and the usual public buildings, but no Aboriginals.

Goulburn River

Renewed labour problems afflicted Goulburn River Aboriginal Station at the end of the 1840s. The original fencing was now so decayed that the plough bullocks broke through it with ease. Dr Horsburgh spent much of mid-1849 searching for lost bullocks, and patching up fences.

About 130 natives were in residence that winter, but they seemed lethargic and unwilling to do much beyond threshing the previous season's grain and making a little flour for themselves. In September the able-bodied left in a group and did not return.

To add to Horsburgh's troubles, white labourer John McBean quit in October, leaving him with little assistance during the busiest season. 'Men are not to be had here', he reported to Chief Protector Robinson. Horsburgh was compelled to treat all the sheep himself for footrot.

The following month he rode up and down the river, pleading with Aboriginals to return and assist him in washing the sheep as preparation for shearing. None would come, even when offered four shillings a day plus rations. Horsburgh managed to build a new sheep wash, but with the continued labour shortage 'I was in the washpool myself from morning to night.'

Finally, a friendly squatter, one of the Campbell clan, sent over his own shearers to get the fleeces off Horsburgh's sheep before they filled up with burrs and grass seeds.

With these additional white men to feed, rations ran short. The government dray had fallen to pieces, and could not be sent to Kilmore with wheat for grinding. 'I am again out of flour,' wrote Horsburgh, 'and in debt to all my neighbours.'

By Christmas 1849 the new season's wheat was ready to harvest. But another of the station's white employees had quit, leaving only one man to assist Horsburgh. With Robinson failing to give prompt directions, 'To whom am I to look for instructions?' pleaded Horsburgh, '. . . I am quite at a loss how to proceed.'

There was also the problem of what to do with the sheep. 'Would the Government wish them to lamb in May or June?' asked the doctor. 'If so, the rams ought to be put into the flock now.'

Horsburgh was finally permitted to engage two itinerant white workers to harvest the crop at 14s. each per week. In February 1850 he was delighted to find two Aboriginals who agreed to work as shepherds for little more than shelter and rations.

With the ending of the Protectorate, La Trobe transferred dealings with Horsburgh on 28 March to the Clerk of Works, Henry Ginn. The doctor's requisitions and pay abstracts were now dealt with rather more speedily.

In April Horsburgh was permitted to make what La Trobe called 'an extraordinary arrangement' with a blacksmith who was willing to erect his own 'substantial dwelling house and workshop' on the station. The smith was able to conduct his own business, using government tools, in return for keeping ploughs and other equipment in good order, and accommodating wayfarers in his new house.

General superintendence of both Goulburn and Loddon

River Stations was handed over to Crown Commissioner Powlett early in June 1850. Powlett visited the Goulburn Station in July. He recommended that a permanent boundary should be marked to enclose its existing area of thirty-five square miles. Although he thought 'little good' was likely to be done for Aboriginals of the district, it was still necessary to have a centre 'to give the aged, infirm and young children, food, blankets &c. in moderation.'

Dr Horsbrough continued determinedly to try to improve the Station. In the spring of 1850 he reported proudly that he had 'succeeded in obtaining 850 lambs out of 900 ewes.' He purchased an old wood-screw wool press from squatter Daniel McKenzie for £4. When the device was repaired and placed in a new wool-shed, the Station's presentation of its wool clip improved markedly.

But Goulburn River Station was doomed after 1851 by the discovery of huge gold deposits not far to the west, with consequent increase in white population and demand for agricultural land along the northern rivers. The almost-deserted Aboriginal Station was surveyed and judged fit for a township, named Murchison after overlander John Murchison who had settled at Yea.

The Aboriginal buildings deteriorated into decaying huts on Murchison Police Paddock, located between Willoughby Street and the river. By the 1880s Murchison had grown into a thriving agricultural town of 500 residents, with eight hotels, three churches, two banks, and a Mechanics' Institute library containing nearly 1000 volumes—none of them telling what had happened to the original occupiers of the soil.

Loddon River

The year 1849 began on the Loddon River Aboriginal Station with continued attempts by neighbouring squatters to encroach on its grazing areas.

W. M. Hunter of 'Tarringower' run, adjoining today's

town of Newstead, had already been evicted from the Aboriginal reserve by Commissioner Grimes the previous year. In an attempt to make sure the land was occupied, Protector Parker agisted 3000 sheep for John Hepburn of 'Smeaton Hill' in 1849.

This did not prevent another settler named John Egan, of 'Corrinilla' run on Jim Crow Creek, from forming an outstation on the southern part of the Aboriginal reserve. He too had to be evicted.

Such squatters had no hesitation in spreading stories that the Protectorate was doomed. The result, said Parker, was that the average daily attendance of natives dwindled from forty to twenty in the second half of 1849.

The ever-hopeful Parker continued to preach Christianity to the natives wherever he could win an audience. With increased attention to religious instruction, he observed, 'cleanliness, industry and general steadiness have taken the place of the ordinary filth, and indolence, and erratic habits of the natives.'

During one memorable trip down the Loddon, arriving at John Bear's 'East Loddon' run adjoining Serpentine Creek, on 14 October 1849 Parker 'held Divine Service in the forest . . . with about eighty of the Mallee and Loddon tribes.'

In mid-1849 Robinson advised Parker that the whole system of Aboriginal protection was again being reviewed. Meanwhile his allowances for rations and forage would be discontinued. This was equivalent to reduction of his income by one-third. Parker protested in vain that his whole family had worked their hearts out for the Aboriginal cause—all on the one salary.

La Trobe applied this saving towards the appointment of Henry and Eliza Judkins* as schoolmaster and schoolmistress at Loddon River Station. They moved into one of the best huts, where they were responsible for the five young black girls, eight young boys and two half-castes undergoing instruction.

* Parents of the noted Methodist reformers W. H. and G. A. Judkins.

A touching footnote says that one of the boys, Yereip, absconded and 'went in search of his father'.

La Trobe visited the station on 14 January 1850 to make arrangements for its future. He confirmed the Judkins family in their position as educators, and they appear to have continued living there for some years.

Parker had already expressed a wish to become a grazier on his own account, especially if this could be allied with other moves to benefit the Aboriginals. Surveyor Robert Hoddle agreed that, if the station were to be reduced from fifty-five to four square miles, Parker might as well be licensed to occupy the remainder.

Parker formally relinquished control of the Aboriginal Station on 28 February. La Trobe permitted him to occupy the southern area around Mount Franklin, on a three-year squatting licence granted without public competition, for a fee of £60 a year. Parker was also allowed to take over the Aboriginal Station's flock of sheep, free of charge, on condition that he supply all mutton required by the school establishment. The former Protector was to give priority in employment 'as far as possible to the Aboriginal natives', and act as visiting magistrate.

Finally, Parker was authorised to erect a homestead and other improvements on his run, 'with the full understanding that whenever it may be held proper to remove him, the sum of £250 will be the utmost limit allowed as compensation.'

Parker was now forty-eight years old, an aged man for those times. He accepted the new arrangements gratefully, and spent much of 1850 'unavoidably absorbed with my own affairs'. Nevertheless, his particular friends among the native families drifted towards his end of the former reserve. 'Since I formed my own establishment in the early part of April,' Parker wrote, 'four natives have been permanently and fifteen occasionally employed in my service.' He paid them £50 in wages, observing that they spent the money 'prudently' on permanent assets.

By the second half of 1850 Parker found himself again

spending much time as teacher and preacher, although now without any government salary. In every moment he could spare from sheep-tending necessities, Parker conducted his own school for several boys and one or two girls. He was especially pleased that some Aboriginals 'sent their sons from a considerable distance . . . that they might have the opportunity of attending the school.'

Each Sunday afternoon was reserved for church services, conducted by Parker in the Loddon River dialect. Children and young adults were his most attentive listeners: the surly aged survivors of untrammelled tribal times 'almost invariably evince opposition to these services', wrote Parker in 1851.

So the brave old former Protector went on, buying into another Loddon River station, called 'Holcombe', at the height of the gold rush, and dying in 1865 mourned by all who knew him.

By the 1880s the old Aboriginal station at Franklinford had grown into a small township with a population of forty-four. Two hundred farming and grazing families in the district supplied enough recruits to support a state school and three churches, while two hotels catered for travellers along the Loddon. A few Aboriginals doggedly survived on the banks of the river, in what would have once been acceptable dwellings but were now regarded as humpies, shunned by all respectable white folk.

Murray and Wimmera tribes

By the end of the 1840s pastoral settlement had spread to the very edges of fertile land in the Wimmera, and down the Murray River.

There were no Protectorate stations in these areas to make regular reports on the condition of Aboriginal inhabitants. Instead, Crown Lands Commissioners prepared annual reports on their observations of native life, gathered as these officers rode from station to station supervising the activities of squatters.

In the Murray District, Commissioner H. W. H. Smythe reported for the year 1850 that the native population consisted of nearly 700 people—270 men, 330 women, and 99 children. In general they were 'idle and disinclined to regular employment'. About fifty were employed by squatters as bark-strippers and boundary riders. Their health was fairly good, 'but when disease attacks them, they soon die.'

Smythe claimed that not a single outrage, of blacks attacking whites or vice versa, had occurred during the whole year. As we saw in the previous chapter, Native Police squads were involved in several deadly confrontations during 1850. Smythe apparently regarded these as none of his business.

In the Wimmera District, Commissioner W. H. Wright reported for 1850 that it was difficult to estimate the numbers of natives in the semi-desert areas of the Mallee. His best guess was a total of 1200 Aboriginals for his entire district. Their health was generally good. Where runs had been established, 'almost every able native is more or less employed by settlers.' They were used for such tasks as carrying water, sweeping yards and herding cattle. 'These are generally honest,' wrote Wright, 'and take a pride in executing properly whatever they are entrusted with.'

Station blacks were regularly rationed and issued with slop clothing. What they appeared to value most was an order on a country store to enable them to purchase whatever goods they fancied. Then, without warning, they might simply disappear on walkabout.

As in the Murray District, no outrages of any kind were reported by the Commissioner during 1850.

21

LEGAL RIGHTS AND LAND RIGHTS DENIED

Many years of attempting to deal with the Aboriginal problem, often in a well-meaning but bumbling kind of way, had taught white men little. Obsessed by the need to impose on the frontier their own kind of social organisation, Anglo-Australian settlers could visualise no other end but that the black people should behave like white people or die out. Yet, in a quite hypocritical fashion, every attempt to allow reasonable legal and land rights to the tribes was rejected by the pastoralist majority in the NSW Legislative Council. Even the most progressive Europeans were almost helpless in the face of this general anti-Aboriginal feeling.

After his arrival in New South Wales, one of the early actions performed by Governor Gipps was to introduce a Bill into the Legislative Council in June 1838, allowing Aboriginal evidence to be heard in court if it could be corroborated by a white witness. The Council delayed matters by adding a clause referring the Bill to British legal authorities. In London the Solicitor-General and Attorney-General agreed that 'To admit, in a criminal case, the evidence of a witness acknowledged to be ignorant of the existence of a God or a future state, would be contrary to the principles of British jurisprudence.' That was the end of the first attempt.

In 1843 Lord Stanley advised Gipps that the British Parliament had passed an Act authorising colonies to make their own laws admitting Aboriginal evidence. Gipps reintroduced the Aborigines Evidence Bill in 1844, but was rebuffed by comments such as those of W. C. Wentworth, that 'it would be quite as defensible to receive as evidence in a Court of Justice the chatterings of the ourang-outang . . .' The Governor was forced to advise London that the new Bill had been 'thrown out on the second reading by a majority of 14 to 10.'

In 1846, after many murderers of both races had escaped scot-free, La Trobe protested to Sydney that these legal difficulties were making a farce of law enforcement. 'Constant murders and acts of violence', with few exceptions, had been allowed to pass. Many of 'the most startling instances of murder' by Aboriginal natives 'have been perpetrated with the most perfect impunity', said La Trobe. Even where police were available, attempts to arrest known criminals were useless, when 'it was clear that no good result, as far as the ends of justice were concerned, would follow such apprehension.'

After La Trobe's comments were passed to London, Earl Grey simply replied that it was up to the local legislature to take advantage of the 1843 Imperial Act authorising Aboriginal evidence to be admitted in court. Attorney-General J. H. Plunkett reintroduced the Aboriginal Natives' Evidence Bill in May 1849. This third attempt was also defeated, although the squatters' majority was now whittled down to one vote.

Meanwhile, a final denial of land rights for Aboriginals took place in New South Wales government circles. This denial had been implicit since the beginning of white settlement, as part of the legal view of Australia as a *terra nullius*— that is, a once-empty land now belonging to the British Crown. When squatters were granted fourteen-year leases over pastoral land by the historic Order-in-Council of March

1847, the Colonial Office proposed that Aboriginals should be legally granted 'the free use of unimproved Crown lands for the purposes of hunting', notwithstanding the existence of squatters' leases over the same land.

In Sydney, however, Crown Law officials advised that since the original Order-in-Council said nothing about Aboriginal rights, it was not legally possible for the local legislature to vary squatters' leases in the manner suggested.

Instead of acting on any matters of substance, the Legislative Council in 1849 adopted the familiar device of setting up a Select Committee to examine Aboriginal affairs. Under the chairmanship of J. F. L. Foster, questionnaires were sent to many leading squatters, magistrates, Crown Commissioners, and the clergy. These observers were almost unanimous in condemning the Protectorate system. Port Phillip squatter George Russell's opinion was typical: he thought the money spent by Protectors might as well 'have been thrown into the sea.'

The Select Committee found itself 'compelled to advise the abolition of the present system'—that is, the Protectorate—but was 'unable to recommend any other as a substitute', except perhaps gradually to educate the white population not to harm Aboriginals. This recommendation, anti-climactic as it was, sealed the fate of the Protectorate. Governor FitzRoy advised Superintendent La Trobe on 3 July 1849 that the Protectors would be paid to the end of that year, and given compensation at the rate of one month's salary for each year of service in the colony.

True to form, Robinson applied for more. On 29 December 1849, La Trobe forwarded Robinson's request to the Secretary of State for a lifetime pension of £200 a year because of his services in Van Diemen's Land as well as Port Phillip.

In London Sir George Arthur supported Robinson's cause. In an almost unheard-of act of generosity, the Colonial Office not only granted the life pension, but gave the Chief Protector £20 a year more than he asked for. Not a bad reward for a public servant who had done as much as anyone to impede the selfless work of most of his assistants. Robinson's last official duty was to visit the Goulburn and Loddon River Aboriginal Stations with Dr Horsburgh in January 1850, pronouncing them to be in a 'highly satisfactory' state. Thus his Australian career ended with a distinct falsehood.

In 1852 Robinson sold for £2500 his beautiful house, 'Rivolia', which he had built in 1843 on twenty acres of freehold land running down to the river in South Yarra. He returned to England with valuable possessions, including four boxes containing 1000 ounces of gold from the colony's new diggings. With this and much other wealth, the former rough-hewn carpenter and Protector quickly established himself in polite society. His first wife, Maria, had died in 1848: in 1853 he married Rose Pyne, daughter of a well-known artist, and had another five children to supplement his Australian family. Robinson died at Bath in 1866, aged seventy-eight.

A question which will always be debated is whether the Protectorate really failed. During his Port Phillip years Robinson himself undoubtedly developed into a mercenary, dilatory, self-interested character. But among his Assistant Protectors were men of great compassion and tenacity, who did their best under often frightful circumstances to stem the destruction of the native race.

Had it not been for these men, and their loyal wives and families, racial conflict in Port Phillip might well have become even more scandalous. It was always unfair to blame the Protectors for not being able to resolve a hopeless situation; a more objective view might be that the presence of Protectors prevented a good deal more harassment and human slaughter on the expanding pastoral frontier.

When the strength of colonial opinion against the Aboriginals was realised in London, Earl Grey took refuge in a repetition of proposals for the formation of new reserves. These were 'to be cultivated, for their benefit, in the various districts open to settlement.' Grey also recommended 'the establishment of industrial training schools, where the natives might be instructed in the Arts of life as well as in the simple rudiments of Education.' Just how these schools would differ from the Protectorate stations on which so much money and effort had been lavished, the Secretary of State did not say.

In Melbourne, Commissioner Powlett reflected gloomily that 'It is now late in the day to form any system likely to improve the condition of the Aborigines.'

Governor FitzRoy sent Grey's vague proposals on to La Trobe late in July 1849. La Trobe answered cautiously that in making any fresh arrangements for Aboriginal welfare, 'the propriety of maintaining reserves for their benefit' would be kept in mind.

FitzRoy replied some months later with a firm instruction that 'a suitable number of reserves of moderate extent' should be allocated 'beyond the settled districts'. This last phrase was extremely important, for it confirmed that the Aboriginals now had no rights at all throughout the lands being utilised by white men. If they wished to take refuge on reserves, it must be well away from white districts—meaning generally on land then considered unsuitable for grazing or agriculture, and likely to support fewer wild animals to be hunted for food.

A further paragraph of FitzRoy's instructions placed selection of sites in the hands of the Surveyor-General and his officers. Crown Commissioners would continue to exercise general superintendence over the reserves themselves. Except in cases of 'extreme emergency', no native would be given food or clothing unless he worked for it. No further funds would be granted for the Merri Creek school, as this was too close to the main centre of white population.

In this document lies the origins of a system of virtual apartheid which saw the establishment of new Aboriginal reserves at such places as Lake Tyers (1850), Lake Boga (1851), Yelta (1855), Ebenezer (1859), Ramayuck (1862), Framling-ham (1865) and Lake Condah (1867).

Even so, government officials still had to keep a wary eye on encroaching squatters. When Edward Thomson of 'Glenfalloch A' run, near Boisdale, applied in 1850 for a lease of eight square miles between Lake King and the Gippsland coast, Surveyor Hoddle told him that the land had already been reserved by Commissioner Tyers for Aboriginal use.

Hoddle also instructed Assistant Surveyor Osgood Pritchard to mark out a small reserve for the Aboriginals at Lake Boga. Hoddle had already written privately to La Trobe, expressing his opinion that 'I do not think large reserves will be of any material benefit to the Aborigines, as it is hopeless to expect they will permanently settle on particular portions of this territory . . . I fear that any large reserves would only benefit the officers employed in their management . . .'

The only Protector who retained a government post was the once-despised William Thomas, for so long harassed and demeaned by the now-redundant Chief Protector George Robinson. In 1850 Thomas reached the advanced age of fifty-seven. For the past twelve years, this former London schoolmaster and his family had doggedly continued to care for Aboriginals around Melbourne. When the end of the Protectorate was mooted, Thomas wrote to La Trobe pointing out that many years earlier in London he had been asked by 'Lady M—', a close friend of Lord Glenelg, 'If I should not like to go abroad and protect the poor blacks.' He had been assured by Sir George Grey that the appointment was permanent, and he had thrown up a lucrative position to come to Melbourne. Closure of the Protectorate would leave him and his large family almost penniless. He pleaded for some other government position. La Trobe's minute on this letter assured Thomas that his efforts 'to benefit the nation' would not be forgotten.

In June La Trobe informed Governor FitzRoy that he had appointed Thomas to a new position, that of Guardian of Aborigines. He would be paid ten shillings a day, with no further allowances, and would maintain 'friendly control and surveillance' of natives remaining around Melbourne. In particular, he would 'keep them altogether out of the town', and 'prevent their encroachment upon the enclosed and cultivated lands.'

Thomas's appointment meant that James Simpson, Crown Commissioner for the County of Bourke, could be released from the usual Commissioner's duties towards the Aboriginals, except to render Thomas 'every assistance in controlling their movements'.

Thomas himself was instructed to make any essential requisitions for food and clothing for Aboriginals through Henry Ginn, Clerk of Works. Cases of sickness should be dealt with by Dr John Sullivan, chief Government Medical Officer. District Surgeons at Geelong and Portland were instructed to deal with cases in their own areas.

In the spring of 1850 some of the Yarra and Mornington Peninsula blacks began attempting to occupy their old camping grounds on the south bank of the Yarra opposite Melbourne. Here they displayed 'intemperate habits', but caused no problems beyond 'noisy conduct when drunk returning to the encampment'. Superintendent La Trobe presented these blacks with blankets and tomahawks, to celebrate the district's imminent separation from New South Wales, and Thomas was able to persuade them to move further upstream to Bulleen.

In his first half-yearly report as Guardian, for July–December 1850, Thomas said that only one serious collision had occurred, when the Yarra and Mornington blacks left Bulleen to go wandering in Gippsland. The Gippsland blacks still regarded them as intruders, and killed three of their number.

This brought the total native population in Thomas's area down to sixty-four. There were 'no young children to fill up the ranks of the dead, which too clearly marks their speedy extinction', the Guardian wrote.

La Trobe's desire to keep Aboriginals out of Melbourne had been fully accomplished, said Thomas. Occasional drunks had been 'speedily removed' to their small camps near Heidelberg, the Plenty River, Moonee Ponds, and Mordialloc. There, blankets and medicines were supplied to all in need.

Thomas believed that permanent central refuges were still needed. He wrote to La Trobe on 31 December 1850 asking for two portions on the north and south sides of the Yarra River to be set aside as Aboriginal reserves. Surveyor Hoddle replied that in his opinion such reserves would of 'as little service' as the former Protectorate reserves. He added that the Aboriginals were 'incapable' of steady labour, and should not be employed even in the police force, except as trackers or guides.

Hoddle believed the only hope was for the children. 'An orphan institution might save the remainder of this unfortunate race', he wrote. 'The children should be removed from their former haunts and away from their tribes'—that is, taken from their natural parents.

Thomas began a series of monthly reports in February 1851. For this month he wrote that the Yarra tribe, now consisting of only twenty-one men and twelve women, had migrated far up the Yarra to 'the Eel Lagoons'. The Western Port tribe, now only fifteen men and eight women, had vanished into the thick bush 'between Mount Eliza and Cape Schanck'.

During March Thomas had so little to do that he spent much of his time on magisterial duties at the Melbourne Police Office.

In April 1851 he was startled when large tribes arrived from the country and camped at various spots around Melbourne 'as tho' to thwart my endeavours to remove them.' He was forced to call on Commissioner Simpson for police help in breaking up drunken encampments on the south bank of the Yarra. Two unnamed blacks were speared to death 'during their drunken fits'.

On arriving home, Thomas found that another group of blacks had surrounded his cottage and demanded 'a poor lubra' named Polly, who had sought refuge with Mrs Thomas. The Guardian's wife had locked all the doors and shutters, and hidden the lubra in the dining-room.

Thomas finally persuaded the blacks to leave. The lubra, he said, was 'one of the most modest, well-conducted females, in many respects highly civilized', who had lived for two years with a shepherd on J. M. Sanger's Avoca run until sought out by her original tribe. Now she was terrified of being seized:

'She grasped hold of me as a dying man would', wrote Thomas. Reconciled with her shepherd, she married him and returned to the Avoca.

After Victoria achieved responsible government during the 1850s, Aboriginal affairs were placed under the Surveyor-General's Department. A Central Board for Protection of Aborigines was established in 1860, Thomas continuing as 'Official Visitor' to the chain of small reserves and supply depots set up in remote parts of Victoria. In 1867, when Thomas was seventy-four, he went blind. He died a few weeks later, survived by only three of his nine children.

22

GENOCIDE, WITH THE BEST OF INTENTIONS

In 1850, following only fifteen years of extensive pastoral settlement, the Aboriginal population of Port Phillip had been reduced to about half its original number.

The precise extent of this depopulation depends on what estimate is accepted for the number of blacks in the district when full-scale white settlement began in 1836. I am inclined to believe the estimates of Aboriginal Protectors and Crown Lands Commissioners, for they were in close touch with most of the tribes, possessed a fair degree of objectivity, and were specifically charged with counting Aboriginal numbers from time to time.

Edward Parker calculated that there were some 7500 Aboriginals in the whole of Port Phillip when whites began to arrive en masse in 1836. His 1843 census of the entire area west of the Goulburn River listed 1100 blacks by name, but he probably missed many in the then little-known Wimmera and Mallee areas.

In 1849 Parker conducted a careful census of the fourteen tribes living along the Loddon River, and concluded that their numbers had been reduced to 271 men, women and children.

William Thomas estimated that before white settlement

the total number of Aboriginals in Port Phillip 'could not be less than 6000'. About 500 lived in the Yarra and Western Port regions, but a number of these were apparently killed in prolonged tribal battles with Gippsland blacks in 1834.

Tyers calculated in the mid-1840s that there were about 3000 Aboriginals in Gippsland alone. Several years later this figure had been reduced to only a few hundred survivors.

In 1850 Crown Commissioners were given the task of estimating the number of Aboriginals remaining alive at that date. Their surveys produced the following results:

Western Port tribes	49
Jajowerong and Mallegoondeet tribes	230
Walidygath tribes	1920
Western District tribes	784
Gippsland tribes	231
Yarra (Melbourne) tribe	10
TOTAL	3224

During the latter half of the nineteenth century it became customary to reduce the apparent genocidal impact of white settlement by reducing the estimates of the original black population.

In the 1870s even such a friend of the blacks as Robert Brough Smyth, chairman of the Victorian Board for Protection of Aborigines, claimed that the total number of natives in 1836 'would not exceed 3,000'. Since there were nearly 2000 blacks still alive in the 1870s, the reduction in numbers seemed not at all serious to such commentators of the high Victorian Age. By manipulating statistics, they were able to satisfy themselves that the pioneering phase had not been so bad after all.

Smyth's estimate of 3000 total black population in 1836 is clearly ridiculous. We know from all the evidence in this book, compiled from first-hand reports, that very severe depopulation had taken place. Smyth was obviously not aware that even in 1850 the Crown Commissioners had counted more than 3200 blacks as still living. And by the time Smyth wrote his version in the 1870s, most of the official documents which disprove his case were buried deep in the Treasury Building in Melbourne, not to emerge until systematic archival research began a hundred years later.

A more careful survey of the evidence available in the 1920s was conducted by A. R. Radcliffe-Brown, a somewhat dogmatic professor of anthropology at the University of Sydney. He concluded that there were 11 500 Aboriginals in Victoria before white settlement. This estimate may be rather too high, although it has been raised even higher by latter-day publicists for the Aboriginal cause. Whatever the true figures, they will now never be known with complete accuracy.

What is undeniable is that large-scale black depopulation did occur during the white pioneering phase, and that it continued throughout the self-satisfied Victorian Age. Outright murder by then had become uncommon, but blacks were still carried off by alcoholism, poor nutrition, disease, and high infant mortality.

By the time the Commonwealth was formed in 1901, and the first national census was taken, an unknown number of mixed-blood people had merged into the general population. Only 271 full-blood Aboriginals remained alive in Victoria. By any standard, this amounted to the virtual extinction of a race of people—commonly known as genocide.

Nothing can now be done to alter, avenge or justify crimes committed so long ago. There seems no point in living persons feeling guilty for the racial devastation caused by ambitious or brutal pioneers. The whole white community, not just the squatters, benefited economically from the development of productive enterprises on the European model. However, it may now be accepted that these enterprises were established on land seized by force from an almost defenceless race of people, and that most of the population is still benefiting from that original seizure. If the Australian ideal of 'fair play' has any meaning at all, it is surely time to redouble efforts to give descendants of the Aboriginal race a better chance in life.

SOURCES

Official Sources

New South Wales. *Acts and Ordinances.* Sydney, 1835–51.
New South Wales Government Gazette. Sydney, 1835–51.
New South Wales Public and Private General Statutes, 1838–46. Sydney, 1847.
New South Wales. Legislative Council. *Votes and Proceedings, 1845* (Select Committee on Condition of Aborigines). Sydney, 1845.
New South Wales. Legislative Council. *Votes and Proceedings, 1849* (Report from Select Committee on Aborigines and Protectorate). Sydney, 1849.
Port Phillip Government Gazette. Melbourne, 1843–51.

The following official records were consulted at the Public Record Office of Victoria, Melbourne.
VPRS = Victorian Public Record Series.

VPRS 10. Superintendent, Port Phillip District. Registered Inward Correspondence relating to Aboriginal Affairs, 1839–51.
VPRS 11. Chief Protector of Aborigines. Unregistered Inward Correspondence, 1847–51.
VPRS 12. Aboriginal Protectorate. Returns, 1840–49.
VPRS 16. Superintendent, Port Phillip District. Registered Outward Correspondence, 1839–51.
VPRS 19. Superintendent, Port Phillip District. Registered Inward Correspondence, 1839–51.
VPRS 20. Superintendent, Port Phillip District. Registered Inward Confidential Correspondence, 1842–43.
VPRS 21. Crown Law Department. Unregistered Inward Correspondence, 1840–51.
VPRS 24. Inquest Deposition Files, 1840–51.
VPRS 25. Gisborne Police Station. Letter and Report Book, 1840–56.
VPRS 26. Aboriginal Protectorate. Sundry Register, 1841–50.
VPRS 30. Criminal Trial Briefs, 1841–51.
VPRS 32. Police Magistrate, Portland. Unregistered Inward Correspondence, 1840–50.
VPRS 34. Portland Police Court Proceedings, 1840–51.

VPRS 43. Police Office, Alberton, Vic. Unregistered Outward and Inward Correspondence, 1845–51.

VPRS 44. Crown Lands & Survey Department. Registered and Unregistered Inward Correspondence, 1840–51.

VPRS 45. Superintendent, Port Phillip District. Correspondence Outwards (drafts), 1846–52.

VPRS 78. Criminal Record Book, 1841–51.

VPRS 90. Victoria Police. Daybook, Native Police Corps, 1845–53.

VPRS 94. Commissioner of Crown Lands, Murray District. Inward Correspondence, 1839–51.

VPRS 95. Commissioner of Crown Lands, Western Port District. Inward Correspondence, 1841–51.

VPRS 96. Commissioner of Crown Lands, Bourke District. Inward Correspondence, 1842–51.

VPRS 99. Commissioner of Crown Lands, Gippsland District. Inward Correspondence, 1849–50.

VPRS 103. Commissioner of Crown Lands, Western Port District. Letterbook, 1839–51.

VPRS 104. Commissioner of Crown Lands, County of Bourke. Letterbook, 1841–51.

VPRS 109. Geelong Police Office. Deposition Book, 1838–41.

VPRS 2893. Superintendent, Port Phillip District. Registered Inward Correspondence from W. Thomas and E. S. Parker, 1850–51.

VPRS 2895. Chief Protector of Aborigines. Outward Letter Book, 1849–50.

VPRS 2897. Superintendent, Port Phillip District. Land Branch. Registered Inward Correspondence re Aboriginal Stations, 1847–51.

VPRS 4104. Superintendent, Port Phillip District. Unregistered Inward Confidential Correspondence, 1842–47.

VPRS 4105. Superintendent, Port Phillip District. Outward Confidential Correspondence, 1839–51.

VPRS 4397. Unregistered Correspondence re Suspension of C. W. Sievwright, 1842.

VPRS 4398. Unregistered Correspondence re Dismissal of W. Le Souef, 1842–44.

VPRS 4399. Chief Protector of Aborigines. Annual Reports, 1845, 1849.

VPRS 4410. Aboriginal Protectorate. Reports and Journals, 1839–49.

VPRS 4466. Unregistered Papers re Native Police, 1848–49.

VPRS 5095. Police Court, Alberton. Cases Heard, 1845–51.

VPRS 6760. Aboriginal Estrays, 1840-60.

Bibliography

Anderson, Hugh. *Flowers of the Field: A History of Ripon Shire.* Hill of Content, Melbourne, 1969.

——· *Out of the Shadow: The Career of John Pascoe Fawkner.* Cheshire, Melbourne, 1962.

Andrews, Arthur. *First Settlement of the Upper Murray, 1835–1845.* D. S. Ford, Sydney, 1920.

Archer, W. H. *Statistical Notes on the Progress of Victoria, 1835–1860.* Government Printer, Melbourne, n.d. [1861?].

[Arden, George]. *Latest Information with regard to Australia Felix . . .* Gazette Office, Melbourne, 1840; Queensberry Hill Press, Melbourne, 1977.

——· *The Separation Question . . .* Arden & Strode, Melbourne, 1841.

Arthur, Edward and Fortescue. *A Journal of Events from Melbourne, Port Philip, to Mount Schank . . .* Sheerness, c. 1844; Sullivan's Cove, Hobart, 1975.

Bacchus, Captain W. H. *see* Osborn [Roberts], B. O.

Baker, C. J. *Sydney and Melbourne . . .* Smith, Elder & Co., London, 1845.

Banfield, L. L. *Green Pastures and Gold: A History of Ararat.* Mullaya Publications, Canterbury, Vic., 1974.

Barrett, Bernard. *The Civic Frontier . . .* Melbourne University Press, Carlton, Vic., 1971.

——· *The Inner Suburbs.* Melbourne University Press, Carlton, Vic., 1979.

Bassett, Marnie. *The Hentys: An Australian Colonial Tapestry.* Oxford University Press, London, 1954.

Bate, Weston. *A History of Brighton.* Melbourne University Press, Carlton Vic., 1962.

Behan, H. F. *Mr. Justice J. W. Willis* . . . The author, Glen Iris, Vic., 1979.

Benson, Rev. C. I. *A Century of Victorian Methodism.* Spectator Publishing, Melbourne, 1935.

Beveridge, Peter. *The Aborigines of Victoria and the Riverina.* M. L. Hutchinson, Melbourne, 1889.

Billis, R. V., and Kenyon, A. S. *Pastoral Pioneers of Port Phillip.* Macmillan, London, 1932; Stockland Press, Melbourne, 1974.

—— *Pastures New* . . . Macmillan, Melbourne, 1930; Stockland Press, Melbourne, 1974.

Billot, C. P. *John Batman* . . . Hyland House, Melbourne, 1979.

—— *Melbourne—An Annotated Bibliography to 1850.* Rippleside Press, Geelong, 1970.

Blainey, Geoffrey. *A History of Camberwell.* Lothian, Melbourne, 1980.

Blake, L. J. *Captain Dana and the Native Police.* Neptune Press, Newtown, Vic., 1982.

—— *Letters of Charles Joseph La Trobe.* Government Printer, Melbourne, 1975.

—— *Vision and Realisation: A Centenary History of State Education in Victoria.* 3 vols. Education Department of Victoria, Melbourne, 1973.

Blanks, Hervey. *The Story of Yea.* Hawthorn Press, Melbourne, 1973.

'Boldrewood, Rolf' [Browne, Thomas]. *Old Melbourne Memories.* George Robertson, Melbourne, 1884; Heinemann, Melbourne, 1969.

Boys, R. D. *First Years at Port Phillip.* Robertson & Mullens, Melbourne, 1935.

Bride, T. F. (ed.). *Letters from Victorian Pioneers.* Government Printer, Melbourne, 1898; Heinemann, Melbourne, 1969.

Brodribb, W. A. *Recollections of an Australian Squatter.* John Woods & Co., Sydney, 1883; Ferguson, Sydney, 1978.

Brooke, B., and Finch, A. *A Story of Horsham* . . . City of Horsham, Vic., 1982.

Brothers, C. R. D. *Early Victorian Psychiatry, 1835–1905.* Government Printer, Melbourne, n.d. [1962].

Brown, P. L. (ed.). *Clyde Company Papers,* vols 3 and 4. Oxford University Press, London, 1958–9.

—— *The Narrative of George Russell of Golf Hill.* Oxford University Press, London, 1935.

Brownhill, W. R. *History of Geelong* . . . The author, Geelong, Vic., 1955.

Bunce, Daniel. *Australasiatic Reminiscences* . . . J. T. Hendy, Melbourne, 1857.

Burchett, W. H. *East Melbourne, 1837–1977* . . . Craftsman Press, Hawthorn, Vic., 1978.

Butler, J. M. *Settler by Succession: A Biography of James Austin 1810–1896.* Neptune Press, Melbourne, 1979.

Butlin, Noel. *Our Original Aggression: Aboriginal Populations of South-Eastern Australia 1788–1850.* Allen & Unvin, Sydney, 1983.

Byrne, J. C. *Twelve Years' Wanderings* . . . 2 vols. Bentley, London, 1848.

Campbell, A. H. *John Batman and the Aborigines.* Kibble Books, Malmsbury, Vic., n.d. [1987].

Cannon, Michael (general ed.). *Historical Records of Victoria,* vols 1–5. Government Printer, Melbourne, 1981–88.

—— *The Exploration of Australia.* Reader's Digest, Sydney, 1987.

—— *Life in the Country.* Nelson, Melbourne, 1973.

—— *Who's Master, Who's Man?* Nelson, Melbourne, 1971.

Carstairs, J., and Lane, M. *Pubs, Punts and Pastures: The Story of Pioneer Irish Women on the Salt Water River.* St Albans History Society, Vic., 1988.

Chambers, Don. *Violet Town or Honeysuckle in Australia Felix.* Melbourne University Press, Carlton, Vic., 1985.

Christie, M. F. *Aborigines in Colonial Victoria 1835–86.* Sydney University Press, Sydney, 1979.

Clark, I. D. *The Port Phillip Journals of G. A. Robinson: 8 March–7 April 1842 and 18 March–29 April 1843.* Department of Geography, Monash University, Clayton, Vic., 1988.

Clarke, Michael. *'Big' Clarke* [W. J. T. Clarke]. Queensberry Hill Press, Melbourne, 1980.

Corris, Peter. *Aborigines and Europeans in Western Victoria.* Australian Institute of Aboriginal Studies, Canberra, 1968.

Curr, E. M. *Recollections of Squatting in Victoria.* Melbourne University Press, Carlton, Vic., 1965.

De Serville, Paul. *Port Phillip Gentlemen.* Oxford University Press, Melbourne, 1980.

Dillon, I. C. *Tracks of the Morning: A Timbertop History Text.* Geelong Grammar School, Corio, Vic., 1989.

Dredge, J. E. *Brief Notices of the Aborigines* . . . Geelong, Vic., 1845.

Dunderdale, George. *Book of the Bush.* Ward, Lock & Co. Ltd, London, 1898; Penguin, Ringwood, Vic., 1973.

Edgar, L. A. *Among the Black Boys* . . . n.p., London, 1865.

Fels, M. H. *The Dandenong Police Paddocks . . . 1837–1853.* Department of Conservation, Forests and Lands, Melbourne, 1986.

—— *Good Men and True: The Aboriginal Police of the Port Phillip District 1837–1853.* Melbourne University Press, Carlton, Vic., 1988.

Fyans, Foster. *Memoirs Recorded at Geelong . . . by Captain Foster Fyans,* ed. by P. L. Brown. Geelong Advertiser, Geelong, Vic., 1986.

Gardner, P. D. *Gippsland Massacres . . . the Destruction of the Kurnai Tribe, 1800–1860.* West Gippsland Community Education Centre, Warragul, Vic., 1983.

—— *Our Founding Murdering Father: Angus McMillan and the Kurnai Tribe of Gippsland 1839–1865.* The author, Ensay, Vic., c. 1987.

—— *Through Foreign Eyes: European Perceptions of the Kurnai Tribe of Gippsland.* Centre for Gippsland Studies, Churchill, Vic., 1988.

'Garryowen' (Finn, Edmund). *The Chronicles of Early Melbourne.* Fergusson & Mitchell, Melbourne, 1888 (2 vols); Heritage Publications, Melbourne, 1976 (3 vols).

Gray, C. M. *Western Victoria in the 'Forties: Reminiscences of a Pioneer.* Hamilton Spectator, Hamilton, Vic., 1932.

Greenwood, G. W. 'Reverend Francis Tuckfield's magnificent failure at Buntingdale'. In *Heritage,* Methodist Historical Society, Melbourne, September 1956.

Gross, Alan. *Charles Joseph La Trobe.* Melbourne University Press, Carlton, Vic., 1956.

Hamilton, J. C. *Pioneering Days in Western Victoria.* Macmillan, Melbourne, 1923; Warrnambool Institute Press, Warrnambool, Vic., 1981.

Haydon, G. H. *Five Years' Experience in Australia Felix.* Hamilton, Adams, & Co., London, 1846 (2 vols); Queensberry Hill Press, Melbourne, 1983.

Historical Records of Australia. See Watson, Frederick (ed.).

Historical Records of Victoria. See Cannon, Michael (general ed.).

Horton, T., and Morris, K. *The Andersons of Western Port.* Bass Valley Historical Society, Corinella, Vic., 1983.

Joyce, Alfred. *A Homestead History . . .*, ed. by G. F. James. Melbourne University Press, Melbourne, 1942.

Kiddle, Margaret. *Men of Yesterday.* Melbourne University Press, Carlton, Vic., 1961.

Kirby, James. *Old Times in the Bush of Australia . . .*, n.p., Ballarat, Vic., c. 1895.

[Kirkland, Mrs K. W]. *Life in the Bush.* n.p., Edinburgh, 1845; reprinted in Hugh Anderson, *Flowers of the Field*, q.v.

Learmont, N. F. *The Portland Bay Settlement.* McCarron, Bird & Co., Melbourne, 1934; Baulch, Hawkesdale, Vic., 1983.

McCrae, G. G. *Recollections of Melbourne & Port Phillip Bay in the Early Forties.* Sullivan's Cove, Adelaide, 1987.

MacFarlane, Ian (comp.). *1842: The Public Executions at Melbourne.* Government Printer, Melbourne, 1984.

——· *Victorian Aborigines 1835–1901.* Public Record Office of Victoria and Government Information Centre, Melbourne, 1984.

Manifold, W. G. *The Wished-for Land.* Neptune Press, Newtown, Vic., 1984.

Massola, Aldo. *Aboriginal Mission Stations in Victoria.* Hawthorn Press, Melbourne, 1970.

——· *Journey to Aboriginal Victoria.* Rigby, Adelaide, 1969.

Meyrick, F. J. *Life in the Bush, 1840–47: A Memoir of Henry Howard Meyrick.* Nelson, London, 1939.

Morrison, Edgar. *Early Days in the Loddon Valley: Memoirs of Edward Stone Parker 1802–1865.* The author, Yandoit, Vic., 1966.

——· *Frontier Life in the Loddon Protectorate: Episodes from Early Days, 1837–1842.* The author, Yandoit, Vic., 1967.

——· *The Loddon Aborigines.* The author, Yandoit, Vic., 1971.

Morton, W. L. *Adventures of a Pioneer*, ed. by J. O. Randell. Queensberry Hill Press, Melbourne, 1979.

O'Connor, T. M. *Edward Stone Parker, Pioneer and Protector.* Spectator Publishing, Melbourne, 1963.

Old Melbourne Gaol 1841. National Trust (Vic.), Melbourne, 1972.

Osborn [Roberts], B. O. *The Bacchus Story . . .* Bacchus Marsh Historical Society, Bacchus Marsh, Vic., 1973.

Parker, E. S. *The Aborigines of Australia: A Lecture*. Hugh McColl, Melbourne, 1854.

Presland, Gary. *Journals of G. A. Robinson: January–March 1840, March–May 1841, May–August 1841*. Victorian Archaeological Survey, Melbourne, 1977–80.

Rae-Ellis, Vivienne. *Black Robinson*. Melbourne University Press, Carlton, Vic., 1988.

—— *Trucanini: Queen or Traitor?* Australian Institute of Aboriginal Studies, Canberra, 1981.

Randell, J. O. *The Pastoral Pattersons*. Queensberry Hill Press, Melbourne, 1977.

—— *Pastoral Settlement in Northern Victoria. Vol. I: The Coliban District*. Queensberry Hill Press, Melbourne, 1979.

—— *Pastoral Settlement in Northern Victoria. Vol. II: The Campaspe District*. Chandos Publishing, Burwood, Vic., 1982.

Reece, R. H. W. *Aborigines and Colonists: Aborigines and Colonial Society in New South Wales in the 1830s and 1840s*. Sydney University Press, Sydney, 1974.

Roberts, S. H. *The Squatting Age in Australia, 1835–1847*. Melbourne University Press, Melbourne, 1935.

Robinson, G. A. *Journals*. (For those published, *see* Clark, I. D.; Presland, G.)

Ryan, Peter. *Redmond Barry: A Colonial Life*. Melbourne University Press, Carlton, Vic., 1980.

Shaw, A. G. L. (ed.). *Gipps–La Trobe Correspondence 1839–1846*. Melbourne University Press, Carlton, Vic., 1989.

Smyth, R. B. *The Aborigines of Victoria*. 2 vols. Government Printer, Melbourne, 1876–78; John Currey, O'Neil, Melbourne, 1972.

Squatters' Directory . . . Argus Office, Melbourne, 1849.

Squatters' Manual . . . Argus Office, Melbourne, 1848.

Sullivan, Martin. *Men & Women of Port Phillip*. Hale & Iremonger, Sydney, 1985.

Tindale, N. B. *Aboriginal Tribes of Australia*. 2 vols. University of California Press, Berkeley, Calif., 1974.

Turner, H. G. *A History of the Colony of Victoria*. 2 vols. Longmans, London, 1904; Heritage Publications, Melbourne, n.d.

Watson, Don. *Caledonia Australis: Scottish Highlanders on the Frontier of Australia.* Collins, Sydney, 1984.

Watson, Frederick (ed.). *Historical Records of Australia, Series I.* Commonwealth Parliament, Canberra, 1914–25.

Waugh, D. L. *Three Years' Practical Experience . . . in New South Wales . . .* John Johnstone, Edinburgh, 1838(?).

Willis, J. W. *See* Behan, Harold F.

GENERAL INDEX

Grampians 63, 82, 96, 112, 116, 119, 146, 148
Grange, *see* Hamilton
Grangeburn Creek 61
Gray, Charles M. 25
Green Hills (Gippsland) 217
'Green Hills' run 96
Grey, Earl 196, 254, 256–7
Grey, Sir George 138, 258
Grice, Richard 37
Griffith, Charles 92
Griffiths, John 95
Grimes, Edward 196, 229, 241–2, 248
Guardian of Aborigines 258–9
guerrilla tactics 29–38, 82
Guinness, Sir Richard 91
Gunbower 232
guns, *see* weapons
Guthrie, James 86

Habeas Corpus Act 104
Hall, C. B. 63
Hallard, Constable William 35
Hall's Gap 63
Ham, Rev. John 160
Hamilton 50, 86, 92, 99, 102, 112, 117, 118, 195, 245
Hamilton, — 31n.
Hamilton, G. D. 117
Hamilton, George 131
Hamilton, James 175
Hamilton, James C. 154–5
Hamilton, James M. 116, 117
Hamilton, Robert 152
Hamilton, T. F. 175
Hamilton, Rev. William 187
hangings, *see* executions
Harden, James 131
Harlin, John 224
Harrow 106, 190, 192
Hartnett, — 214n.
Hawdon, John 94
Haydon, G. H. 172
Hayes, Thomas 23
health problems, *see* disease
Heart Inn, Port Albert 211
Heidelberg 15, 32, 38, 60, 71, 159, 259
Henning, Thomas 221
Henty family 56, 96, 102, 144
Henty, Edward 59, 154
Henty, Francis 49–50, 115
Henty, John 48, 62
Henty, Stephen George 50, 51, 57, 62, 102
Hepburn, Captain John 129, 130, 248
Hexham 60
Heywood 190–1

Hickling, William 89
Higgins, William 143–4
'Highland Brigade' 171–2
Hill, Richard Guinness 91–5
Hill, Thomas 214n.
Hoddle, Robert 204, 244, 249, 258, 260
Hogg, James 141
'Holcombe' run 250
Holker, Wilson 184
homosexuality 135–6
Hopkins River 60, 64, 89, 97, 108
Horrell, Charles C. 244
Horsburgh, Dr James 136, 184–5, 230, 245–7, 256
horses and horse-racing 9, 32, 42, 45, 50, 55, 60, 61, 86, 87, 97, 116, 126, 132, 140, 148, 159, 161, 165–7, 186, 190, 222, 223, 231, 235–6, 238
Horsfall, James 152
Horsham 148, 149, 155, 193, 230
hospitals
  bush 17
  Melbourne 134, 160
hostages taken, 34, 213–16
hotels, *see* public houses and publicans
Hotspur 100, 120
Houlston, Mrs — 56
Howitt, Richard 43
humanitarianism 2, 7, 79, 85, 179, 220, 242
Hume, Mrs Elizabeth 229
Hume, John Kennedy 229
Hunter, Hoskin & Davidson's run 86
Hunter, Alexander 43
Hunter, James 98, 100
Hunter, John 86, 88, 98
Hunter, W. M. 247–8
hunting grounds, *see* land
Huon family 220
Hurst, Rev. Benjamin 53, 61–3, 138, 199
Hutcheson brothers 97
Hutcheson, Peter 89
huts 10, 15, 18, 22, 24, 26, 31, 42, 48, 52, 59, 69, 86, 96, 99, 132, 134, 147, 152, 156–7, 160, 169, 175, 182, 197, 200, 202, 221, 225–6, 228, 243, 248, 250
Hutton, Captain Charles 41
Hutton, William 244

immigrants, white 9, 56, 62, 64, 66, 133, 152, 177, 224
import duty 176–7
Indian stockmen and labourers 83, 175, 183–4, 223
influenza 163, 165, 168, 184, 230
'Ingliston' run 33

INDEX TO ABORIGINAL NAMES TRIBES, WEAPONS AND PHRASES

Many of these entries represent names or nicknames attached to Aboriginals by white settlers. Unfortunately the true tribal identities of these people are now rarely known. Inevitably the one English name (e.g. Billy) could be attached to several different natives in different areas. The reader should not assume that any entry in this index invariably applies to the one individual.